Sky Mothers
Born of Shadows Book 4

J.R. Erickson

Copyright © 2018 J.R. Erickson

All rights reserved.

This is a work of fiction. Names, characters, places, and incidents either are the products of the author's imagination or are used fictitiously. Any resemblance to actual persons, living or dead, businesses, companies, events, or locales is entirely coincidental.

ISBN-10: 1718729308
ISBN-13: 978-1718729308

DEDICATION

For Hannah

ACKNOWLEDGMENTS

Thank you to all of my family and friends, who have been my avid beta readers, and to my wonderful husband who has supported this re-commitment to my writing. Thank you to my amazing editor Michal Anderson who made this book better and wasn't afraid to give me real - and often funny – feedback. Finally my gratitude to Rena at Cover Quill who designed my beautiful covers for the Born of Shadow's Series.

CHAPTER 1

"All packed?" Abby found Sebastian in their room sitting on the bed. He held a long white candle in his hands.

He looked up and grinned.

"Three t-shirts, two pairs of shorts, and my sandals."

Abby cocked an eyebrow.

"No pants?"

Sebastian pointed down.

"Wearing them and my sweatshirt too. All long sleeves will be carried on the body for this adventure."

Abby frowned.

"So, you'll have a backpack and I'll have a giant rolling suitcase and a duffel bag?"

He laughed.

"No, I'll have a backpack, a giant rolling suitcase, and a duffel bag. You'll have our coffees."

He stood and set the candle gently on the bedside table. Grabbing her hand, he pulled her toward him.

"I'm so excited to travel with you," he murmured. His blue eyes sparkled with the same excitement she felt reflected in her own. A little shiver coursed through her body. Lately, she had begun to feel Sebastian's energy. She wondered if this meant that his powers were growing stronger.

In the month since Dafne's death, Abby and the other witches of Ula had been busy. They sifted through the Asemaa files in a frenzied search for the magic that might destroy the amulet. Coming up empty, Elda and Faustine went to the cave of elders and sought advice. The leaders offered little insight and ultimately it was decided that the Coven of the Sky Mothers in Australia would be their best option. Abby, Sebastian, Julian, Oliver, and Helena would make the journey. Lydie had wanted to go and nearly cried when she learned that she would be excluded, but Elda insisted that she stay at Ula. She was months behind in her apothecary studies and Bridget wanted to teach her how to grow magical plants. Ultimately, she gave in, but Abby worried about her mental health while they were away. After Max's death, she had been sad, but since Dafne's she'd grown despondent.

Abby tried to push thoughts of Lydie from her mind and focus on the day ahead.

"I feel like a little kid flying for the first time," she admitted. "Excited, nervous, like I have to pee a lot, though that may be the baby."

Sebastian rested his hands on Abby's shoulders and looked into her face.

"You're a bad-ass witch, no silly plane ride is going to get under your skin."

She screwed her eyes shut and peeked at him through the slit in one eye.

"If you'd attended Psych 101 and heard Mr. Frasier's lecture on human error in airline pilots, you might feel differently."

"At this point, I'll take human error any day of the week."

She nodded.

"True, the odds are probably significantly better than going up against evil demons that actually intend to kill you."

"Infinitely better," he said. "And I'll give you the window seat."

He jumped onto the bed and danced around.

"No, please! I need the aisle so I can pee."

He laughed and back-flopped onto the bed.

"Future wifey, you can have anything you want."

****

"Ugh, another backpack guy? Did you even fit a toothbrush in there?" Abby asked, grimacing at Oliver's meager luggage.

"Toothbrush, board shorts, all-terrain tear-away pants, two t-shirts, sunglasses, headphones, and a book!" Oliver exclaimed triumphantly.

"Did you bring a pony?" he gestured at Abby's suitcases propped on the ground next to her.

She swatted at him.

"No, I actually intend to change my clothes while we're there."

"Don't sweat it, honey," Helena called. She sailed through the airport in a flowing purple dress and turquoise shawl. Peacock feather earrings dangled from her ears and she had pulled her hair up into a French twist.

"Wow," Sebastian echoed Abby's thoughts.

"You like?" she asked with a curtsy. "I haven't traveled in ages! I'm doing it with style."

She pulled an equally vibrant, huge yellow suitcase through the terminal, the handle braided with red ribbon.

Julian followed behind her. He wheeled a medium-sized black leather bag and carried a laptop case over his shoulder.

"He looks like a CEO," Abby whispered to Sebastian.

"You three are like a band of misfits," Sebastian told them as they sidled up next to them in the check-in line.

"The plan was to not draw attention to ourselves, but as you can see…" Julian gestured toward Helena. "Only Oliver listened."

Oliver winked and unzipped his coat behind Julian's back. He wore a t-shirt with a picture of several unicorns farting glittery rainbows. The caption beneath it read *Unicorn Squad* in pink block letters.

Abby and Sebastian burst out laughing.

Julian whirled around.

"Ugh," he sighed. "Where did you get that?"

"That truck stop off I-75 on our way down. I thought this seemed more appropriate than the t-shirt covered in sparkling kitties."

"What did that one say?" Sebastian asked.

"Show me your kitties." Oliver grinned and Sebastian snorted.

"Just check in already," Julian moaned, waving Oliver ahead in the line.

****

When they landed in Cairns, Australia, Julian rented a Range Rover and they piled their stuff in the back.

The flight had been tiring and Abby felt the pressure finally subside when she stepped foot on solid ground. Two connecting flights, twelve trips to the bathroom, and a bout of nausea during their bumpy ride from Sydney to Cairns had left her ready to give up air travel for life. She'd also dreamed of Kanti. It had been a death dream as she'd begun to think of them. She'd had three now. In this dream, Kanti raced through a series of tunnels with a fire close behind. Smoke began to fill the space and she couldn't see, could barely breathe. Just before Abby woke, Kanti had collapsed in the tunnel and lay gasping for breath. She had not told Sebastian about the dream during the flight because he'd been snoring softly beside her.

"Oh, heavenly sun," Oliver shouted, holding his arms out to either side and twirling around. He got down on his knees and pretended to kiss the dirt.

Helena shielded her eyes. "Why didn't I join the Sky Mothers? Warm year round, flowers bursting from every tree, fresh mangoes…"

"Kangaroos," Abby added. "Let's move here?" she grabbed Sebastian's hand.

"And give up the deep character carved out by long brutal winters in Northern Michigan? Never!" he joked, but tilted his face into the sun.

"Steinbeck said, 'What good is the warmth of summer, without the cold of winter to give it sweetness?'" Julian remarked, slamming the back door on the Rover.

"Hogwash," Oliver mumbled from the ground.

"It does feel painfully good. Can we put off the work and hit the beach for a few days?" Sebastian asked, winking at Abby.

Julian climbed behind the wheel.

"Nope. But don't worry, Sky Mothers has it all, beach, ocean, sunshine, you name it."

****

They drove for hours, winding around steep cliffs in the forest.

"You sure this is a road?" Oliver asked, peering out the window at the dense foliage.

The Rover hugged the trees on one side because the other slid steeply into the forest far below.

After an arduous descent, Julian pulled to a stop in front of a wooden gate crawling with ivy.

"You've been here before?" Sebastian asked Julian.

"Twice," he told them, leaning out of the window and pressing his palm against a large opal embedded in the wood.

"How does that work?" Oliver asked, curious.

"Not a clue," Julian confessed. "I asked them during my last visit, but the Sky Mothers are rather…secretive. Especially when it comes to their security."

After several minutes, the gate swung open and Julian drove through. A hard-packed dirt road twisted through a half mile of Eucalyptus forest.

Abby watched out the window, feeling like a tourist, searching for a koala bear or an exotic parrot. Sebastian looked equally starry-eyed.

"Oh my," Helena breathed.

Abby turned forward.

A lush garden surrounded a sparkling pool of water. Waterfalls cascaded into the lagoon from a high mossy ledge. Perched above the waterfalls, Abby saw a sprawling menagerie of glass and sandstone structures. The largest building boasted a tall arch, shaped like the rustic goddess statues that Abby had seen in anthropology books during college. The sun reflected off the windows creating a mirrored wall of light.

"This way," Julian said, leading them toward a manicured path that wove around the waterfall and up the slope.

A witch in a white silk robe, the hood covering her hair and part of her face, emerged from the arch. She drifted toward them like an apparition.

Except for Julian, they all stopped and stared.

"Julian," the witch said warmly, taking his hands. She slipped the hood down, revealing her youthful face and satiny rose gold hair. Huge baby-doll blue eyes sparkled in her elfin face.

"Mattie," he pulled the beautiful witch into a hug. She laughed and kissed his cheek.

"You missed me, then?"

"You, or Kit's buttered prawns, I regularly dream of both."

She laughed and the sound echoed like tinkling bells.

"Come meet my friends," he told her.

Julian led Mattie back to the group.

Helena stepped forward, smiling graciously. She held out her hand.

"I'm Helena." She grasped Mattie's slender fingers in her own.

"Matilda," the witch told her, looking deeply into her eyes for several seconds.

Abby watched the exchange, wondering what sort of information Matilda gleaned from staring.

"Helena of Aepa in the Mediterranean Isle." Matilda nodded her head. "I see them in you. The almond-shaped eyes. Now, this style of yours makes me think you were related to Antheia."

A look of surprise passed over Helena's face.

"Antheia was my mother."

"Yes, of course she was. She was like an exotic flower."

"I haven't heard her name in a hundred years," Helena breathed, looking excited and out of sorts.

"Perhaps we can reminisce about her later then? I too love an occasional walk down memory lane."

Matilda moved to Oliver.

She took his hands and held them.

Abby watched the tiny flecks of light in her eyes. Her pupils looked less like black orbs than portals into another universe. Abby braced her hand on Sebastian's arm, suddenly feeling faint.

"I'm Oliver," he said. "This is quite the set-up you have here." He nodded toward the structure beyond.

"You like it?" Matilda asked with genuine curiosity.

"It's like a dream."

Matilda nodded and glanced back at the arch.

"It is our dream made manifest." She turned to face Sebastian. "And you too are a powerful manifester," she said. "And a non-witch. Tisk, tisk Julian, you did not properly reveal yourself."

"I'm sorry, Mattie," Julian admitted. "It slipped my mind."

Though Abby wondered if it had. Julian did not seem absent-minded, ever.

"Did it now?" Matilda said, but her eyes gleamed as she spoke.

She glided toward Sebastian and took his hands. She cocked her head as she looked deeply into his eyes. Her beauty radiated from every pore. Abby felt a pinprick of jealousy and shifted her gaze to the falling water. It immediately soothed her.

"An interesting specimen, you are…"

"Sebastian," he offered.

"Sebastian, yes. Binda will love to get to know you better."

Abby bristled and Matilda turned to her, smiling.

"Not that way, lovely, I promise." She winked at Abby. "And look at you, so young." She took Abby's hands.

Abby felt an intense warmth spread out from the woman's silken touch.

"Oh my, and a life already threaded with your own. A daughter, no less. A gift that we Sky Mothers cherish above all others."

Abby nodded, though she didn't quite know why. Matilda had a powerful presence and put Abby immediately at ease. No, it was more complex than ease. Matilda felt like the mother Abby had always wanted, but never had.

"Come inside, dear friends," Matilda announced, releasing Abby's hands. "You've had a long journey."

They followed Matilda through the archway and into a long hallway with ceilings that soared. Enormous bamboo fans whirled overhead. Thick, soft couches and chairs sat clustered along the hallway, surrounding glass tables strewn with pink flower petals and flickering candles. A tunnel of wind moved through the hallway as they walked, somehow not disturbing the flowers strewn about. Beyond the corridor, the ocean stretched before them in sparkling waves. Abby savored the salty breeze on her face.

At the opposite archway, Matilda gestured toward a shimmering infinity pool that seemed to vanish into the ocean. Flanking the pool, Abby saw a stretch of the whitest sand she'd ever laid eyes on.

"Look," Sebastian whispered, nudging her.

Abby followed his extended fingers.

"A kangaroo," she shrieked, growing red as the other witches turned to stare.

"Carlos," Matilda told her. "Go pet him, he's a ham. But watch out for Lolita, the big one with extra scruffy ears, she likes to sneak up and nip you."

Abby and Sebastian walked down marble stairs into the grass. Carlos hopped over to them and waited expectantly.

"I think he's looking for a treat." Sebastian laughed, scratching his neck.

"He's so big," Abby said, amazed. Close up, the kangaroo stood a foot taller than her. She ran her hand over his chest.

"Ouch," Sebastian yelped, spinning around.

Another kangaroo, larger in stature and personality, had a clump of Sebastian's black hair in its mouth.

"Nice to meet you, Lolita," Abby told the kangaroo, laughing.

****

"Where are all the men?" Sebastian asked Julian that afternoon.

They sat in the hallway that Abby had deemed the wind tunnel, snacking on fruit and cheese, and resting up from their flight.

"The Sky Mothers are all women. They do not allow male witches in their coven."

"Say what?" Oliver asked, incredulous. "Why?"

"They're highly devoted to the sacred feminine. They believe that the male element disrupts the purity of a female witch's power. It's too focused on separation and disparity."

"Wow, isn't that sexist?" Oliver asked. "I thought inclusion was a big part of the witch's law."

"Inclusion is important, but it doesn't encompass all things, such as living quarters and covens. The truth is that witches are very human in that way. They choose what feels right to them. The Sky Mothers have lived this way for more than two-hundred years."

"I think it's refreshing," Helena said. "No offense," she patted Oliver's knee. "But I can see the appeal. A sisterhood."

Abby smiled and nodded. She too could see the allure, but a life without Sebastian? No thanks.

"No children then?" Sebastian asked.

Julian shook his head.

"It is a sacrifice the witches of the Sky Mothers make when they enter the coven, but they are not celibate and they are not eternally bound by the choice. There are witches who have left the coven to have a partnership with a man. Though I believe it is rare."

"How many witches are in the Sky Mothers?" Oliver asked.

Julian shrugged.

"I don't know. I've met five of them during my two visits here, but there are spaces where men are not welcome. Don't worry," he assured them when Sebastian frowned. "You won't stumble into one of those areas. They are bewitched to repel male energy."

"Wait, I'm going to open a door and get blasted on my ass?" Oliver asked, a sparkle in his eye.

"Ha-ha," Julian said dryly. "You'll never even know the room is there. That's how effective their spells are."

"So how do you know they're not celibate?" Oliver grinned.
Julian narrowed his eyes and shook his head.

****

"Beautiful hair you have," Binda murmured, touching Sebastian's curls lightly.

"Thanks," he told her, surveying the room.

He sat on a stool in a circular glass chamber filled with sunlight. Five doors opened to views of the ocean, the gardens, and the beach.

Matilda had taken the other witches to retrieve the ax while Sebastian got carted off to meet Binda, the founder of the Sky Mothers.

"Close your eyes," Binda told him.

She was a tall, foreboding woman with thick graying black hair tied in a white scarf. Like Matilda, she wore a sheer white robe that billowed in the wind. Unlike Matilda, she had intense masculine features and a rigid demeanor that put Sebastian on edge. She scanned him like an interesting sea creature she had found on the beach.

He felt her hands move over his scalp and neck and shoulders. He could not imagine what she might discover by touching him, but he had decided to play along. His curiosity about his developing powers forced him to be open to all manner of probing.

"Open your eyes," Binda commanded.

She held a large opal in her hand.

"Stare at the opal please."

He gazed at the shimmering stone. It was a large raw purplish mineral with a dazzling rainbow of colors sparkling from its depths. Binda watched him closely.

"Am I supposed to see something in this?" he asked, glancing at her.

"It is I who sees," she told him. "Don't break your gaze, stare deeply."

He did. He had never looked all that closely at an opal before. The colors swirled and shifted, refracted and expanded. He started to feel dizzy and clutched his stool with both hands.

Binda abruptly pulled the opal away. She folded the gem within a piece of white silk and tucked it into a leather case.

"Have you discovered my life's purpose?" he asked, cocking an eyebrow.

"You are a conflicted spirit, Sebastian. I sense deep love in you, but also great anger. You are vengeful, insecure, and obsessive."

Sebastian frowned. He'd been joking.

"You also have powers that defy ordinary man. We have come to call your kind hybrids."

"Hybrids?"

"I believe that a hybrid is created when the desire for power-for magic, if you will-creates an opportunity for transformation. If the individual meets the power that he desires, he will assume some of it."

"That makes me sound power hungry."

"You are," she said shortly, and left him alone in the room, contemplating her words.

CHAPTER 2

"It is fifty thousand years old," Matilda told them, pulling the curtain back to reveal a warped and ancient-looking tree. It twisted and curled toward the light shining through an opening in the domed roof. A sliver of iridescent water ran in a moat around the tree and thousands of hairline cracks spider webbed toward the trunk.

"It's beautiful," Helena whispered, stepping closer.

Matilda put an arm out to stop her.

"It's enchanted. The water, the air. Best not go farther. Only Binda and I have access here."

Abby watched the tree warily. Beautiful was not the word she would have used to describe it. Creepy maybe, definitely eerie.

"Why do you keep the ax here?" Oliver asked.

In his tone, Abby sensed her own feelings mirrored. The tree made him uncomfortable.

"The ax was found with this tree. The Mother Tree, we call her."

"And you transported it?"

Matilda laughed.

"Goodness, no. When you discover such eternal magic, you do not uproot it and steal it to make it your own. You uproot yourself and move to be with it. Binda built our coven around this tree. This tree is one of the greatest mothers of all time. Can you imagine the seedlings that have populated the earth from this ancient beauty?"

"Hmmm," Helena murmured, awash in a glow of reverence that matched Matilda's.

Abby, soon to be a mother herself, did not share in their admiration.

"Makes my skin crawl," Oliver whispered to her from the side of his mouth.

Abby held out her arm so Oliver could see the prickling of goose bumps there.

He shuddered in response and they took a couple steps away from the tree.

Julian walked through the doorway behind them.

"Ah, the great slayer. She looks youthful and vibrant as always."

"Slayer?" Oliver grumbled.

Matilda stopped at the water's and carefully slipped her fingers through the air over the stream. Abby realized that the water was not merely a moat, but a wall of water surrounding the tree. She looked around for the source. Matilda stepped through the water. As she moved closer to the tree it seemed to sense her presence and shift toward her. She walked to the trunk and laid her head on the charcoal colored bark. She stood that way for a long time.

"She secretes a poison through her bark. We believe the original bearer of the ax fell prey to her charms and perhaps rested against her trunk. He never woke up."

"You found his bones, then?" Helena asked, backing away from the tree as if she suddenly saw it in a new, more sinister, light.

"One shard, embedded in the bark."

"So, the tree ate him?" Abby asked, feeling a sudden chill.

Matilda pulled her hands from the tree and rinsed them in the cascading water.

"I believe that she did, yes."

A gleaming ax with a spiraled bronze handle and a black razor-sharp blade stood propped against the tree. A shimmer of red undulated down the blade when Matilda touched it.

"It hasn't been used in well over a decade," Matilda told them, lifting the ax.

She looked at the weapon with a tenderness that Abby found rather unnerving.

"I wish you had brought your magical item here, Julian. I am reluctant to part with this."

Julian nodded.

"I understand, but as I mentioned, the item in question houses an evil spirit. I hardly wanted to contaminate your sanctuary and risk leaving some remnant of her behind."

"Oh, there is no risk of that," Matilda continued. "This weapon lets nothing escape."

"How are we getting it on a plane?" Oliver asked. "I have a feeling the scanner might pick that one up."

Matilda laughed.

"Always joking," she said merrily. "Why do you hide your fear behind jokes, Oliver?"

She turned her inquisitive blue eyes on Oliver, and Abby noticed the color rising in his cheeks.

"The case will be enchanted," Julian cut in. "They'll never detect it."

"Right you are," Matilda agreed.

****

"Why do they call themselves the Sky Mothers if there are no children?" Sebastian asked Julian that afternoon as they lounged by the pool.

"Coven names are generally not chosen, but given," Julian explained. "Take Ula, it means jewel of the sea. When Faustine came to America to start his coven anew, he spent many months wandering the shores of Lake Superior. He saw a gleaming quartz stone sticking from the sand and picked it up. A fisherman happened upon him that morning, gestured to the stone and said, 'Ula-Jewel of the Sea.' It was an answer. A coven should not choose its own name. It is spoken in the old ways as an egoic misdirection that will likely lead to egoic pursuits. The name should be chosen for it. From what I know, the Sky Mothers were originally a small group of witches deep in the outback, midwives, healers, hunters. And then Binda, during a walkabout, had a visit from a spirit beyond the veil. This spirit directed Binda to the ancient tree they call the Mother Tree. She told Binda that she would have a vision and know it was time to build her coven, a coven of women."

"So Binda is the original? Now I see why she seems a bit old and cantankerous," Sebastian muttered.

"Don't say that to her or she'll have your hide. Literally, I'd imagine."

Sebastian laughed, but Abby squirmed at the comment.

Binda had put her on edge as well. She gave off a hostile and inquisitive energy. Abby felt a bit flayed after a few minutes with her. Her questions alone seemed to go beyond her general thoughts and into some subconscious chamber that she had intended to keep closed to herself, and most definitely to Binda.

"She called me a hybrid," Sebastian said.

"Like if a Dalmatian and chihuahua had a baby?" Oliver asked.

Abby punched him lightly on the arm.

"Interesting," Julian responded. "I know very little of hybrids. I've surely never met one. Until now of course." He winked at Sebastian.

"You've heard of them, though?"

"Over the years, sure, in various circles. In a way, they are like urban legends for witches. They are humans and witches. They are considered dangerous because they tend to be emotionally vulnerable and less in control of their powers."

"I hate to say that it makes sense," Sebastian continued. "I'm definitely not in control of my powers."

"You opened the earth when Kanti attacked us so that we could escape," Abby argued.

"I didn't, though. I mean, I did, but I wasn't visualizing the earth splitting and trees falling. Do you think I would have killed that big oak tree? I wanted to hang a tire swing from that one! I just concentrated all of my energy on making something happen and it did."

Julian nodded.

"You see the challenge with the idea of a hybrid, Sebastian, is that we don't have a classification. There aren't tens of thousands of hybrids that we can look at and say, 'Yep, they have these powers and abilities and this weakness.' We witches have been around for thousands of years. We have a specific timeline. We begin exhibiting powers at a certain point, we are defined by our element of power, and we can learn to direct that element. But witches have other superhuman capabilities that we all share. Then there are powers beyond those universal capabilities, but they don't differentiate us in a substantial way."

"Why did Lydie exhibit powers so young?" Oliver asked suddenly. "I've wondered about that. I mean, I was seventeen, Abby was twenty-four. Helena told me she was fifteen."

"I was nineteen," Julian confessed. "Lydie is special. She has always been special. But it's not unheard of."

"I saw small children at the All Hallow's Ball doing magic," Sebastian added.

"You did?" How did I miss that?" Oliver asked, looking bummed.

"Not many, a group of five or six."

"Some years you will see a handful of children. Usually, the covens frown on children under ten attending the event, but some covens are more lenient. Sorciére is one of them because they have Cherie."

"Cherie?" Oliver asked.

"A young witch. She is four, I think. She is the child of two witches. She and her parents did not actually attend the Ball. Galla told me they were in Japan visiting an ill friend. However, I believe they allowed several other covens to bring their young witches because they originally thought that Cherie would be there and it would be good for her to meet other young ones."

"I'm not sure I would have liked that," Abby admitted. "To have powers when I was four."

"It's not ideal," Julian admitted. "Accidents are much more likely, and for toddlers, that's already a problem."

Abby thought of their daughter. Would she exhibit unnaturally early powers? Or would she never be a witch at all? Sometimes it hurt her brain to think about it. Mostly because she inevitably found herself afraid for her unborn child. She wanted to give her everything, but most of all happiness. Lydie often seemed troubled. Abby did not want that for her daughter. She wanted to protect her against all the evil in the world.

****

Lydie woke with a start. She blinked in the darkness of her room, and tensed, waiting for the sound to come again. Something had woken her, something foreign in the otherwise quiet night. It would be all too easy for the Vepars to attack Ula again while Julian and the other witches were in Australia. Clenching her teeth to keep them from chattering, she shoved her blankets off and stepped out of bed.

French doors opened to her balcony. As she stepped out, she felt the crisp air that signaled an end to winter and a transition into spring. It was a different kind of cold, still bone-jarring in the Upper Peninsula of Michigan, but the winds of change were less bitter. As a fire element, she hungered for summer. Some fire witches loved the winter. It cooled the hot energy always flowing, but Lydie found the cold stifled her energy, her creativity, her whole self.

A sliver of moon did little to illuminate the lake or sky. She watched and waited, but saw and heard nothing. Nightmares were not uncommon for her so she attempted to dismiss the noise and turned back to her bed.

The sound came again. An echo across the water like crying, or more like wailing, that rose and then disappeared. She went to the rail and squinted into the darkness, but could see nothing.

She walked to her bed where her cat Garfield, a ball of orange fluff, slept in a pile of blankets. She ran her fingers down his back and then sighed.

"The trials and tribulations of a witch," she muttered.

Her shoes were next to her bed and she slid them on and grabbed Dafne's red cloak from the hook on the back of the door.

Outside the castle, the cliff protected the lagoon from the biting lake breeze.

Lydie could wake Elda or Faustine, or even Bridget. She should wake them, but she didn't.

She climbed into one of the rowboats, eyeing Faustine's fleet of military boats warily, and rowed beyond the castle cliffs. She could see a vortex of angry wind lashing the lake into a small cyclone. It was an isolated event and the rest of the lake was untouched. Lydie knew what it meant. Someone was trying to get to Ula and the protective spells around the island were forcing the intruder to reveal themselves. Lydie had never intercepted a visitor. Faustine felt it prudent, and safer, that he do it himself.

Lydie waited for the cyclone to subside. As an eerie calm descended over the lake, she heard the cry again, louder this time and unmistakably in pain.

The truth was that Lydie did not feel afraid and if whatever lurked in the lake intended to do her or the witches of Ula harm, she would know it. She had keen intuition, always had, and she trusted those feelings first and foremost.

She rowed quickly and saw the silhouette of another small boat begin to take shape. It appeared empty. As she drew alongside the battered little boat, she heard the cry again, muffled beneath a dark blanket. Lydie glanced around, searching for anything amiss, and then climbed into the boat. As she began to pull the blanket back, the woman beneath it cried out and shrunk farther into the boat.

Rail thin, most of her hair fallen out, with patches of red welts covering her body, the woman looked near death.

"It's okay," Lydie whispered, squatting in the boat and finding a space on the woman's arm that didn't look bruised and angry to touch. The woman shivered violently and Lydie had her first regret at not waking Elda.

"There, there, you're not alone anymore. I'm here to help you," she cooed.

The woman twisted around and looked at Lydie. Lydie saw recognition in her eyes but she did not know the witch beneath her.

At night, Faustine rarely connected with the witches of Ula telepathically. It was disruptive to his sleep if he did so, not to mention theirs. Still, Lydie reached out to him. She was not telepathic, but Faustine had taught her years ago that intense concentration on another person, even without special abilities, could convey a message. With someone like Faustine, whose mind was open and receptive in a supernatural way, that was much more likely to happen. Within seconds, she felt him.

"What's happened, Lydie?" he asked.

Lydie did not respond, but looked at the witch in the boat, knowing that Faustine would sense her.

"Adora," he said. "Stay where you are. I'm coming."

CHAPTER 3

Set high in the forest, on a cliff overlooking the ocean, the Sky Mothers had five yurts for their visitors. A beautiful open-air kitchen with a tree growing in its center offered them a place to gather for their first morning at the coven.

Sebastian worked on preparing a French press of coffee while Abby wandered the kitchen, touching things.

"Everything is so deliberate," she said. "Look at this table."

The table was a mosaic of broken glass in a hundred different colors and shapes. It formed a goddess pattern in the same shape as the archway into the Sky Mothers' central house.

"I like it," Sebastian said. "And at the same time, I don't. Maybe it's the whole 'no man' thing, but I feel like more of an outsider here than anywhere I've ever been."

"It's not just you," Abby admitted. "I feel that way too. Like we've stumbled into an alien civilization. Ula is different than the typical world, but there's something very human about it. Everything here feels sort of…"

"Perfect," Sebastian finished.

"Yes, perfect. And cold."

"I dig the yurts though," he said. "Making love to you with the whales calling in the ocean. I could have died a happy man last night."

Abby smiled, remembering.

It had been hopelessly romantic. Through the skylight in the roof of the yurt, they could see a billion stars. The whales sang in their deep baritone cries. Abby felt like she melted with Sebastian. Afterward, she slept better than she had in months.

"Waking up to pee was a bit harrowing," she confessed. "I was scared I would plummet over that cliff in the dark."

"That's why I peed in the bushes," Sebastian told her.

The community bathroom on the cliff was tucked near the woods. The walk only took a couple of minutes, but in the dark with the rush of the sea far below, it had been an unnerving journey.

"Is that coffee I smell?" Helena twittered, gliding into the yurt. She wore a long dress that reminded Abby of the cosmos. Dark turquoise and purples created whorls and spirals within the fabric.

"Coffee coming right up," Sebastian told her. "Cream?"

"Yes, and honey?"

Sebastian delivered Helena her coffee and slid onto the bench next to Abby.

"My head hit the pillow and I didn't move until five minutes ago. I can't remember the last time that I slept so good," Helena said, sipping her coffee appreciatively.

"Us too," Abby agreed.

"I swear I saw one of those ghostly Sky Mothers sneaking out of Oliver's yurt last night." Sebastian grinned.

"No, you did not," Abby exclaimed. "Did you?"

Sebastian shrugged. "That or he's staying in a haunted yurt."

As if on cue, Oliver lumbered in wearing only a pair of surf shorts and a vaguely guilty expression.

"Yes! The coffee gods have blessed us," he moaned, grabbing a mug hanging from a rack carved from driftwood.

"Anyone else bless you last night?" Helena murmured, stirring her coffee and eyeing Oliver mischievously.

He cocked an eyebrow and then looked at each of their faces.

Abby grinned and tilted her head.

A tiny something tugged at her heart, but she ignored it. She loved Sebastian. Any feelings she had toward Oliver were strictly platonic. Why on earth would she care if he had a fling with one of the Sky Mothers? Though she had to wonder how he managed to get one of them into bed after only a few hours.

"My lips are sealed," he told them, pouring an enormous ration of sugar into his coffee.

"Oh, come on," Helena teased. "Just give us a name. How can I concoct a story in my head without a face to go with it?"

"No way, no how," Oliver said. "Plus, I don't even know what you're talking about. I had a perfectly amiable conversation with one of the ladies last night and there's nothing more to tell."

"Who on earth was doing all the moaning last night? Good grief, I thought a monkey was in labor in the forest," Julian complained, walking into the kitchen and heading for the last of the coffee.

Oliver turned red and Sebastian guffawed.

"An amiable conversation, huh?"

"Thanks, Julian," Oliver grumbled.

"What?" he asked. "It wasn't a monkey?"

Abby saw the gleam in Julian's eye.

"Matilda said breakfast in the big house at nine."

"Thank the Goddess, I'm starving," Oliver quipped.

"I bet you are," Helena teased.

****

They ate breakfast in the wind tunnel. The long hallway that opened on the garden at one end and the ocean on the other. A constant soft, salty breeze rushed through the space.

Once settled on the chairs and couches, the wind seemed to rush above them, but they were shielded from the sensation.

"Wheatgrass, goat's milk smoothies, and poached eggs," Matilda announced.

Two other Sky Mothers brought trays of food, setting them on the glass tables and departing without introductions.

"Is anyone else joining us?" Oliver asked, looking around expectantly.

"No." Matilda smiled warmly. "It is Sunday. Our Coven's day of prayer, meditation, and fasting. I am merely here to bid you good morning and then I too must excuse myself. We'll see you tonight for a bonfire."

****

In the healing room, Adora slept fitfully. Bridget had given her a sleep aid and treated her wounds. A shimmering sheet, enchanted with healing light, lay draped over Adora's emaciated form. Elda and Lydie helped Bridget crush herbs and seeds and prepare poultices.

Faustine stood close to Adora, trying to intercept some of her passing dreams.

He touched his temple gingerly and shook his head.

"Her mind is very jumbled. It hurts my head trying to sort through her thoughts."

He stood and looked down at her for another moment before breaking away.

"Bridget, let me know when she wakes up. I'm going to the tower to send a message to Julian." He left abruptly.

Lydie watched him leave and wondered if he was angry that she had not sought help before going to Adora.

"Such a shame," Bridget murmured, walking to the bed and slightly parting Adora's lips. Using a dropper, she placed a tiny amount of a dark liquid inside her mouth.

"What are you giving her?" Lydie asked.

"Bit of birthroot to help with bleeding on the inside," Bridget told her.

"Thank the Goddess you found her," Elda said, handing Bridget an amber glass spray bottle.

"I heard her crying," Lydie admitted. "It woke me up."

"Apparently we need to modify our spells. When a person or witch triggers the protective spells around Ula, Faustine should receive an energetic message, but he felt nothing until you reached out to him, Lydie."

"Will she die?" Lydie asked, not sure if she wanted to hear the answer.

"Not if I have anything to say about it," Bridget assured her.

"How on earth did she escape?" Elda asked, thinking out loud.

****

That evening, Matilda built a great bonfire on the beach. Five Sky Mothers joined them in total. Matilda, Binda, Kit, Grace, and Jesse.

Abby sat on a cloud of air wrapped in a silk liner. The chair bobbed and undulated beneath her, seeming in rhythm with the movement of the ocean.

Sebastian kissed her head as she watched the dancing flames. The fire shifted and twirled with the conversation. When one of the witches' voices rose, the flames leaped higher and brighter. When the conversation lulled, the flames turned to embers.

Oliver walked to the water's edge.

"It's glowing," he called out.

"Plankton, luminescence," the witch, Kit responded.

She had black dreadlocked hair tied back with a piece of twine. Her mocha skin was freckled and glowed pale in the light of the moon. She wore piercings in her nose, eyebrow, and lip. Unlike the other Sky Mothers, she did not wear a simple white robe. She dressed in dark linen pants and a snug black tank top that showed strange markings, like henna tattoos up and down her arms.

"Kit, those symbols on your arms are beautiful, what are they?" Helena asked, leaning forward for a better look.

"They are part of my aboriginal ancestry. My grandfather was a medicine man. My initiation into the medicine lineage included a branding of sorts."

Helena grimaced.

"That sounds painful," Sebastian said.

"It was," Kit admitted. "Especially at fourteen, but I'd spent my whole life preparing. The pain was a gift, in a sense. Until that point, there was so much value placed on the initiation, without the pain and the markings, I'd wake up the following morning no different than the day before. With these," Kit held up her arms. "I was changed. There is fire in my blood, there is a memory of great pain and an even sweeter memory of surviving. I felt like a warrior when I woke up."

Julian smiled and nodded as if agreeing.

"I believe that's important and perhaps missing for many people."

Kit looked at him.

"Not everyone is meant to be a warrior," she said simply. "Though I see that you are, despite the marks that you do not have. I think your scars are on the inside. And yours as well," she tilted her head toward Sebastian.

He stared back at her.

"Yeah, but I didn't feel like a warrior when I got them."

"Well, that is an experience of a fourteen-year-old girl. It was vanity. I hadn't become a warrior yet, I just looked a bit more the part. My true scars came later as well. Most of them are visible only to me."

Abby felt a rolling sensation in her womb. She pressed a hand on her stomach and smiled.

"Is she talking to you?" Grace asked, tilting her head toward Abby's belly.

"Dancing, I think," Abby told her.

"Pregnancy is so beautiful," Grace murmured dreamily. "It is one of our greatest acts of service - to usher a child into the world. Helena says that she is your midwife?"

"Yes," Abby smiled at Helena. "We're lucky to have her."

"And she, you," Grace agreed. "I delivered twin brothers only last week. Such a miracle with their shining blue eyes and tufts of blond fuzzy hair. It was hard not to take them home."

"Perhaps too much energy has already been spent reminiscing about that birth," Binda told her sharply.

Grace looked as if she intended to say more, but closed her lips and looked sadly toward the lapping waves.

Matilda rested a hand on Grace's arm, comforting her.

Abby got the sense that Grace had more than a service-driven love for babies.

Kit stood and gathered several more logs. She arranged them carefully on the fire. Abby saw the flames lick her hands, but she seemed unaware.

Oliver watched her from the shore and Abby realized that Kit must have been the witch in his yurt the night before.

Kit gave him little notice. She glanced his way and then settled back into her chair, watching the flames intently.

Abby thought about Ezra back in Chicago, another fierce witch that Oliver seemed drawn to. She wondered what part of him had been attracted to her. She could not have been more different than Ezra and Kit.

"Want to go for a swim?" Sebastian asked, his face glowing in the firelight.

Abby looked toward the water. She could see the shimmering green luminescence as it washed over the beach.

"Race ya," she told him and catapulted out of her chair.

She stripped off her dress as she ran, still wearing her swimsuit from earlier in the day.

"Cheater," Sebastian yelled, but he quickly caught up with her. In her witch body, she should have been able to outrun any human, but more and more Sebastian seemed to be gaining similar abilities.

They dashed into the ocean. A million flecks of glowing green and blue water splashed around them. Sebastian dove first and Abby watched his beautiful body, naked except for boxer shorts, slice through the glowing water. She dove behind him. They swam hard and fast into the ocean. They both came up for air and treaded water far off the shore.

"Look at that sky," Sebastian said, tilting his head back.

Abby looked up.

She had never seen so many stars. Even at Ula, perched on an isolated cliff in the vastness of Lake Superior, the stars could not compare to the scene above them. Abby felt like a drop in an ocean of sky. She and Sebastian were just tiny stars embedded in a vacuum of sparkling space.

She felt Sebastian's leg brush against hers and a shiver ran along her spine. *He is mine*, she thought and felt giddy at the notion. A year ago, Abby would not have fathomed the trajectory of her life. She would have admired a man like Sebastian from afar with his shaggy curls and his intense blue eyes. She would have wondered what it would be like to kiss his full lips, to look into those mysterious eyes, to stay up late talking about their dreams.

"And now I know," she told him, wrapping her arms and legs around him in the water.

"You know what?" Sebastian asked, kicking his legs and running his hand along her slick back.

"You," she said, kissing him and pushing back with a rush into the water. She dove deep and swam into the glittering luminescence.

She had gone swimming in the ocean twice in her life and both times she had been overwhelmed by the sense of infinite mystery that surrounded her. She remembered each experience with the kind of clarity that punctuates major catastrophes or intense moments of joy. She remembered wading into the water with Sydney. She was seven. The waves swept onto the shore in a constant barrage of frothy power. Sydney held her hand the whole time. She promised not to let go as the waves pushed them back and the undertow tugged at their feet.

The second time she had gone with Nick, a decidedly different experience. Nick hated salt on his lips and the stiffness in his hair after an ocean swim. He went in the water one time, up to his waist, for two minutes. Afterward, he rinsed in the public shower, slathered with sunscreen, and read from an enormous law text. Abby swam alone. For hours she ran in and out of the surf. Thinking back, she wondered if that had been the day the seed of doubt about her and Nick took root. How did he see the ocean with such small eyes?

Abby burst through the surface. She saw Sebastian in the distance floating on his back, staring at the sky. She wondered if he thought about his own memories of the ocean. Had he gone swimming in the sea with his parents and Claire? Were his memories buried in grief?

She dove beneath the water and swam to him slowly. The abyss spread out beneath her, and beyond the moonlight and effervescent plankton, an infinite darkness awaited.

CHAPTER 4

No sooner had Oliver closed his eyes than the dream assailed him. He stood again at the edge of the snowy forest behind Abby's house. Paralyzed, he watched as Dafne lifted the dragon blade and thrust it into her body. The dark red of her blood saturated the snow quickly. She reached for him, but his feet denied his demands to run to her.

He woke in the cliff-top yurt. His breath struggled to get out as if someone had clamped a hand around his throat. He fought the pressure away.

"Hey," a groggy voice murmured beside him. "You're thrashing like a stuck fish over there."

Kit.

He reached out his hand and brushed her arm, felt the curve of her naked hip. Settling back against the pillows, he took a long, deep breath and let it out in a rush. The vision of Dafne dying came to him night after night. He hadn't told anyone. Each night, after the dream ended, he wanted it gone from his thoughts. By the light of day, he usually succeeded.

Kit shifted beside him and he felt her hand in the darkness slide over his stomach and between his legs. He moaned and rolled toward her, pulling her against him.

It had been more than a year since Oliver had taken a lover. The appearance of Abby and Sebastian had changed the routines at Ula and the desires of his body had fallen to the back of his thoughts. In the past, Oliver left Ula every few months to seek out a physical connection. Sometimes he went to a bar on the mainland. That was easy. Other times, he wanted more challenge so he opted for chance encounters at a library or grocery store. He could be anyone during those excursions and so could they.

Lately, though, he wanted a witch. The random women were never meant to be more. Observing Abby and Sebastian had caused a longing in Oliver that he had not expected. If he was flat-out honest, he wanted Abby, but she loved Sebastian-end of story. Beyond wanting Abby, he wanted a union that traveled beyond a motel room and a night of sex. He wanted a companion. Perhaps Dafne's death had more to do with that than he cared to admit. Though he and Dafne had never been intimate, there had been a bond between them. She was his teacher, his friend, and often his confidante. Not that she ever confided anything to him. She rarely spoke of anything personal, but she listened as he rambled about the family he missed, his brother in particular.

When he met Kit the first day at Sky Mothers, he felt an immediate chemistry. Kit also made it clear that she preferred casual and discreet, two aspects that Oliver generally preferred as well. But the dreams of Dafne left him feeling empty and alone. He wanted someone to fill the void. Perhaps then the nightmares would stop.

Kit climbed on top of him. She kissed him hungrily. Her mouth moved from his lips to his neck, and he pulled and pushed against her slick, naked body. She was not delicate and soft. Her muscles were taut and close to the surface. She did not make love so much as ravage and use him. He liked it. It allowed him to do the same. Lost in the sensations of her body, Oliver forgot about his dream.

After Kit returned to sleep, Oliver left the yurt and walked the edge of the cliff. The water churned below and he climbed down, savoring the energy boost of the huge rock wall in front of him.

****

Sebastian stepped into the forest, following the sound of rushing water. He had noticed it the night before when he crept out of the yurt to relieve himself. Abby had joined Matilda and Grace to talk about secret women things. He didn't mind. Sebastian thrived on alone time. He and Abby both needed their quiet spaces to reflect on the ever-changing world around them.

The forest smelled fragrant and damp. He examined eucalyptus trees and watched for exotic birds. Underfoot, a floor of ferns and tiny brightly colored flowers spread beneath his feet.

As he walked, the water sound grew louder until it filled his head. The trees opened to reveal a dark lagoon. The water shimmered and reflected the morning sun, and gray rocks filled the pool and lined the edges. A powerful surge of water crashed from the cliff overhead. It dropped in a crystalline sheath and sent a frothy spray into the hot, dry air.

Without a thought, Sebastian stripped off his shirt and shorts and waded into the pool. He sucked in a breath at the icy water. Gooseflesh tightened his skin, and he sighed, long and deep. It was an ecstasy of sorts, immersing the body in frigid water as the hot air buzzed around him. He went under and surveyed the depths of the shadowy blue lagoon. Points of light streaked into the pool and cast the rocks beneath the surface in glittering silver.

Breaking the surface, he felt the cold drain from his face and shoulders. He went under again. In and out of the water he dove, and then flung himself back into the dazzling sunlight and warmth. His mind emptied as he moved. The only thing that existed was the sensation in his body, flooding every cell. When he finally ended his game, he climbed onto one of the hot gray rocks and lay back, feeling the rivulets of water snake down his cool skin.

"Fierce, isn't it?"

The voice startled him and Sebastian sat up, instantly aware of his nakedness.

A woman sat on the rock just beside him. She had not been there when he emerged, but had he really been paying attention?

Wavy sandy blonde hair fell from the loose bun piled on her head and framed her face. She smiled at him, big and open, and her gray-blue eyes smiled too. She wore a simple white robe, Sky Mothers attire, but it was short with a braided hemp rope wrapped around her waist.

"I'm Hannah," she told him.

Sebastian discreetly placed a hand over his groin. She watched him, amused.

"Umm, do you mind?" he asked, gesturing for her to turn around.

She smiled wider.

"Of course not." She turned, and Sebastian scrambled off the rock and shuffled into his shorts, feeling the blood rising into his face. He wanted to splash cold water on his skin and hide his blush, but she'd already turned back to him.

"It's just a body, a nice one too."

"Thanks," he said, awkwardly. "You're a Sky Mother then?"

"I am that," she nodded. "And so much more, and nothing at all."

He cocked an eyebrow and she winked at him.

She stood and allowed her robe to drop to the rock. He stared at her naked body. Curves and small perky breasts and golden thighs filled his vision before she turned and expertly dove into the lagoon. As she broke through the surface, the reverie vanished and Sebastian looked toward the woods, nervously. He expected to see Abby standing behind him, a mask of fury and hurt etched into her face, but no. Only the forest returned his gaze. He glanced back at the pond, at the ripples still fanning across the surface where Hannah dove in. Before she emerged, he walked into the woods, heading back to the Sky Mothers compound, trying to shake off his guilty feelings.

****

Sebastian found Abby at the eternity pool with Matilda. He paused at the glass doors and watched her.

She sat perched on the edge of the pool, facing the ocean. Her long golden-brown curls fell down her bare back. He studied the curve of her face, her small pouty lips in profile, and her little perfectly formed ear. He had kissed her ears, her neck, her lips. How many times already in the few short months that he had known her, had he gotten lost in the curve of her neck and the soft hollow of her throat? Watching her, all guilt at having seen Hannah vanished. With Abby, nothing and no one else existed.

He pushed the door open and she turned, seeing him.

"Hey there, handsome."

He kneeled beside her and kissed her shoulder, and then her lips.

"Has it been enlightening?" he asked, referring to her time with Matilda.

She nodded and returned her gaze to the ocean.

"Very. They performed a blessing on the baby and gave me a whole bag of herbs and oils to help with the pregnancy. Matilda also taught me how to create bubbles that carry things. She's a water witch too. Here, watch."

Abby stood and closed her eyes. Whispering beneath her breath, she drew water from the pool and formed a bubble the size of a beach ball. She opened her eyes, concentrating on the bubble, and slipped her sunglasses from her head.

"Water, wind, strong as glass

Help this bubble travel fast.

Deliver these glasses straight and true

To Julian who waits for you.

Blessed be."

The bubble sailed off toward the compound.

Sebastian laughed.

"That's awesome. We never have to trudge through snow to get the newspaper again!"

"We don't get a paper," she teased him.

"But now we can."

She laughed and pretended to push him into the pool.

"You're already wet," she said, touching his hair.

"I found a beautiful waterfall back in the woods," he told her, feeling the admission about meeting Hannah on his lips.

"Abby, we found that cookbook," Grace called, walking toward the pool.

Sebastian let the information die on his lips.

****

The Sky Mothers cooked together. Nearly every meal was prepared communally, and they invited their guests to join them in an enormous open-air kitchen where they prepared quinoa, roasted vegetables, platters of fried plantains, fresh fish caught from the ocean, and heaps of fresh fruit. Sebastian joined with fervor.

"To ensure that dinner is edible, I'm going to stick with cutting up pineapple. Care to join me?" Oliver asked Abby.

Abby laughed and nodded.

"Yes, my talents don't extend to the kitchen, and honestly, I'm so engrossed by the process that it's hard not to just sit and watch."

"Well, I'll hold the knife then so you don't lose any appendages."

A beautiful young witch stood at a butcher block carefully scaling fish. Her wavy golden hair was tied on top of her head and partially covered with a white lace scarf. She wore a white robe that flowed over her shapely body and cascaded to the floor. Abby noticed her because she seemed to be sneaking glances at Sebastian at every opportunity.

"Who's that?" Abby asked, nudging Oliver and inclining her head toward the woman.

Oliver glanced at her and shook his head.

"Not a clue, but she's gorgeous."

"Yes, she is."

The woman waved her fingers and the scales swept up and into a trash bin. She picked up another hunk of fish and again her eyes darted toward Sebastian who worked silently, focused on the enormous bowl of black bean hummus that he was making from scratch.

Helena and Julian helped Kit fry plantains and Helena laughed gleefully every time Kit blew the tips of her fingers like they were a smoking gun.

Matilda created a row of floating dishes that she walked from the kitchen toward the outdoor dining table.

The witch watching Sebastian stepped closer to him, and peered into his bowl.

"I didn't catch your name earlier. Sebastian, is it?"

Abby saw a flush turn Sebastian's neck crimson. Her own body tensed and she felt a wave of jealousy. A huge aquarium holding the day's fish exploded. Water and glass spurted in every direction. Both Matilda and Julian threw their arms up and the water and glass froze in mid-air. Together they directed the shards toward a series of wastebaskets.

The witches stopped what they were cooking and several gasped or cried out.

"Ouch," Helena murmured, touching her shoulder where a piece of glass had embedded in her skin.

Kit plucked the glass from her shoulder and pinched the skin together. It singed and closed at her touch.

"Not a drop of blood spilled," she said triumphantly.

"Is that a new kind of magic? Exploding aquariums?" Julian asked, smiling, but looking concerned at Matilda.

"Obviously not," she turned and gazed among the witches. Her eyes rested briefly on Abby, but she said nothing.

Abby also felt Oliver's eyes, though he did not look at her directly. Sebastian left his post and hurried over to her.

"It didn't hit you, did it?" he asked, scanning her body for abrasions.

"No, I'm fine," she promised, avoiding his eyes.

She did not want to admit that her emotions had caused the explosion.

Over Sebastian's shoulder, Abby saw the beautiful witch watching them. She smiled and turned back to the table.

****

They ate dinner at a long wooden table next to the waterfall that they first encountered when they arrived at the Sky Mother's Coven. The table could sit at least fifty people. An arch of twinkling white lights, braided with bright red flowers hung over the table and created a fairy-like atmosphere that put Abby in a practical dream state. Or a would-be dream state if not for the witch across from Sebastian who took every opportunity to catch his eye.

Matilda had introduced them before dinner. Her name was Hannah and she clearly had taken a liking to Abby's future husband.

"This is delicious," Hannah told Sebastian, scooping hummus onto a piece of freshly baked sourdough bread.

"Thanks," he told her and then directed his attention to Abby.

"How are you feeling, babe?" he asked, lifting her hand to his lips. He kissed her knuckles.

Abby glanced at Hannah across the table. She watched them, smiling. Her expression revealed little, but something in her eyes made Abby uncomfortable.

"Good, great. I feel like we're in a wonderland." She gestured to the twinkling lights suspended just above them.

"We should do something like this for our wedding. What do you think Helena? Could we recreate this at Ula?" Sebastian called down the table and Abby noticed that Hannah's smile faltered, just a little.

"You're engaged to be married?" she asked Abby.

"Yes," Abby told her, studying her face and trying to get a sense of her intentions.

"And having a baby," Sebastian added.

Abby knew that he too sensed Hannah's interest and obviously intended to deter her, but something about his eagerness bothered her.

"What is this arch made from?" Helena asked Matilda, studying the canopy of lights and flowers above them. They seemed to be embedded in a gauzy white fabric, so thin, they could see the stars.

"Spiderwebs. Look." Matilda pointed and all of the witches craned upward.

Abby did not exactly see the spiders, but a subtle shifting in the fabric itself. As if the fabric got the chills and shuddered.

"I saw them at the All Hallow's Ball," she murmured.

"A journey they didn't appreciate," Kit told her. "We had to send them first class by air. The mirrors are too dangerous for such delicate creatures." She lifted her hand to the fabric and a line of spiders scurried down her arm.

Oliver recoiled.

"Sorry, it's not personal, guys," he told the spiders. "But my skin crawls just looking at you."

Kit smiled and cocked an eyebrow.

"Do you know that the silk in a spider's web is five times stronger than a strand of steel that is the same thickness? Spiders are magic in nature. These are all female. There are males, of course, but they don't colonize with our beautiful ladies. They just come in to grab a scrap of food now and then."

"Do you feed them?" Helena asked.

She watched the spiders with a curiosity that, like Oliver, held an edge of discomfort.

Kit laughed.

"Spiders are one of the most adept species on the planet. They've survived well over three hundred million years. What would they become if I fed them? Slovenly, disinterested, eventually extinct. What is wild is meant to be wild, take the creature out of the forest and he is no longer a creature."

"You've managed quite well," Hannah quipped.

Kit narrowed her eyes at Hannah but smiled, coolly.

"This papaya is amazing," Julian interrupted, cutting the tension that had begun to rise.

"Plucked direct from our own trees," Matilda told him warmly. She glanced at Hannah and her eyes looked stormy.

*****

"He can do it!"

Abby paused. The angry sounding voice had come from behind a closed door.

"Hannah, you can't possibly know that. Don't you wonder if you're projecting Liam onto this stranger, vainly hoping to-"

"No," Hannah hissed.

Abby spun away and slipped behind a huge potted tree just as the door flew open and Hannah stormed out.

Kit followed, but turned and walked toward the ocean rather than chasing Hannah.

Abby waited another minute and then crept back into the large hall. The marble floors were cold beneath her feet, but a warm breeze seemed to always flow through the open windows and doorways. She shivered and stared in the direction that Hannah had retreated.

They were talking about Sebastian, she knew, but why? And who was Liam?

CHAPTER 5

"The day they took me," Adora started and then abruptly stopped. She took another sip of the tea that Bridget had prepared. "I was watching the well from a tree. It started to snow. I could barely see, and then I had a horrible sense they had found Abby in the car. I moved through the trees, and saw her, Abby. She was walking blindly through the snow. I could feel the heat just pouring off her. She began to get sick and then sat down in the snow. I started to go to her when Tobias walked out of the trees. Abby saw him, but her eyes were glassy and vacant like she was dreaming. He held a glass bottle in his hand and he handed it to her, whispering in her ear. I couldn't hear what he said. I jumped from the tree onto his back. I might have had him, but he wasn't alone. Another Vepar attacked me from behind. I remember them dragging me through the snow and my whole body had gone numb. I lost consciousness. When I woke again, I was in a lair. I felt the weight of the earth all around me. I had no power. I don't know how they stifled it, but I couldn't astral travel, I couldn't summon my element. I grew weaker. They were biting me to keep me unconscious, but it was more than that. I had memories of being in my body, memories not from my life. Somehow, they were stealing my body. Does that make sense?"

"Unfortunately, yes," Faustine admitted. "Continue and then we will fill you in on all that we know."

"I had memories of running through the woods. I remembered standing on a cliff and watching Lake Superior below me. There were all these black creatures flying in the sky."

"Skin-walkers," Elda whispered.

"The memories were brief, snippets really, but I had the sense that each time they used my body, I became weaker. I couldn't walk, could barely lift my head at one point. I think they expected me to die. The memories stopped and I started to regain a bit of strength. Barely, enough to sit up, and then eventually to stand up. One night, I woke in my cell and my head was clear. It was the first time since I'd been taken that I couldn't feel their venom inside of me. I knew that I had to escape, it was my only chance. I started to draw on my power. It felt like ages before something broke through their barriers. I managed to draw a few shards of rock together and pop the lock. I got out of the room. It was a typical lair, a mind-numbing series of dark tunnels. I felt like I ran through them for hours before I finally smelled fresh air. I raced toward it and emerged on a cliff. I ran into the woods, but I was so weak. I gained as much distance as possible and then I found a little cave that I could fit inside. I crawled in and slept. I recognized Lake Superior. I knew if I could just find the strength to get to the island, to Ula, but I couldn't. I spent weeks in that cave trying to gain enough strength to come here, but I didn't seem to be healing. She touched the red welts on her head. Whatever they'd done to me, my air element seemed almost cut off, like I didn't have access to my power."

****

Matilda led Julian into the greenhouse to collect seeds. They grew a strain of plant that Kit had discovered and named he Peace Keeper. Seeds from the plant, when crushed, released an intoxicating aroma that rendered everyone who breathed it languid and blissful.

"I am sensing a strange energy from your witch Hannah directed at Sebastian," Julian told her.

Matilda stopped at a large bushy plant whose dark glossy leaves cascaded over its pot.

"I tried to create an errand for Hannah during your visit," Matilda confessed. "After Binda told me that Sebastian was a hybrid, I asked Hannah to travel to Sydney to retrieve some elixirs that a friend of mine makes, but she resisted. I believe she sensed the power in Sebastian and wanted a chance to know for sure."

"Why is she so interested in hybrids?"

"We have a secret place here," Matilda started and then paused, as if reluctant to explain. "We call it the dream wood,"

"The dream wood?"

"Hannah fell in love with a man, Liam, who disappeared into the dream wood. A hybrid man."

"I'm not following."

"The dream wood is a strange bit of magic. Witches cannot go there, though it was created by one of the original witches who founded the Sky Mothers. Her child was a hybrid and being hunted. She bewitched a portion of the forest to allow only his kind to enter. Liam stumbled upon it accidentally. Of course, we both know that it was not truly an accident. Did it call to him? Perhaps. He told Hannah of the things he saw and felt. In the dream wood, Liam could see into the past and the future, he could touch the trees and watch them become gold beneath his fingertips."

Julian frowned.

"I still don't understand."

"Nor do I, but it is believed that the hybrid child of the witch who enchanted the forest, spent his years in isolation there honing and playing with his magic. He created a sort of wonderland that is accessible only to those who share his cellular structure."

"Have you known other hybrids who entered the space?"

"One, a young man. His name was Fin and he went into the dream wood more than fifty years ago. He never came back out."

"Is that what happened to Liam, then? He disappeared?"

Matilda nodded and pulled her shimmering blond hair over one delicate shoulder. She had a fairy-like ethereal appearance. In her presence, Julian often felt light-headed and romantic. He knew it was one of Matilda's powers and not something she emitted intentionally.

"Liam went back several times. He grew addicted to the experiences in the dream wood. I told Hannah to warn him of the dangers, and she did, I'm sure, but she is impulsive. I fear that she too grew obsessed with his stories and perhaps with the possibilities. To see the future is a rare gift and it is easy to become entranced by it."

"But then he never came out," Julian mused, frowning. "What then? She hopes to send Sebastian to the dream wood to search for Liam? Impossible! Sebastian has too much at stake. Absolutely not."

"I agree with you, of course. However, I cannot prevent Sebastian from going into the dream wood any more than you can if he were to choose that."

"He wouldn't. Abby wouldn't allow it and honestly, I would prefer that he never heard of the dream wood at all."

"I fear it may be too late for that."

****

"Are you sure she came this way?" Sebastian asked, sensing that the witch leading him into the forest had an ulterior motive, but lost for what it might be. Why would she lure him into the woods?

He stopped and glanced back at the Sky Mothers' compound.

Hannah turned and smiled. Her golden hair hung loosely over her bare shoulders. She wore a sheer white dress with tiny straps made from pearls.

Sebastian swallowed. Hannah was beautiful and eager. He felt desire when he looked at her, followed immediately by guilt. He didn't want to be attracted to her, but he couldn't help it.

"Come on, not much farther."

She held out her hand and he nodded, but did not touch her. He wondered if she used some form of magic to enhance his desire. He thought touching her might increase the effects and he had no interest in going there.

As they walked, the canopy from the huge trees grew thick and no light penetrated. The forest looked as if it had never been logged. It would take three of him standing fingertip to fingertip to wrap his arms around one of their massive trunks.

Another ten minutes passed, and then twenty. Abby would not have walked alone so far into unknown woods. They had been walking on an incline for a long time. He could see the forest sloping down and back toward the ocean.

Hannah stopped and turned toward him.

"Okay, I lied," she admitted. She stared at him with huge inquisitive eyes. Her gaze shifted along his body and she stepped closer to him, trailing her fingertips over his bare arm. "You're not sweating at all."

Sebastian brushed away her hand and turned back.

"Wait," she said. Her voice had changed subtly. He heard fear and desperation.

"What? Why have you brought me here?"

"Do you see that footbridge?"

Sebastian gazed in the direction that Hannah pointed. Through the trees, he spotted a tattered footbridge that appeared to extend across a gorge.

"Yeah, so?"

"I need you to cross it."

"Is this like a test of some sort? See if the human is stupid enough to fall to his death on a fraying rope bridge?"

"You know better than that, Sebastian." She moved toward him and took his hands. "I can't go beyond that bridge, but you can. It was created for someone just like you, a hybrid. It's a magical place, more amazing than anything you've seen in this world. You can do things there, see things, know things, fly if you want, change forms. The possibilities are limitless. You will be limitless."

Her eyes sparkled as she spoke and Sebastian knew that she believed every word she told him.

"Why can't you cross the bridge?"

"A witch created that forest for her son, for her hybrid son. He was in danger. She bewitched the space so that no witch or human could enter, only a hybrid. And that bridge," she nodded toward the fraying walkway, "is merely an illusion. There's a bridge, of course, but it is so strong it could be made from steel. It's a deterrent, you see."

"What happens if you try to cross it?"

"I just can't. My body stops. It's like I am paralyzed. I can turn and walk away, but I can never go forward."

"What is it that you want?"

Hannah bit her lip.

"A year ago, the man I loved went in there and never came out."

Sebastian stared at the bridge and the forest beyond. He searched for any clue that something extraordinary lay on the other side, but he saw only more forest identical to that which they had just walked through.

"Why did you bring me out here alone? Why didn't you just ask me in the open?"

"Because Matilda preferred to keep you away from this forest. It is unknown to us as witches. She cannot protect you once you cross that bridge, but I see you differently, Sebastian. I don't believe that you need protection."

****

"Have you seen Sebastian?" Abby asked and grimaced at the words. The question and the niggling feeling behind it reminded her too much of the previous October when Sebastian disappeared from the All Hallow's Ball.

Oliver looked up from where he stood hunched over an ancient looking text filled with tiny, cramped writing. He squinted at Abby and then shook his head.

"He hasn't come this way, though who would unless they were into mental strain and torture."

Abby laughed and glanced around the small library. It was very different from the space at Ula with its soaring ceilings and roaring fireplace. The Sky Mothers' library occupied a narrow alcove. A pair of wooden chairs sat in the center of the space and shelves with old, crumbling books pressed in.

"This is their library?" Abby murmured, touching one of the books and looking at the streak of white dust on her fingertips.

"No, it's their archives and antique books. They don't have a library. Matilda told me that they spread the books all over and when you stumble upon a book, that's the one you're meant to read."

"What if they need a potion for poison ivy?"

Oliver grinned.

"I asked the same question, substitute poison ivy with bed bugs."

Abby laughed.

"And?"

"And she said, 'only witches live here,' and walked away."

"What does that mean? No bed bugs for witches?" Abby scratched absently at her arm.

"I think she meant witches can find what they're looking for without having it organized in a library."

Abby rolled her eyes.

"Not this witch, I just spent ten minutes looking for my sandals."

She pointed to her bare feet.

Oliver laughed and shook his head. "They're by the pool."

Abby's eyes widened in surprise.

"How do you know? Did you just see that in your mind?"

"No, I walked by them twice this morning."

They both burst into laughter and for an instant, Abby forgot her sense of misgiving. She returned to her questions.

"You haven't seen him? Didn't hear Julian say they were taking a walk, anything like that?"

"No, are you worried? This place is huge. He probably just took a stroll to check things out. Do you sense something?"

Oliver looked at Abby intently and she knew that he too searched for an energetic rift, some proof that Sebastian was in trouble.

"Yeah," he nodded. "Something is off. I'm not feeling danger, but…"

"Me too," she agreed, relieved that she hadn't imagined it, but more concerned to have her fears confirmed.

"Let's go find Julian and Helena."

****

Sebastian gingerly placed a foot on the bridge, ready to spring back if it collapsed. The bridge held firm, more than firm, it did not sway as he placed his weight on it. The boards that looked rotted did not sink beneath his feet and the frayed rope did not suddenly spiral apart. He walked easily across the bridge. As he stepped into the forest, the world before him shifted. The forest flickered and a strange series of other worlds slid into place and then vanished, to be replaced by another and another. He saw soaring snow-capped mountains and dense jungle forests. He closed his eyes and when he opened them he stared at futuristic world suspended in the stars.

"Pick one," a voice said, startling him in the stillness. He followed the voice and staggered back when he discovered Claire, his baby sister, grinning from the high branch of a tree. She wore white shorts and a yellow t-shirt. Her brown hair stuck up like she'd just climbed out of bed.

He blinked and rubbed his eyes, afraid that when he opened them, she would be gone, but no, she watched him still. She swung her legs back and forth.

"Pick one, silly," she said again. "Which world do you want to explore?"

He looked straight ahead and again the worlds flashed by. He lifted a trembling hand.

"That one," he said, finding it hard to speak.

He had simply chosen, not looking all that closely at the changing landscapes.

A mystical forest materialized. Mossy boughs hung from the trees and a glittering mist shone in the sunlight slanting through the branches. In the distance, he could see huge limestone buildings in various stages of decay. Wide stone steps, some of them crumbling, led to an enormous archway. It looked like an ancient city in Greece hundreds of years after it had been abandoned.

"Shall we?" Claire asked him, leaping from the tree and holding out her hand.

****

Julian did not look surprised when Abby and Oliver burst into the greenhouse. Instead, he looked angry and shot Matilda a venomous glare. Matilda held his gaze, but Abby noticed that she too seemed to be expecting them.

"What's going on?" Abby asked.

"Apparently, Hannah lured Sebastian into the woods."

Abby scowled, looking back and forth between the two witches.

"What does that mean?" she snapped.

"Lured? Is she trying to seduce him?" Oliver cocked an eyebrow.

"No, she is not trying to seduce him," Matilda explained. "There is a place not far from here, it is called the dream wood. Only hybrids can enter. Hannah wants Sebastian to go in there because…"

"Liam," Abby interrupted her. "She wanted him to find Liam."

"How do you know about Liam?" Matilda asked, surprised.

"Who's Liam?" Oliver asked.

"He's Hannah's lover and he was a hybrid. He went into the forest a year ago and never returned," Julian answered.

Abby closed her eyes and didn't breathe, just for a moment, just long enough for the panic to subside.

"Is there something dangerous in the dream wood?" Abby whispered.

"We don't know," Matilda admitted, not looking Abby in the eye. "A witch cannot enter the dream wood, only a hybrid. There is no way for us to know what happened to him."

"Maybe he just walked through and out the other side, caught a ride going south," Oliver remarked. "This isn't exactly a coven for men, right? Where did he live?"

"Who cares?" Abby shouted. "Where is the dream wood? Maybe we can stop them."

"I will go," Matilda said. "I can go fast, it's not safe for you to run at such high speeds Abby."

"Me too," Oliver added.

"Yes, and I will also go," Julian concluded. "Abby, Helena is with Grace in the garden. Go to them. We will return the moment we have found them."

Abby shook her head.

"Not a chance. I've played helpless victim before. I can't go as fast, but I can still go. Tell me where I'm going."

Matilda explained quickly and then she, Oliver, and Julian sprinted into the woods. They disappeared from her sight within seconds.

The walk would have been beautiful if Abby didn't feel ready to strangle Hannah. She had sensed Hannah's interest in Sebastian-watched it with her own eyes, but had done nothing. She should have refused to let Sebastian out of her sight. Anger at Hannah felt better than the fear of losing Sebastian again. That thought, she did not entertain. He would be fine.

CHAPTER 6

"Are you real?" Sebastian asked Claire as they walked, side-by-side, through the sparkling ferns and trees.

She looked real, but he had not touched her. He merely watched her from the corner of his eye. He saw the tiny mole next to her left eye. He noticed how she sucked on a bit of her straight brown hair if it brushed her mouth. Everything about her seemed real, but of course Claire had been dead for over two years.

Claire cast her big blue eyes on him and smiled.

"Do you remember Rumi?" Claire asked.

"Of course," Sebastian said.

Rumi was a thirteenth-century Sufi mystic who wrote about the divine. Their father used to read his translated poetry to their mother each night before bed.

"Rumi said, 'This place is a dream, only a sleeper considers it real. Then death comes like dawn, and you wake up laughing at what you thought was your grief.'"

Sebastian considered her quote. He did not remember their father ever reading that one. Did that make her real? That she had knowledge she did not possess during her lifetime?

"What is this place?" Sebastian asked. "A dream, then?"

"It's all a dream, Sebastian. Our life with mommy and daddy. Your life now with Abby-she's lovely, by the way. I too wish that I could hold Vidya when she is born. Maybe she'll be a hybrid and you can bring her here."

Sebastian stopped.

"Vidya?"

"That will be her name, but don't worry, Abby will come to it on her own."

Sebastian wanted to ask Claire a thousand questions, but he couldn't seem to do it. He feared that any moment she might vanish into thin air. He stared ahead at wide, limestone-covered steps, leading into one of the ancient structures. The first building loomed before them, a beautiful old church with a face of stained glass.

"What is this place?"

"What is not important, brother. This place is an experience of another world. If you keep analyzing it, you will never arrive. Let's look inside."

They walked under a shadowy archway and into a vaulted room filled with splintered pews. Marble statues of saints lined the walls.

Claire kneeled on the floor and pressed her forehead to the stone. Sebastian watched her, curious.

He rubbed a hand across his brow and sighed.

"I can't stay for long. Abby doesn't know I came at all."

"Sshhh...."

As Claire bowed on the floor, Sebastian walked to another archway that led out of the room. He followed a stone walkway that narrowed and moved higher. The floor next to the walkway fell away and soon he looked down on a river that flowed through the building.

"I miss swimming," Claire said, startling him.

"You can't swim anymore?" he asked.

"It's different," she admitted. "Sometimes it is like everything is swimming, but here, it's not safe to swim."

"Not safe?" he asked, but she'd already continued along the stone pathway. Through the high, beautifully crafted windows, Sebastian could see more old-world buildings and then forest that seemed to stretch forever. He touched the stone walls and the glass of the windows. It all felt real. Nothing about the space around him seemed like an illusion, but how could it be real? He watched Claire's head bob as she walked as if moving to her own internal tune.

They came upon a set of pathways that led in different directions. One crossed high over the river and continued to the other side of the building. Another forked into a set of dark stairways that disappeared around shadowy corners.

"Where do they lead?"

Claire gestured to a set of stairs leading down to the right.

"To the future."

She pointed left toward+ the path across the river.

"To the past."

She gestured straight ahead, along the path they followed.

"Right now."

Sebastian stared at the path to the right, the black stairwell.

Had Claire not been his guide, he would likely have chosen the path to the past, but with her beside him, he turned toward the stairs.

She put a hand on his arm.

"Whatever is seen cannot be unseen."

"Are you telling me that I'm going to see something bad?"

She smiled a small crooked smile that revealed the tiny chip out of her left front tooth. She had broken it when she was eleven. She had been trying to catch a stray cat that she spotted behind a fast food restaurant. When the cat darted under a car, Claire tripped and hit her face on a concrete parking barrier. She had cried and bled, but refused to give-up on the cat. Eventually she coaxed him into a cardboard box, and only then did she allow her parents to take her to urgent care. She hadn't needed stitches, but she named the cat Stitches just the same.

"I don't know what the future will show you. Maybe it will be beautiful, or perhaps terrifying."

"Sounds like the past."

"There is always the choice of now."

Sebastian shook his head.

"I have to. I don't know why, but I have to."

They walked down the stairs together, descending into blackness.

Sebastian smiled and saw a bright orb of fire floating before them. It appeared and chased away the darkness.

"Wow!"

He changed the color of the fire to red, and then blue, then neon green, and finally unmellow yellow-like Claire's childhood room.

"Unmellow yellow," she laughed. "Or lemon, according to Mom."

"Do you see Mom?" Sebastian asked suddenly, realizing that if he was speaking to Claire, he might also speak to their parents.

Claire nodded.

"Of course, my world is boundless, Sebastian. This version of me is just a tiny piece. And the Mom and Dad that we knew in life are available, but I rarely call on them in that way. I would love to bestow you with the infinite truth of the life you get the instant you cross to the other side, but I can't."

"It's against the rules?"

"It's unfathomable to the human mind. And it's meant to be. Part of your purpose is surrendering to the mystery."

"This conversation is making me feel like my little sister has left me in the dust."

"Literally," she laughed. "But you choose the questions, Sebastian. We can talk about childhood if you'd rather. I can argue with you about who's going to load the dishwasher."

He smiled and shook his head.

"No, I like this evolved version of you. I guess it just makes me sad for the past."

Sebastian noticed that the darkness in front of the light orb had begun to dissipate. A glowing blue light cast shimmering patterns on the stone walls.

The steps ended in a cavernous room, empty except for a huge glass cylinder filled with blue light. The cylinder stretched from floor to ceiling.

"What is it?" he asked, mesmerized by the glittering light.

"Beats me," Claire admitted.

"How does it work?"

"You just step inside."

"Is there a door?"

"The glass will permit you."

Sebastian walked to the cylinder and felt scared for the first time since crossing the bridge into the strange land. He had a sudden thought of all that was at stake. Abby and the baby waited for him with the Sky Mothers. If something happened to him, how would she go on? It would break her heart, and for what? A glimpse into the future. But the thoughts grew more distant as he watched the sparkling rays swimming behind the glass. He stepped forward into the light.

****

Abby found them arguing in the forest. Julian's face looked red with anger, and Hannah's own features were set in stubborn defiance.

"Hannah," Matilda said to the witch. "I told you not to bring him here. How could you defy me?"

Hannah did not look at Matilda. She stared at a tattered bridge beyond them.

At the thought that Hannah had tricked Sebastian into crossing that rickety bridge, Abby flew into a rage. She raced at the witch and shoved her with all her strength. Hannah's eyes opened wide at the last second and Abby saw her try to grab hold of Abby's arms, but she did not move quickly enough. She flew backward and landed hard on the ground. Abby pulled moisture from the trees and created a whirlwind of rain and ice that pelted the witch from every direction. Hannah screamed and fought at the oncoming ice, but she could not push it away.

Finally, Matilda cast a bubble around Hannah, blocking her from Abby's wrath.

Abby fell against a tree, gasping. Some of the rage drained out of her and she released the water back to the earth.

Oliver looked at her, shocked and maybe a tiny bit delighted.

Hannah stood, soaking wet, her defiance replaced by fury. She started to lift her hand as if to cast against Abby, but Julian flicked his fingers at her. Seemingly nothing happened, but a tremor passed through Hannah's body and she stood very still.

"Hannah, Julian will release you, but if you attack Abby, we will be carrying you back to the compound as a statue," Matilda told her.

Hannah's eyes looked wild, but she blinked hard as if to signal her compliance.

Julian freed her and she stumbled forward a step. She narrowed her eyes at Abby, but said nothing.

"He walked across the bridge on his own. I didn't shove him. He wanted to go," she told them, angrily.

"He would never have found this place if you hadn't led him here," Julian reminded her. "You had no right to do that."

"This is my coven," she hissed at Julian. "I don't take orders from you."

"You do, however, take orders from me if you want to continue as a part of the Sky Mothers. You are one of us Hannah, and I cherish you, but there are rules that we abide by, rules that when broken create ruin in the covens. Do you want that for the Sky Mothers?"

"Of course, I don't, Matilda, but…you understand. I know that you do. You must have thought of the dream wood when you realized he was a hybrid."

Matilda sighed.

"I thought of it, of course. I cannot control every thought, but I knew my intentions the moment the thought arose. To keep him as far away from the dream wood as possible. He is part of another story, Hannah. He is going to be a father soon. You've put his family in danger."

Abby had stopped listening. As she drew closer to the ancient looking bridge, she felt a subtle shift in the air. It seemed to grow thicker. Her stomach lurched as she tried to step onto the bridge. She could not set her foot down. It hovered in midair, but would not lower. She took a few steps away and ran at the bridge, jumping at the last minute, believing that the enchantment would not reach high enough to stop her. It did. She didn't hit a wall, but her jump failed to propel her forward, she landed at the start of the bridge, no closer to the dream wood.

"You can't get across," Hannah called to her. "I promise that I have tried a thousand times. I've slept here and tried with the new moon and the full moon, during lightning storms and dry spells. I've used every bit of magic I've ever learned to get onto that bridge and I've never made it."

"It's true, Abby," Matilda told her, walking closer. "Every Sky Mother has tried to penetrate the barrier around the dream wood. I do not believe that it can be done by a witch."

"Who created it? How does it exist?" Oliver asked, joining Abby and trying to step onto the bridge. He frowned, whispered an incantation and tried again.

"Her name was Meghan and she was an original Sky Mother, one of our founding Mothers. Her child, Clyde, was a hybrid. She created the dream wood to protect him."

"A Sky Mother with a child?" Oliver asked, surprised.

Matilda offered him a sad smile.

"Meghan is part of the reason we decided that the Sky Mothers should not have children. They can, of course," Matilda quickly added at the looks of dismay on Abby and Oliver's faces. "But they must leave the coven and build their life elsewhere if they choose that path. You see, Meghan already had a son when she and Binda created the Sky Mothers. He was not a child, but a seventeen-year-old man when she came to Australia. She created the dream wood to protect him and then she created the Sky Mothers to protect herself. Only Meghan could enter the dream wood. Unfortunately, both she and Clyde disappeared into it more than two hundred years ago."

"Have other witches tried to get in? Other than Sky Mothers?"

"No," Hannah interrupted. "It's a secret and we intend to keep it that way."

"Good job doing that," Oliver told her sarcastically.

Hannah ignored him.

Matilda placed a hand on her arm.

"We don't know if a witch were to destroy the enchantment, if the worlds created within the dream wood would vanish. What might happen to Liam and to others…"

"Others?" Abby fumed, trying not to act on her anger a second time.

"Clyde was the first. Then Meghan went in after him and never emerged. Two more hybrids went in and never came out. A young man visited us here, more than fifty years ago now. He came with two witches from a coven in South America. We did not know he was a hybrid. He disappeared on his last night. Only after he vanished did one of the witches mention that he had been exhibiting interesting powers, but did not appear to be a witch. They actually brought him here to see if we might detect it as well."

"How do you know he went into the dream wood?" Julian asked.

Matilda looked him in the eye.

"The same way that I knew Abby was pregnant the moment I met her. The same way that we know when something dark is approaching or that our sister who lives on the other side of the world is sick."

They all nodded. Even Abby found herself nodding though she had less experience with her powers of intuition. Still, they popped up again and again, just as they had an hour earlier when she sensed something had happened to Sebastian.

Abby felt the baby shift and she placed a hand on her stomach. When she looked up, she saw Hannah watching her. The witch had tears in her eyes and she abruptly broke Abby's gaze.

"I might be sick," Abby blurted and walked behind a tree. She felt suddenly hot everywhere and saliva filled her throat and mouth. A hand touched her back, gently and then more firmly. In an instant, the nausea passed.

Abby glanced behind her to see Hannah.

"One of my many talents," Hannah told her, beginning to look ashamed. "When I'm not destroying other people's lives, that is."

Abby nodded and stood up. She had not forgiven Hannah, not even close, but she did feel grateful that the witch kept her from retching. Morning sickness had been minimal with the pregnancy, and usually she had one of Helena's tinctures handy if it did come on. But when it hit her, it was a tidal wave of discomfort.

"I'm sorry about Liam. You obviously loved him a lot."

"Love him. I love him, a lot. He's alive, Abby. I would never have done this otherwise. I know it in my heart, in my bones, that he's alive and he's in there."

"Did he ever come back out? Or just go in one day and disappear forever?"

"He came back. He went in several times. He told me stories, amazing stories. They were so vivid that I dream of them sometimes. He could choose the world or create the world any way he wanted to. He could fly." Hannah smiled, remembering. "He loved it, of course. But he never would have stayed. It was the best of both worlds, we thought, at first. He had the dream wood and I had the Sky Mothers. Together, we have a house on the beach about twenty miles from here. That's where we were building our life together."

"You were leaving the Sky Mothers?" Abby asked, realizing that Hannah had been doing exactly that.

"Maybe, eventually, yes. Liam wanted children. I did too, I just struggled to say it out loud because I knew that would take me away from the Sky Mothers once and for all."

Though Matilda had heard everything Hannah said, she did not comment. Obviously, Matilda too had perceived that Hannah intended to leave the coven. Perhaps she supported the choice.

****

Sebastian felt an unbearable cold descend over his body. It bit his skin and then sank deeper. The cold reach his muscles and they spasmed and grew taught. It traveled to his bones and blood. It moved into his organs. He felt the blood slowing and thickening in his veins. It hurt to breathe, to exist. He wondered if the cold would kill him. He had a momentary suspicion of Claire and the whole world he'd been so entranced by. Had she merely lured him to his death?

Gradually, painstakingly, the cold transformed into a vibration. Every cell of his being shook until he felt lighter than air. He no longer felt his body at all, just a sense of himself as nothing and everything. He relaxed into the sensation as the boundaries of the physical world vanished. He realized that he could direct his energy. Around him, endless silvery light reached into eternity. He had no concept of time or space. How could he choose where to go?

"With your thoughts, silly." Sebastian heard Claire's voice in his head.

"How do I have a thought about a future that hasn't happened?"

He thought he heard her giggle and then sigh.

"Will we destroy the amulet?" he asked. The question came to him from nowhere, and as a vision materialized before him, he realized that it had been concerning him ever since they had taken the necklace. So much of his and Abby's happiness rested on destroying the amulet and ridding themselves of Kanti forever.

He saw the towering castle of Ula slide into view. The turrets cut into the perfectly blue sky. The image moved closer. He saw the stone slab at the second lagoon. He stood on the slab, Abby clutching his hand. Oliver, Julian, Faustine, and Elda stood in a circle. The amulet lay on the stone. The golden snake glinted in the sunlight. The red jewel lacked the vibrancy that he remembered from the night Kanti placed it around his neck. In fact, the whole amulet looked less, somehow. Less what, he didn't exactly know.

Overhead the full moon shone bright and eerie, wisps of cloud drifting over its surface. Faustine swung the bronze-handled ax high and brought it down. The amulet shattered. Bits of stone flew in every direction. The gold snake lay severed. They all stared and waited. Shouldn't there have been an explosion? A blast of dark energy leaving the amulet? Something.

Sebastian looked up at the faces of the other witches.

"There's something wrong," Julian said.

CHAPTER 7

The vision of Ula slowly vanished and Sebastian felt the cold return. The space around him grew firm and with a loud thwack pushed him out of the cylinder. He stumbled into the stone room, watching the dazzling lights, and trying to make sense of the vision.

"The amulet broke apart," he told Claire as if she knew completely what he referred to. "But it seemed so easy. It was too easy."

Claire nodded.

"I need to leave," he told her.

Sebastian had mixed feelings about leaving the dream wood, mostly because he might never return and see Claire again. But on the other side of the bridge, Abby waited. She might have noticed him missing and grown anxious and upset. He wanted to stay with Claire. He wanted to investigate the dream wood. But most of all, he wanted to hug Abby and tell her about the vision of the amulet.

"Sure, you do," Claire agreed. "And she knows you're missing, and she's very upset."

"How do you know?"

Claire gave him a funny look that he remembered from childhood. It seemed to ask, "are you serious?"

"Okay, yeah, I guess you're probably all-knowing now, huh?"

"Not exactly, but I have a few tricks up my sleeve."

"Why did you go with Tobias, Claire? I'm not blaming you," he said quickly, ashamed at his question. "I've just always wondered, what made you trust him?"

Claire tucked a piece of dark hair behind her ear and looked at him with such innocent blue eyes that his heart sagged in his chest.

"I was fifteen, Sebastian. He was beautiful and funny and clever. He could do magic. I thought it was destiny. I never saw him coming. I wish I could have known better. Not for me," she added. "I kind of like life on the other side. But for your sake. My death shifted the course of your life. I'm happy it did because you found Abby, but I'm not happy for the shadow it has cast over your heart."

Sebastian stepped forward and wrapped Claire in his arms. She felt so familiar, it hurt. In that hug, Sebastian could be her big brother again. They could have a single moment where he protected her and she allowed it. She did not vanish. She stayed solid in his arms and sighed.

"I sure have missed arguing with you over who's going to pump the gas," she told him.

"I miss your eight million colors of toenail polish lined up on the bathroom sink," He laughed.

She pulled away.

"Since you brought it up," she looked at him slyly. "I know you threw away my Cat Scratch Fever Orange Polish."

He grimaced and looked sheepishly at the floor.

"No use denying it?" he asked.

"You said yourself, I'm all knowing."

"In my defense," he protested. "It was on the floor and I stepped on it. I didn't just toss it in the trash out of spite. There was orange polish everywhere. I felt like a murderer cleaning it up and hiding the paper towels."

She laughed.

"I don't blame you. I was pretty serious about my nail polish."

Sebastian turned for the stairs, but Claire stopped him.

"Let's take a different way."

He followed her across the room, beyond the cylinder of light, and they came to a series of doorways.

"Which one?" he asked.

"Your world, your choice."

"This doesn't feel like my world," he grumbled. "And I really need to get back to Abby. Which one?"

Claire shrugged.

"I can't choose for you. It's part of the deal if I come to a place like this. I can come, I can even have a body again, but every choice is yours."

Sebastian sighed and stepped toward the center door.

It opened into a forest. The shrubs and trees looked black and gnarled. The ground released a coppery smelling mist when they stepped out of the building.

"Can we choose a different door?" he asked sarcastically.

"Sure," Claire said, following him out.

Sebastian thought if he turned back, the other doors would be gone.

"We can get back this way?"

"Yes, you can get back any way. It's your world."

Ahead of them, Sebastian saw beyond the forest, the face of a cliff that he recognized. The bridge was up there. As they walked, Sebastian studied the plants, mostly dead, or dying. He wanted to water them. Or pull them from the ground and replant them in a place that didn't seem toxic. He knelt down at a tiny patch of blue flowers, but when he reached toward them, they shriveled away.

A splash drew his attention and he looked up to see a dark pond. The surface glistened in oily swirls. Huge black lotus flowers sat on the surface of the water.

"Creepy," he whispered to Claire as they passed by.

He noticed more ripples in the water, farther out on the pond and studied the surface. It took a moment, but he realized that something was protruding from the water. A round shape that nearly blended into the darkness surrounded it. As he watched, he recognized two glowing red eyes. The rounded shape was the top of a woman's head and she was submerged from the lips down. He could see only her black hair fanning out on the water and her two glowing eyes watching him.

Sebastian turned to Claire. She too watched the woman and Sebastian saw fear on her face.

"Best to keep walking," Claire whispered.

They turned back to toward the cliff and Sebastian glanced behind him several times, but as they drew farther away from the pond, he could no longer distinguish the woman from the water.

"What was that?" Sebastian asked.

"I don't know," Claire admitted. "Something not good, I can tell you that."

When they reached the base of the cliff, Sebastian looked up. The rock wall was nearly flat with bits of vine snaking down the surface, though clearly not strong enough to hold him.

"How do we get up?"

"Your world," she grinned. "Climb, scale a tree and leap over. If it were me, I'd fly."

"Fly?"

Before Claire could answer, Sebastian took a running start and leaped into the air. He expected to flail and land back on the ground with a thud. Instead, he zoomed upward as if he wore a jetpack strapped to his back. He flew up and beyond the cliff. As he rose higher he saw the bridge, and he thought, beyond the bridge, he saw Hannah with several other witches. But already they grew tiny as he drove his body toward the sky.

****

Abby nodded off against a tree.

Kanti ran through tunnels lit with crude torches. Her bare feet, raw from scraping against rocks, bled openly. She spun and stared into the darkness behind her, hearing the beast that pursued her. He had turned into something inhuman, a monster with wings and fangs and grossly sharp fingernails. He would eat her. She would die before the baby could be born. She murmured and cried and tried to be silent, but fear made her call out to her mother, her father, her tribe. After a seeming eternity, she burst from the underground prison onto a grassy cliff. She ran to the edge and paused for only an instant at the dizzying drop to the choppy waters below. She jumped.

"Sebastian!"

Abby heard someone call his name and her eyes snapped open. She did not know who uttered it, but there he was.

Sebastian walked across the bridge and when he saw Abby, he broke into a run. He kneeled at her side and gathered her into his arms.

"Are you okay? Have you been hurt?"

"No, no," she shook her head, still groggy and disturbed from her dream.

"You made it out," she told him. Relieved, she buried her hands in his hair and kissed him.

Beyond him, she saw Hannah continuing to watch the bridge as if she expected her lost love to come trailing out as well. No one arrived.

Sebastian helped Abby to her feet.

"What happened in there?" Julian asked before Abby had a chance to voice the very same question.

Sebastian widened his eyes and looked back at the bridge, but mostly to the woods beyond.

"I don't even know how to describe it."

"Perhaps we should return to the compound before we hear Sebastian's story," Matilda interrupted. "I'm sure everyone is hungry, and tired too." She winked at Abby who leaned heavily against Sebastian.

She pressed her hands into his back, clutching him, and thanking the divine for his safe return from the dream wood.

"Sebastian?" Hannah asked, her voice small.

Sebastian sighed and shook his head.

"I'm sorry, Hannah. I didn't see him, but I think Matilda is right. Let's go sit and we can talk about this. I have a plan."

****

They sat in the wind tunnel. Grace brought platters of fresh fruit and pitchers of tea.

Sebastian described his experience in the dream wood, leaving out a few critical pieces: Claire and the vision of the amulet.

"You could choose the world?" Oliver asked, popping a strawberry into his mouth and immediately reaching for a handful of nuts.

Sebastian nodded.

"The worlds appeared before me, just for an instant, and then disappeared. I chose in my mind and that world stayed."

"Was this a place you've been before?" Julian asked. "This old, crumbling city?"

"No, and honestly, I don't think it's a place that exists in the natural world. There was a river running through the buildings. The light was different."

Matilda nodded.

"We have heard many stories of the worlds within the dream wood."

"Liam went there," Hannah told them. "He described a cathedral filled with saints. Their eyes were bleeding."

Sebastian frowned.

"I was in the cathedral and saw statues of saints, but their eyes weren't bleeding."

"How did you get out?" Abby asked. She had other questions and she also sensed that Sebastian was holding back. She thought he would confide the rest to her later.

"I just walked out. I came back the same way that I went in. I didn't have any trouble."

A shadow passed over Hannah's face.

"So what is this plan that you were talking about?" Julian asked.

Sebastian looked at Abby, reassuring her with his gaze and then kissed the tip of her nose.

"I saw something as I was leaving, someone in fact. She was in the water, watching me."

"Another hybrid?" Abby asked.

"I don't think so. She didn't seem of this world, for lack of a better explanation. There is a place in the dream wood where I can look into the past. I think that I need to take something of Liam's with me and I'll ask to a see a vision of his final moments. The weird thing is, I feel sure this woman in the water knew him."

"You;re sure it was a woman?" Abby asked, blushing at the edge in her voice.

"Yeah, at least her head looked like a woman, I don't know what was beneath the water."

"That place sounds more like a horror movie than a dream," Oliver joined. "A dead forest and an old cathedral full of stone saints? No thanks."

Helena smiled and patted Oliver's knee.

"This from a Vepar hunter," she teased.

"Vepars, I can handle, water monsters, not so much."

"I didn't hear an actual plan," Julian interrupted. It's all fine if you see what happened to Liam, even if you talk to this water creature, but then what? What if she took him? Killed him?"

Hannah gasped across the table and Matilda put a hand on her arm to stop her from disrupting the conversation.

"I will check the vision first. If he's dead..." He looked apologetically at Hannah. "I'll leave, end of story."

"And if not?" Julian asked. "If you see that this water creature abducted Liam?"

Sebastian shrugged and broke eye contact.

"Then I'll follow my intuition, Julian. You have been teaching me, after all. What's the purpose of all the training, if it's never tested?"

****

Sebastian lit the torches outside of the yurt. He and Abby walked to the cliffs at the edge of the ocean and the fires lit the forest behind them. Sebastian laid out a blanket and they sat for a while in silence.

"I saw into the future, Abby."

She studied his profile as he stared at the horizon.

"What did you see?"

He frowned and shook his head.

"Something goes wrong with the amulet."

"The ax won't destroy it?"

"No, at least not in my vision. But maybe it's false. Maybe it wasn't the future and instead my worst fears reflected back to me."

"You want to go back," Abby said after several minutes.

"Yes," Sebastian admitted. "But not because I'm intoxicated by the dream wood. I liked it, don't get me wrong, I've never experienced anything similar, but I believe that Hannah is right, Liam is trapped there and I want to try and find him."

"Do you always have to be the hero, Sebastian?"

Sebastian stiffened, and Abby almost apologized, but couldn't bring herself to deny the feelings. It scared her that Sebastian intended to return. It also made her angry. What about their baby? What happened if he disappeared in the dream wood too?

"I have to try, Abby. I didn't want to say it in front of the others, but Claire was there, she was helping me."

Abby studied his face. It always came back to Claire.

"How was she there? In your mind? As a spirit?"

"In her body. Solid, real. I hugged her. She walked with me. She talked about life after death."

Abby started to chew on her thumbnail and stopped. It was an old Abby behavior, chewing her nails when she got anxious. She closed her eyes for a moment and let her thoughts, and more importantly, her feelings slide away. She felt the soft breeze as it rushed from the ocean. She heard it travel over the grass and rustle the ferns and leaves in the forest. She tuned in to the huge body of energy that surrounded her. As all her fear and anxiety ebbed away, she allowed the thought of Claire to return. She imagined the pictures of Sebastian's sister and felt into that space. Only warmth greeted her. No ominous premonitions rose up at the image of Sebastian's beloved Claire. Perhaps she really could help him.

"Okay," Abby conceded, trying to sound convincing.

Sebastian sighed and looked out at the ocean.

"I really needed you to say that right now. A part of me thought you might not believe me, or think I'd gone nuts."

Abby laughed and leaned against him.

"There's an ancient evil spirit haunting us. I can hardly doubt that your sister has found a way to come back and help us."

"Yes, us. I wish I could take you in there to meet her."

"Me too," Abby said.

She watched the water crash against the cliffs far below and shuddered, remembering her dream of Kanti. Like Kanti in the vision, Abby was pregnant. Could she jump to save her child? Herself?

CHAPTER 8

Sebastian returned to the dream wood the following morning. He held a hemp belt that belonged to Liam. He tied it around his own waist as he crossed the bridge. He had also brought a knife from Matilda. It sliced through stone and metal. Julian had sent him with a compass, goggles, a snorkel and handful of protective stones.

He stepped off the bridge and looked directly at the tree where Claire had greeted him the day before. It stood empty, and he felt his excitement shrivel and die.

"What's in there?" a voice whispered in his ear.

He spun around to find Claire standing behind him, also looking critically at the tree branch. "A rare Australian vampire bat?"

He grabbed her in a hug.

She laughed and hugged him back, before tickling his sides.

"Hey," he laughed. "Mom said no tickling."

Claire bent over laughing.

"Dad hated that! He asked how he was going to punish us if there was no tickling."

"She said to use a belt like her father did," Sebastian guffawed. "As if, do you remember her dad? He probably weighed ninety pounds soaking wet."

"Grandpa Hershey," Claire grinned.

They had called their mom's father Grandpa Hershey because he always had a pocket of Hershey kisses he would give them in exchange for hugs.

Sebastian continued laughing, but as he watched Claire, the humor started to drain out of him and a horrible sense of loss drifted at the corner of his thoughts. What happened after he found Liam? He left Claire again, forever?

She grabbed his hand.

"I'm with you all the time big brother. I know it's different here. You get to see me, but I'm out there too. I'm at your house in Michigan. I'm at Ula. I'm everywhere."

He took a deep breath and nodded.

"A part of me believes that and another part can't forget what it feels like not to talk to you every day. I was so excited to come back here today and see you."

"I know," she said. "Me too, but even in this space, my time is limited, Sebastian. I won't be hanging around here after you're gone."

"Where will you go?"

"Everywhere, silly. Now tell me what you have in that bag."

Sebastian lifted the rucksack that Matilda had given him.

"A knife, a compass, some swim gear and stones."

"So, this is a regular adventure we're on?"

"I'm looking for a man named Liam. Know him?"

"I showed up here when you did."

"Is that a no?"

Claire smiled and looked far away.

"That's a no," she said.

"I want to go to the place that lets me see the past."

"Choose your world," Claire reminded him.

"If I choose a different world, will I still be able to see the past?"

"Yes, visions of the past and the future are available in all the worlds."

Sebastian looked beyond the cliff into the forest. The worlds began to shift in and out of focus. As a vision of a copper city suspended in clouds passed before him, he nodded and the world fell into place.

"Good one," Claire agreed.

Sebastian looked at the turrets and structures capped with mushroom shaped copper roofs. Bridges stretched between the structures and Sebastian could not see the ground. Clouds drifted through open windows.

"A floor of marshmallows." Claire grinned.

"Where is the ground?"

Claire looked over the edge of the cliff they stood on.

"What ground?"

Sebastian too leaned over the side, and the dizzying emptiness nearly made him lose his balance. He stepped back from the ledge. There had been nothing. Only miles of empty blue sky with bits of white cloud scattered throughout.

"I can fly," he said out loud. "I'm not going to fall because I can fly."

"Sure can," Claire said.

But instead, they walked.

****

Abby wandered the woods, aimlessly. An hour had passed since Sebastian entered the dream wood. Nerves prevented her from any kind of deep thought. Each time, she found herself contemplating the curse, Kanti or even the upcoming baby. Then she thought about Sebastian, which quickly segued into the fear that he might never come out of the dream wood. That thought caused every muscle in her body to grow tight. In response, the baby rolled and shifted in her womb. The movement made Abby feel nauseous and crampy.

"If you're going to spend the day nervously combing the forest, let's at least be comfortable," Oliver said, surprising her.

"You didn't have to come out here," she told him.

She had assured the other witches that morning that she didn't mind waiting for Sebastian alone.

"Don't be silly," Helena trilled, emerging from the trees. "What kind of midwife would I be if I left my only patient alone in the woods. And we've brought refreshments."

"Among other things," Oliver added.

He took a square of folded white nylon from a bag slung over his shoulder. He threw the nylon into the air and it popped apart, expanding into a huge canopy. From his bag he also removed several bundles of what looked like sticks, but again when he threw them, they transformed into three reclining wood chairs and a small table.

Helena produced her own bag and Abby watched, amazed, as she removed a pitcher of iced tea, four glasses, a container filled with sandwiches, a plate of fruit, and several books.

"Where were those magic bags when I was packing for this trip?" Abby asked, thinking about her unwieldy luggage that Sebastian had wrestled out of the trunk of their car.

"These are Sky Mothers' bags. We have a few at Ula too, but every now and then they eject all of their contents so we don't use them much," Helena admitted.

"Books?" Abby asked, touching one of the titles.

"Reading material provided by Julian," Oliver laughed. "He's not one to waste time."

"What if Sebastian doesn't come out?" Abby asked, voicing the fear playing in her mind.

"He will," Helena assured her, passing her a sandwich. "I read the tea leaves this morning. No foul omens in any of my twelve cups."

"Twelve?" Abby asked.

"Yes, overkill perhaps, but I wanted to be sure and if you haven't tried Grace's cocoa peppermint tea, you simply must!"

"I'm with Helena on this one," Oliver agreed. "No sense of ill tidings whatsoever."

Abby wished she felt as confident. It was hard to distinguish a sense of anything with her entire body wound like a rubber band. She had tried meditating as she walked, but found clearing her mind nearly impossible.

"We've got a visitor," Oliver commented.

Abby twisted in her chair and saw a small bird with bright blue feathers on his back and a plume of copper on his chest approaching them on the ground. Another landed behind it. The original bird hopped beneath the canopy of the tent and stopped next to Abby's chair. Several more birds landed. Each of them tentatively made their way to Abby. The first flew up and landed on the table near her elbow.

"Oh my," Helena whispered.

"Abby-the bird whisperer," Oliver said.

Abby held out her hand and the bird on the table plucked at her fingers. It ruffled its feathers and then settled into its wings and closed its eyes.

Another of the birds jumped on the table. A third flew into Abby's lap.

"Oh," she gasped as one of them flew up and landed on her shoulder.

"This is amazing," Helena said. "They're drawn to you."

"So were the crows," Oliver murmured.

Abby saw the sorrow in Oliver's eyes. Helena looked similarly distressed at the memory. The night when the crows had protected her against Kanti-except Kanti was in Dafne's body and Dafne had died.

"I believe they're attracted to the baby," Abby admitted, gently running her fingers along the smooth feathers of one of the birds.

"She will be strong," Helena said. "If she already commands the birds, then she is a force of nature."

****

"What's this room made of?" Sebastian asked, staring at an enormous gold and black coffin. It sat in a room comprised of glistening white crystalline walls.

"Salt," Claire said touching the wall and licking her finger.

Sebastian did the same. Sure enough, he tasted salt.

"Please tell me I don't have to get in that thing," Sebastian muttered.

"You don't have to," Claire replied happily. "Though if you want to see the past…"

Sebastian groaned.

"This is funny to you? My climbing in a coffin?"

Claire winked.

"Kind of like old times. Remember when you dared me to go into that crawlspace at the church Mommy took us to for potlucks?"

Sebastian grimaced and nodded.

"I closed the door and it got stuck," Sebastian recalled. "Mom was livid. Sorry about that."

"It was kind of fun, after I stopped crying anyway." She giggled. "Seriously though, it was okay, Sebastian. I know you felt bad. You probably still feel bad, but I loved telling the story later."

"So, I should view this as a great future story?"

"Could be."

Sebastian climbed into the coffin. The moment he closed the lid, he felt a warm rush like water filling the space. He immediately panicked and tried to fling open the lid, but when he reached his hands up, the lid had disappeared. It was as if he had sunk into an abyss. The warm liquid moved over his body and soon covered his face. He couldn't breathe, but as quickly as the terror gripped him, a placid calm stole him.

In his mind, he said, "Show me Liam in the dream wood on the last day Hannah saw him."

The darkness edged away.

Though he didn't close his eyes, a veil of black fell over them. The black grew thick and heavy until his entire body spasmed with the tension of trying to see.

After seconds that felt like hours, a vision of the past filled the darkness before him.

He watched Hannah and Liam embrace. The man was tall, nearly as tall as Sebastian, with blond wavy hair tucked beneath a blue bandana. He wore white linen pants and a matching shirt, similar to the Sky Mothers' attire. Liam grinned as he traipsed into the dream wood. Sebastian looked for his guide when he entered the dream wood and he was not disappointed. Though instead of a person waiting to greet Liam, a beautiful red fox stood just beyond the bridge.

Liam spoke to her and the fox responded in a softly musical and very human voice.

"I want to speak to the water witch," Liam told the fox.

"It is unwise to seek out the water witch, dear Liam. She is surrounded by darkness."

"But I can do anything here. She can't possibly hurt me."

"Foolish words from a smart man," the fox replied looking toward the shifting worlds.

Liam chose the world and the forest shifted into a palace of snow and ice. He and the fox slid down a hill of snow, both laughing. Liam clearly knew the way. He ran through the snow and then squatted down and jumped, like a movie superhero, onto the ledge of a tall ice-capped roof. He scaled the roof and the fox easily kept pace. He slid down another roof and landed in a courtyard filled with mirrors. Running full speed, Sebastian almost yelled "Stop," as Liam rushed into the glass, but the moment it shattered, the mirrors were whole again.

Beyond the mirrors, Sebastian watched Liam walk into an ice cave. A door stood on the other side. Thousands of holes were dug into the cave walls and Liam walked to one, bent down, and retrieved a key from its depths. He unlocked the door and walked through, the fox on his heels.

Past the door, the snowscape had vanished, and Liam moved into a dark forest. Sebastian recognized it from his visit to the dream wood the day before. Every aspect of the dream wood appeared to change with the worlds, but this forest looked identical.

Liam moved slowly as he circled the black pool. When a shape began to break through the surface in the center of the pond, he paused. She revealed only the crown of her head, her eyes, and her nose. Two glowing malevolent eyes watched Liam hungrily. Beside him, the fox whimpered and backed away.

"Best to turn back now, Liam," the fox trilled.

"I've come with questions," Liam told the woman. "I can offer you gifts in return- anything from the world outside the dream wood."

The woman's eyes did not move from his face. Stillness and silence stretched beyond the pond.

A tiny ripple disturbed the water as her hand broke the surface. She curled her fingers back, beckoning to him, and then slowly sank beneath the surface and disappeared.

"I have to go in," Liam whispered.

"No," the fox shook her head from side to side.

"What's in there?" he asked.

But the fox retreated several more steps.

"Better not find out. Better to go back to Hannah and life on the other side of the bridge."

But Liam had already slipped out of his shoes. He walked to the edge of the pond and leaned forward, touching it with his fingertips. Before he could back away, slimy white arms reached from the dark water and grasped his shoulders, pulling him forward.

He screamed and reached behind him where the fox had raced forward, but he vanished into the water before she could reach him.

****

The vision drained away and Sebastian lay against the cold silk of the coffin. He thrust his hands up and the lid flung open. Sweating and unnerved, he climbed out and lumbered away from the box, sitting roughly on the floor.

"Did you find him?" Claire asked, watching anxiously.

He noticed that she no longer wore the same shorts and t-shirt. Now she donned a pair of their mother's painting pants-blue scrubs streaked with yellow and red paint. She wore one of Sebastian's old shirts. A concert t-shirt from Rusted Root that he had bought the summer before his parents died in the crash.

"How do you change clothes?" Sebastian asked, trying to shake the lingering fear the vision had inspired.

"I can appear any way that I want."

"Must save loads on laundry, no pun intended," he joked and then laughed a dry bark that sounded miserable to his own ears.

"What did you see?" Claire asked.

"The water witch pulled Liam into the pond," he admitted.

"Do you believe he is dead, then?"

Sebastian shook his head.

"No, there's a part of me that wishes I did. I suddenly want to get out of this place, but I wish I could take you with me."

"You do, I just don't look as fashionable out there. Think warm breezes and butterflies."

"You appear as warm breezes and butterflies? I tend to think it's you when a lightning storm is happening."

"Those too," she promised.

"He wanted something from the witch."

Claire looked thoughtful.

"What could she give him?"

"I don't know," Sebastian admitted. "And Hannah didn't mention it. What could be so valuable that…"

"He'd risk everything to get it," Claire finished.

"Exactly."

****

It took Sebastian hours to find the pond. He walked through doorways and down hallways. Claire could not offer any guidance because the world was as unfamiliar to her as to Sebastian. When at last he found it, he'd nearly given up. They had discovered a floating garden nestled within a group of buildings. As they walked through the garden, Claire pointing out flowers, Sebastian noticed a dark mist emerging from a grove of trees. He had to fight through tight, twisted branches that scratched his face. On the other side of the grove, he discovered the pond. The black water did not reflect the blue sky overhead. It remained dark and motionless.

"I would like to speak with you," he called across the water, not sure if the witch would hear him, or if he wanted her to.

A ripple broke across the water and Sebastian watched the top of the woman's dark head break the surface. Her two red eyes fixed on his own.

"I'm here for Liam," he told the witch.

Claire took his hand and tugged him away from the water's edge.

"Don't get too close," she whispered.

Sebastian took the belt from his waist. As he held it over the pond, the water began to ripple and then churn. For an instant, the water took on the shape of Liam's face, the mouth opening in a scream.

"Help Me!" The scream burst from the water and echoed around them.

Sebastian stumbled backwards and nearly fell.

Claire clutched him uneasily.

The witch continued to watch them.

"I have to go into the water," Sebastian said.

"No, no," Claire shook her head from side to side. "You're not responsible for him. Think about Abby."

"I am," Sebastian murmured. "And I just know that I have to go in there."

"I can't go with you," she told him, tugging on his shirt. "I can't follow you into the water."

"Just wait for me, right here. Okay? I'm coming back out."

He took out the snorkel, goggles, and the knife. He had no idea what to expect as he stepped to the edge of the pool, but could not shake the vision of the slimy arms reaching out to grasp Liam. No arms reached for him. Gingerly, he stepped to the edge of the pond, intending only to check the depth, but his foot found no ground and he twisted around for a final look at Claire before the water swallowed him whole.

CHAPTER 9

"Any sign of him?" Hannah asked, leaving the trees and ducking beneath the canopy.

Her long blonde hair was woven into a series of braids that created a crown around her head. She wore a semi-sheer white dress, ankle-length, that showed off her curves. Though her smile looked tentative, her eyes shone with the desperation Abby had seen the day before.

"Nope," Oliver said curtly, making his opinion of her known.

She ignored him and took a chair near Abby.

"I'm sure he's okay, really."

Abby felt Hannah's need to make amends with her and found it hard to ignore. Sebastian had chosen to go back into the dream wood. Had he never returned the day before, she would have blamed Hannah. She may have even hated her. But he went back knowing the risk. It was no longer on Hannah what happened to him.

"Tell us about the dream wood, Hannah," Helena asked, passing her a cup of tea. "I've never heard of anything like it, and to be truthful, I'd never even heard of a hybrid before we came here."

Hannah took the tea gratefully.

"I've been hearing about hybrids since I became a witch."

"And when was that?" Abby interrupted, always curious how long other witches had been in the world of magic.

"Well, I was sixteen when I first started exhibiting powers. Matilda found me just a few months later and I'm thirty-eight now, so twenty-two years."

Abby eyed Hannah appraisingly. She looked twenty. Abby had assumed she was a young witch due to her impulsiveness, but no, she had been a witch for more than twenty years.

"Anyway," Hannah continued. "Clyde had disappeared long before I joined the Sky Mothers, but he had become a myth of sorts. Only Binda knew him and Meghan. The other two witches who had been a part of the Sky Mothers during that time had left. One died shortly thereafter. Matilda came to the Sky Mothers twenty years after Meghan and Clyde disappeared. In those days, apparently Binda was still desperately trying to get into the dream wood. It became clear to Matilda that they would never get inside. Matilda once told me that she thought Clyde murdered Meghan in the dream wood. Though she didn't know him, Binda had told her that he had a dark, cruel nature."

****

The instant he disappeared beneath the water, Sebastian emerged in a dark forest. There was no drowning or thrashing for air. He looked up. Far above him, rather than a sky, he saw the murky underside of the black pond. He could not see the world beyond the pond or Claire. He watched a dark shape moving through the water. The shadow slid from the black water into a tree. Sebastian thought he saw the two red eyes of the water witch.

His feet sunk into the marshy ground and a smell of rotten eggs and seaweed emanated from the earth. He turned in a circle, scanning the gnarled trees and the ferns slumped over and beginning to rot. Looking back toward the sky, he tried not to contemplate how he would get out if he did find Liam. He still had the knife re-sheathed against his leg, but he no longer held the goggles or snorkel, not that he needed them. But the transition unnerved him. He had not fallen from the pond above, but simply appeared on the forest floor. Sebastian rarely questioned the magical world. Since Claire's discovery that she was a witch, he had accepted that the rules of life he'd been shown were wrong, simple as that. Still, he didn't like how seamlessly he moved from what appeared to be one world into another, without actually intending to do it.

Sebastian walked for a long time. The smell and weak light had started a throbbing behind his eyes. He turned often, seeking a sign of life, but the dead forest seemed to stretch into eternity. He squinted into the growing darkness before him. He thought he could see the faint glow of lights, but didn't trust his eyes as the headache grew. He continued walking until he felt sure that lights glowed in the distance. As he grew closer, the earth suddenly vanished. He stood at the edge of the soggy forest where a ramshackle plank bridge suspended across a dark void. He looked down but could see no ground. The bridge did not have a handrail and appeared, much like the bridge into the dream wood, to be in the later stages of decay.

At the end of the long, tattered bridge stood a dilapidated house. Sebastian felt as if something or someone peered at him from the dark windows. Two torches flanked the stone steps that led to the front door, where a bouquet of black flowers hung.

"What was I thinking?" he asked out loud.

He thought back to the night before, standing with Abby outside the yurt. He had felt so confident in his need to return to the dream wood and seek out Liam. Now, standing at the edge of a haunted house, likely stuck in a dead world that he could not escape, he wished to turn back the hands of time and make a different choice.

He glanced a final time at the dead forest behind him and then turned back to face what lay ahead.

****

As day turned to dusk, Abby grew anxious. Their tent was filled with birds and Helena and Oliver fed them bits of fruit and gave them names like Jack Sparrow and Quackie Chan. Abby tried to join them, but could barely find a smile, let alone a quirky bird name. Hannah had left hours earlier and not returned. Likely Matilda had warned her to stay away from Abby and the witches of Ula.

"What time is it?" Abby asked.

Helena glanced at the sky.

"Just after six, give or take a few minutes."

"He's been gone for nearly ten hours."

"Watch out, Polly Pardon's eyeing your sandwich," Oliver told Abby, nodding at the uneaten sandwich on her plate.

Abby broke a hunk off and threw it to the bird.

She stood and walked from the tent. At the start of the bridge, she met the invisible wall and fought the desire to pound her fists against it and scream Sebastian's name.

Another half hour passed and then an hour. The sunset lit the sky in streaks of pink and orange, but was soon replaced by the milky dark of evening.

Abby had not moved from the bridge and her legs had begun to ache.

"Still no sign of him?" Oliver asked, startling her.

Abby shook her head, afraid to say the words out loud.

"Maybe he just got carried away. If I could fly, I would probably disappear into that place for a week."

She nodded but remained silent.

Helena moved next to Abby. She had packed up the tent and other items in the bottomless bag. She touched Abby's elbow.

"I know that you can't imagine leaving right now, but for the baby's sake, you need to come back to the yurts."

Abby bit her lip and stared harder into the forest. Had something moved?

"I can't, Helena. What if he comes out and he's injured. I have to be here."

"I'll be here," Julian said, walking up behind them from the woods. "I'm going to take the night shift."

Helena smiled at Julian and tried to take Abby's hand.

Abby pulled it away, unable to shift her focus from the forest beyond the bridge.

"Set the tent back up," Oliver told Helena. "I'll go back to the Sky Mothers for some hammocks. Camping!"

He ran off into the forest.

Abby smiled after him and then returned her watchful eyes to the trees.

"You're not looking at the dream wood, Abby," Julian reminded her. "It's an illusion, just like the bridge."

Helena pulled a chair from her bag and opened it for Abby.

"Sit down, honey."

Abby sat and folded her shaking hands in her lap.

She tried to keep her eyes open, but they felt thick and heavy. She leaned back in her chair.

Kanti struggled in the arms of the giant, but it was no use. He outweighed her by three-hundred pounds, maybe more. He held her high, her feet kicking out for his shins or his groin, with her arms pinned behind her back. The hole before them yawned long and narrow. She knew that hole. She had watched the people in her tribe dig similar holes when an elder grew ill and passed into the spirit world. The white man sat on the edge of the hole with his treasures spread around him like a greedy child. He touched the strange charm on the gold rope, a serpent with a bloody heart. The man stood and brushed the dirt from the seat of his pants. As the giant held her and she writhed and kicked, the man kissed her hard on the mouth. He tasted of salt and rotten things. He tasted of dead and evil and darkness.

When he placed the golden rope with the snake over her head, she tried to jerk away from him. She did not want the jewel against her naked chest. He gripped her hair and held her head in place.

"You will wear it or return to the box."

She glanced beyond him to the forest where she knew the giant had tied their houses. The box was wooden, long and narrow, much like the hole before her. Slits in the side allowed air and a sliver of light, but there were times she laid in it for hours. Before they placed her in the box, the giant always stuffed her mouth with bits of dirty rag so that she could not call out for help.

She grew still, terrified at returning to the box.

The man placed the snake over her head. The weight pressed into her chest and felt hot and heavy against her clammy skin. Another sensation accompanied the heaviness, a steady drum, as if the snake had a heartbeat.

The giant tied her hands behind her back, tied her ankles together, and covered her mouth and nose with a handkerchief. She stood at the edge of the hole and stared down. Rough hands shoved her from behind and she fell into the hole like a piece of board, unable to break her fall. She started to cry as the shovels of dirt landed on her back.

Abby woke gasping and crying. She swatted her hands in front of her, trying to fight off the man and the giant who had disappeared with her dream.

****

"This is delicious, Bridget," Elda said over dinner.

Their large dining table at Ula seemed empty with many of their coven in Australia

"Thank you, dearie. I found the recipe in an old book of shadows, believe it or not. That Astral book that Sebastian brought. The witch who wrote it called it Soul Summoning Porridge. Ha, I love a witch with a sense of humor."

Faustine looked up sharply and stood up from the table, knocking his chair to the floor.

"What's happened?" Lydie gasped, her eyes darting to the candles as if she expected one to be extinguished.

Elda stood and opened her arms wide, allowing a wave of calm energy to move across the room.

"I saw something," Faustine said, not looking at anyone, but into the distance as if trying to see another place, perhaps another time.

Elda went to him and rested a hand on his forearm.

"What is it, Faustine? Has someone been hurt?"

"No, no." He shook his head. "It was in the memory of the Lourdes of Warning. I didn't recognize it at the time…" he trailed off. "I have to go to the tower."

He left the room abruptly without another word.

Lydie looked shaken and on the verge of tears.

"I'm going to my room," she spat and stomped out as well.

Bridget pursed her lips and then shrugged, returning to her seat and spooning more porridge into her bowl.

After a moment, Elda did the same.

"I am going to take Lydie to Florida," Elda told Bridget.

"You are? What on earth is in Florida? Just trying to cheer her up a bit?"

Elda smiled.

"No, though I hope it does cheer her up. I received a letter from her aunt. I've been contemplating telling her and now I feel the time is right."

"An aunt?" Bridget asked, looking suddenly sad. "She won't leave us Elda, will she?"

Elda shook her head.

"No, I don't believe so, but she is coming to an age where she needs a connection to her roots. This aunt has a blood connection to Lydie. It's important for Lydie to have that."

****

Sebastian placed each foot gingerly on the soft boards as he walked across the bridge. He held his arms out to either side and fought the urge to get down and crawl. Heights didn't generally scare him, but the dizzying drop on either side of the bridge never ended. That scared him.

When he finally made it to the house, he jumped from the bridge onto the stone steps with a whoop of laughter. The sound echoed through the chasm below and circled back in a haunting cry.

Touching the door handle, he paused, absurdly thinking he should knock. What if someone lived on the other side? He couldn't just barge in.

He knocked twice and waited.

No one appeared at the door and not a sound emerged from within the house.

He turned the handle gingerly. It screeched and he pulled his hand away as if burned. The door swung open with a shriek of rusted hinges. The smell that hit him nearly sent him staggering back to the bridge. He pulled his shirt up to cover his nose and mouth.

He walked into the darkness, trying not to gag at the putrid odors that assailed him. It looked like a typical old house. Sagging furniture coated with dust and cobwebs sat on threadbare rugs. He moved down a hall to a stairway that led to the second floor. Whatever lay in the house would be upstairs, he felt sure.

At the top of the stairs, he faced a long, dim hallway lined with doors. He considered listening at each one but then decided hesitation would not serve him in this awful place. He unsheathed his knife and pushed open the first door, finding an empty room with a small bed pushed against the wall. The bed was lined with ragged stuffed animals. Button eyes dangled from the faces of bears and puppies by strings. Their mouths were sewed in jagged black stitching. A rocking chair sat in the corner and it rocked gently as if someone sat holding a baby.

He moved to the next door, more spooked by the empty room than he cared to admit. He pushed the door open and immediately a terrible wailing met his ears. It was not merely a cry, but a head-splitting sound that seemed to come from everywhere. He dropped his knife and clamped his hands over his ears.

The instant he lost his weapon, something lunged at him from the dark room. He felt the weight of it strike him and drive him back into the wall. He grabbed at the figure, cloaked and snapping at his face with yellowed, stinking teeth. He shoved it away. The thing was actually very light, skeletal even, like an emaciated person. It scurried away, tucking itself into a shadowy corner of the room.

Sebastian touched his lip and his fingers came away wet. He could taste coppery blood and he wiped it away. Bending down, he picked up the knife and moved into the room slowly, not shifting his eyes from the creature. It looked up at him, the cloak falling away from its face, and he realized he was staring at an old man. The bones of his face jutted through translucent skin.

The man's eyes, once green, looked yellow and bloodshot. They shifted from Sebastian to the doorway beyond him and his eyes bulged. He snarled, pulling his thin lips away from his teeth, and tried to back farther into the corner.

Sebastian saw a inky phantom out of the corner of his eye. He spun around, knife raised, but the black enveloped him. He vanished into the darkness.

CHAPTER 10

"The book that Dafne retrieved from the L'Osbcurite. I know where it is," Faustine told Elda later that evening when he retired to their room.

"You do?" she sat up in bed and set her book about magic in the Middle Ages on the bedside table.

"The Lourdes has it."

Elda frowned.

"How on earth would she get it?"

"That I don't know, but it was in her lair. I'm sure of it."

"But we didn't even know the title, how could you have recognized it?"

"I've meditated on those pages a dozen times. During each session, the word 'Yarrow' drifted into my thoughts and I kept assuming that the herb was in the title or perhaps just a recipe for some malady within the text, but tonight at dinner, as Bridget spoke of cookbooks, a memory came to me. There was a book on the Lourdes's vanity. I barely paid it heed, but my subconscious must have retained it. When I went back through her memories, I saw it again. The author is Yarrow, not the title. Joseph Yarrow!"

"I will contact Galla at Sorciére and ask her to search for a copy."

"There is no copy. The L'Obscurite don't just deal in rare books, Elda, many of their texts are one of a kind. Yarrow's book was written and bound by himself. The information was too dangerous to publish."

"Then you will return to the Lourdes?" Elda asked, frowning.

"Unfortunately, yes."

****

Sebastian stood outside his own home, his home with Abby. Night had fallen. The cold had edged from the bitterness of winter to the brisk winds of spring. He could hear Lake Michigan, turbulent, beating against the shore. A glow emanated from their living room window and he walked onto the deck and around the house to peer inside.

He could have simply walked through the front door, but he didn't.

At the window, he paused and took a breath. Abby and Oliver lay entwined on the shag rug before the fire. They were not making love, but somehow their embrace felt more intimate. They lay facing each other, staring deeply into one another's eyes. He could see only Abby's face. She smiled and laughed and touched Oliver's lips tenderly with her fingertips.

Sebastian rested his head against the glass. His stomach had turned into a ball of steel. Equal parts fury and despair trembled through his body. He tilted his head back and then drove it forward, smashing it into the glass.

The vision melted and now he stood in the oratory at Ula. The stone walls were muted and blurry. From the corner of his eye, he saw shelves of books of shadows, a desk littered with papers. But his eyes saw only the metal box. It shone as if lit from within, but the room was void of light, the darkness outside seeping in. He touched the box, smooth and cold beneath his fingers. Deftly, he put in the code and lifted the lid. He reached inside, lifted the black cloth, heavy with the weight of its treasure. Folding back the fabric, he sighed with pleasure. The amulet lay on the black cloth. The red stone pulsed and the eye of the snake locked with his own.

A tremor of pleasure moved through him as he lifted the amulet out and slipped it over his head.

Instantly, the room vanished and Sebastian stood in another castle. His castle. He stood at the head of a long table. The chairs were filled. Claire, his parents, Abby and others. He was the master of this universe. In a dungeon in the heart of the castle, Oliver hung chained to the wall. A smile curved Sebastian's lips at the thought of Oliver, powerless, while he ruled supreme.

Abby looked at him with adoration. He touched the amulet on his chest and felt the power surge through his body. He lifted his hands and the ceiling ripped open, revealing the night sky. A thousand skin-walkers soared above the castle. They waited for their master, Sebastian, to guide them. The power had shifted. The light had been snuffed out.

He blinked away the visions. More would come if he didn't force himself back to reality. The images hurt. Like dreams, they did not feel false. He embodied each completely. In the final vision, he had been a Vepar, the greatest, most powerful Vepar that ever existed. A shudder of pleasure and fear coursed through his body.

"Interesting dreams you have, hybrid."

He looked toward the voice and his head lolled on his neck. Every muscle and tendon in his body seemed weak and useless. His eyes blurred and then cleared.

The water witch sat in a glittering opal chair. The curves and edges of the chair sparkled in a rainbow of colors reflected by the light from a huge crystal chandelier. Sebastian lay on a floor of glass. Beneath the glass, he could see only sky and clouds. The witch looked different. Her red eyes were shaded with a purple veil, and her long black hair hung over one shoulder. She wore a shimmering black shift, and silver bracelets lined her arms nearly to her elbows.

Sebastian struggled to his hands and knees and then stood, shakily.

Looking at the floor made him dizzy and he stumbled to a wall and pressed his hand against the cool limestone.

"What do you want?" he asked.

"To make your dreams come true, of course. What do you think the purpose of this world is, after all?"

Sebastian touched his head gingerly and found a soft spot matted with dried blood.

"Who hit me?"

"You had a little fall."

He shook his head and searched the room for a door. There was none.

"You have something that belongs to me," the witch continued, and Sebastian heard barely disguised fury, and envy, beneath her words. "You intend to destroy it."

She had seen the amulet in his dreams.

"How do you know that? What did you do to my head?"

The witch laughed. Smoothing her hand along the opal chair, she trained her steely gaze on Sebastian's.

"Do you fancy yourself a witch, hybrid? An impenetrable fortress? I am a witch. I could fillet your mind with a thought. I have seen all that you are and I am not impressed."

"The amulet is dangerous. It holds a spirit. She'd make mince-meat out of you." He didn't know why he spoke the words, surely not to save himself. He knew she would grow angrier and she did.

Beneath him the floor vanished and he plummeted into the sky. He might have screamed. He thrust his arms above him, but the glass floor had already disappeared. He flailed in terror, unable to breathe as the wind rushed by. With a smack he hit the ground, but it wasn't the ground, it was glass. He opened his eyes to find the glass floor restored beneath him and the witch watching him with satisfaction. She had meant to scare him. It worked.

He shifted onto his back and breathed, feeling his heart kicking against his ribs. The rise and fall of his chest had never felt so good.

"In this place, I own you. And the only way you leave is if I let you. Understand?"

He nodded.

"Good. I'm not surprised to hear you've underestimated the true nature of the amulet. Your kind always does. Those who consider their magic superior scoff at the true magic of this world."

"It's not here. It's in America."

She said nothing, but Sebastian felt his head grow stuffy and thick.

"I see," she said after a moment. "Then you will bring it back to me."

"Why would I do that?" he asked, pushing himself up to sitting. He still felt the sensation of falling, and looking at the glass floor made his stomach turn.

"Oh, a slip of the tongue, I fear. You will not bring it with your own two hands. You will stay here with me in the dream wood. Your lovely Abby will bring it to me or perhaps the handsome Oliver. Maybe they could fetch it together."

Sebastian narrowed his eyes. He wanted to get angry and rush the evil witch but knew too well the power she had over the dream wood. If she intended to kill him, it would take only a thought.

"I've left on my own before. How can you hold me here?"

The witch smiled and her red eyes shone beneath her veil.

"You crossed the barrier. Down here, you are mine."

He understood. When he went into the pond, he left the dream wood that was controlled by hybrids and entered another world, a dark world.

****

"Someone's coming," Oliver shouted.

Abby jolted awake and blinked into the dark forest. Where was she?

At first, she thought herself back in her house in Trager, dreaming in her bed. She looked around wildly, trying to get a grasp on reality. Dark hulking shadows slowly materialized into trees. Overhead the dark sky held thousands of stars and the moon shone.

She stood quickly and a wave of dizziness almost buckled her. Julian grabbed her arm and steadied her.

A figure crossed the bridge and Abby's heart leaped and then fell as she saw the small, hunched person who moved toward them.

Julian lit a torch and held it before them.

"Help," the stranger croaked.

"You have to cross the bridge," Julian called. "And then we can help you."

The figure moved closer and Oliver stepped in front of Abby.

"Go back toward the trees Abby, just in case."

Abby didn't move. She watched as the man, clearly not Sebastian, stepped from the bridge and sank to his knees.

The old man looked at them with sickly yellow eyes from a gaunt face lined with wrinkles. His hair hung limp, revealing bald patches.

Julian knelt and took the man's hand. Helena hurried to their side.

The man hung his head.

"I have a message from the water witch. If you want to see Sebastian again, you must bring her the amulet."

****

"How is he?" Julian asked when Matilda met him and Helena in the apothecary.

The Sky Mothers kept their tinctures and potions in a circular room connected to their greenhouse.

Helena was busily folding herbs into a poultice.

"He is alive, but I fear not for long." Matilda sighed. "Something continues to drain him. I've performed several healing charms and given him every potion in our stores, but still, he declines."

"He is Fin, then? The hybrid who disappeared fifty years ago?"

Matilda frowned and nodded.

"Yes, he has aged greatly. At first, I did not recognize him at all."

"Has he said more?" Helena asked, handing the poultice to Matilda.

"Very little that has been coherent. I can't tell what are dreams and what are real experiences. He talks a lot about the water witch, whoever that is. Liam never mentioned her and surely Meghan would not have created an evil witch in the dream wood."

Julian sighed and ran his hands through his silver hair.

"I'm starting to think the universe is working against us on this curse," he mumbled.

Helena touched his arm but felt a similar defeat.

"What will you do?" Matilda asked.

"I will retrieve the amulet and bring it back. What other choice do we have?"

"And you will just hand it over to this dark witch?"

"Of course not. I'm not sure what we will do. I would like some time with Fin. I believe that our only hope is to know more about the dream wood."

Matilda crossed her arms and looked away. Helena wondered if she might resist allowing Julian access to the frail man.

"Let's give him a few more hours of rest and then you can attempt to speak with him."

****

Abby waited until Matilda closed the door firmly behind her and walked toward the ocean.

She pressed the door open and peeked into the room.

The old man, Fin, lay on a table covered in white linen. A mist surrounded the bed, seeping from a series of pores in the floor. A mobile of crystals dangled just above the man's chest and cast patterns of rainbow light across the sheet covering his emaciated body.

"Fin?" Abby whispered, moving closer to the bed.

She gently lifted the washcloth away from the man's eyes.

He opened them, blinking at Abby several times as if he could not see. His eyes were still yellow, but some of the white had begun to return. The corners were thick with a milky crust.

"I'm Abby, Fin. Sebastian is my fiancé."

Fin stared at her, but no recognition dawned.

"Did you meet Sebastian?"

Fin pressed his lips together and his eyes darted toward the door.

Abby glanced behind her, but no one had entered.

"Please, it's urgent."

Fin tried to speak, but his voice came out in a barely audible croak.

Abby found a pitcher of water and quickly poured him a glass. She held the cup to the man's parched lips and tried to steady her shaking hands.

"Met him," Fin whispered. "You can't save him."

Abby clutched the man's hand, alarmed at the paper-thin skin and bird-like bones beneath.

"What do you mean? Why can't I save him?"

The door swung open behind her and Abby whirled around.

Binda stood in the doorway. She narrowed her eyes at Abby, but did not chastise her. Carrying a tray of slimy looking slugs, she walked to the edge of the bed and surveyed Fin.

"Leaches, my dear."

Fin's eyes were closed. He had fallen back asleep.

"I can help," Abby told Binda, watching the older witch carefully arrange the leeches on Fin's bare chest.

Binda did not speak or look at her.

"My blood can heal him," she continued.

Binda paused.

"This man cannot be saved, Abby."

"What? Why?"

Binda pulled the sheet lower and Abby jumped back. From the waist down the man's skin had grown gray and putrid. The smell made Abby gag and she ran from the room, vomiting on the stone walkway outside the door. She did not return to the room, but walked toward her yurt, tears streaming down her face. What had happened to the man? And did the same fate await Sebastian?

Sky Mothers

CHAPTER 11

Elda knocked on Lydie's door and waited. Lydie had spent a good deal of time in her room since the others had left for Australia. Elda had little experience with pre-teens. It had been decades since she'd experienced the evolution of a child as they transitioned into adulthood and she felt, honestly, unprepared.

Lydie opened the door.

"Hi," she said, with a hint of defiance.

Elda sensed that Lydie wanted to act out, but fought the urges. Though Lydie was young, she had been raised in an old castle in the ways of an old world and teen rebellion didn't exactly fit.

"Can I come in?"

Lydie held the door open and retreated to the couch at the end of her bed. A worn paperback lay open on its spine.

"Are you upset that I asked you not to go to Australia?"

Lydie bit her lip and broke eye contact with Elda. She looked sad, angry, hurt-a torrent of emotions that all wanted their time in the light.

Finally, she nodded and swiped a curl behind her ear. She picked absently at a fraying string on her sweatshirt.

"I'm sorry that it hurt you, Lydie. I want you to know that I have a reason."

Lydie looked up with a mixture of curiosity and challenge.

"Did you know that your mother had a sister?"

"A sister?" Lydie apparently had not known.

Elda nodded.

"Your mother mentioned her once many years ago, but then never again. I believed she had died or perhaps they were estranged. After your parents' deaths, I briefly looked for her sister, but could find no address or information about her whereabouts. Then a year ago, I received this."

Elda held up an envelope.

"It was addressed 'To Whom It May Concern' at your parents old home. I had their mail forwarded to our post office box many years ago. After a couple of years, the mail slowed and then stopped altogether. Until this letter, of course."

Lydie held out her hand.

"Can I see it?"

Elda handed it to her.

She studied the envelope. The return address said Camilla Baker, who lived on West Sixteenth Street in Dunedin, Florida.

"Aunt Cammy," Lydie whispered under her breath.

Elda widened her eyes, surprised.

"You did know her?"

Lydie wrinkled her forehead and shook her head.

"I don't know. I guess I must have. Seeing her name just now, I suddenly remembered my mom standing in the kitchen saying that we were going to bake a cake for Aunt Cammy's birthday. I don't remember the woman though, or the birthday for that matter. Though I do remember my mom letting me lick the bowl. It was strawberry cake batter."

Elda smiled.

"Your mother had a special skill in the kitchen. She made the most divine coconut cake."

Lydie smiled and then frowned.

"My memories of her are so flimsy. I get a glimpse, a smell, an image, but nothing of substance. I want to close my eyes and get transported back there, but I just can't."

Elda took a deep breath and moved closer to Lydie on the couch. She put an arm around her and leaned her cheek against Lydie's soft, sweet-smelling curls.

"I know sweetie. I still miss my mother and I've been without her for a very, very long time. I cling to those bits of memory too. You'll keep those for the rest of your life, but when people are gone, they're just…"

"Gone," Lydie finished.

"Would you like to meet her? Your aunt?"

Lydie sat up and swiped at her eyes. She stood and crossed her room, looking at a collage on her wall. It contained pictures of her parents together with quotes and images that she and Helena had cut from magazines.

"Yeah, I think so."

****

Sebastian woke in the dilapidated house. The soft rotting floorboards creaked as he pushed onto his hands and knees. His head ached and he tasted the coppery metallic of blood on his lips. He had no recollection of the witch moving him to the house, but maybe she hadn't. In a world of illusions, space and matter abided by different laws, or perhaps no laws at all.

His stomach growled and he smiled at the normality of the feeling. He wanted desperately for typical sensations, otherwise he might succumb to the sense of hopelessness nagging at the corners of his mind.

"Food. One thing at a time."

He stood and surveyed the room. He did not have high hopes.

In the kitchen, most of the cupboards hung open and empty. He turned the faucet handle and a spurt of black water rushed out, followed by the groaning cry of empty pipes. No water was a much larger problem than no food.

He walked back upstairs, pushing doors open to find empty bedrooms.

After he felt sure the house lay empty, he returned to the front door and the unnerving path that led to the woods. He walked the bridge slowly, unable to avert his eyes from the empty void that lay to either side of the decayed planks.

He followed the same path that led him to the house. Perhaps he could climb the tree that he had seen the water witch slip out of.

When he found the dark water floating eerily above the soft earth, he scanned the tree that rose into the water. Like the rest of the tress, it looked black and gnarled. When he jumped for a low branch, it snapped and fell to the ground. Thousands of blazing red ants swarmed away from the ashy bark. He tried for another branch, which also broke. When he tried to climb the trunk, the bark slid away and revealed more ants, millions of ants. They swarmed over his hands and forearms and he felt the sharp sting as they bit him.

"Oh shit," he cursed, rubbing his arms vigorously. Even as he rubbed them away, he felt more streaming up his legs. He whirled away from the tree and dropped to the ground. The soft earth sank beneath his weight and he writhed against it, scrambling to remove the ants intent on devouring him. He kicked off his pants and struggled out of his shirt, scooping handfuls of the stinking ground, muddy beneath the surface, over his inflamed body. After several minutes of violently applying mud, he lay still.

"Dream wood, my ass," he whispered. "Nightmare wood is more like it."

He looked up at the murky water suspended above him and wondered if Claire stood on the edge, peering into the black water, searching for him. More than that, he thought of Abby. What had she done when he never returned from the dream wood? What was she doing at that moment?

Gradually, the pain subsided and the mud began to dry.

Sebastian stood and wiped the dried mud from his skin. Shaking out his clothes, he slipped them back on, and attempted to ignore his thirst as he moved away from the pond. More bent, blackened trees lined the marshy ground. When he heard the sound of trickling water, his heart leaped. It was strange how desperately he wanted water now that it was unavailable. Would his mouth feel paper-dry if he were strolling through the dream wood, rather than locked in a dead world beneath it?

"The Underworld had rivers, shouldn't this place?" he asked, mostly to hear his own voice. In his life before Claire's death, Sebastian studied mythology. Not in any serious way, but as a hobby of sorts. He had found the idea of an underworld intriguing, but highly unrealistic. He simply didn't believe that people were destined to spend eternity in a world clearly created by the small mind of man.

The trickling grew louder and the ground beneath him grew harder. The marshy earth gave way to slick black rock. The terrain became steep and slick and he moved slowly, to avoid slipping.

He found the water leaking from a crevice in a wall of black rock that would be impossible to scale. Sebastian pressed his face against the surface. It had an acrid, sulfur taste, but the water was ice cold. He drank hungrily until his belly felt like it might burst. He stripped off his clothes and cupped his hands beneath the water. It ran slowly and took a long time to fill his palms, but the sensation as it splashed over his body nearly brought him to his knees. Air-dried, he put his clothes back on and followed the rock wall. A half-mile down, he found a cave that disappeared into darkness. He had to duck to enter and looked behind him at the already dim light. He did not have a flashlight or any way to produce fire.

He could not see how far the cave traveled, but he had to try. Though he doubted the cave offered a pathway out of the witch's world.

He couldn't shake the feeling that she knew exactly where he was, but he blocked the thought. He felt along the wall, walking hunched over, until the path opened above him and he could stand straight. Images of sleeping monsters popped into his mind to replace the blackness before him. Giant bears with bone sharpened teeth, or worse, creatures that only existed in a world of nightmares, came unbidden to his mind. He had always had an active imagination. At that moment, it served him in the worst way.

He smacked into a rock wall and stumbled back, falling on his butt. A sharp pain shot up his spine and the breath whooshed from his lungs. The darkness was getting to him. What if he got turned around and never made it out of the cave? He knew better than to allow the thoughts ricocheting through his mind. In extreme situations, people's fears usually killed them, not the experience. Rock climbers, deep-sea divers, hikers lost in the forest- he'd read enough stories to know that he had to pull his shit together if he wanted to get out alive. Not only the cave, but the dream wood, too. Several hybrids had gone in and never emerged. Were they dead?

When his heart slowed, he crawled on hands and knees to the rock wall that he'd run into. Fumbling blindly, he realized that the cave divided into two tunnels. He stood, slowly, and closed his eyes. The level of darkness didn't change with his eyes closed, but his level of calm did.

"Which way?" he whispered.

He didn't question his sudden movement toward the right tunnel. Was he guided or merely making a choice? He honestly didn't know.

He walked and breathed and counted his steps. Ten steps into the right tunnel, twenty, eighty, one hundred fifty, and then a subtle change. The black seemed less black. He walked faster, still counting, two hundred and ten steps, and then light. The tunnel widened and opened into a spacious cavern. Stalactites grew down from the cave ceiling like a mouth full of teeth, but the freakish imaginings no longer bothered him. He could see again. Several torches lit the interior and he walked toward one, slowly.

As he moved through the cavern, a rough hand shoved him from behind. He sprawled forward, too surprised to get a hand out and break his fall. He landed on his chest and his face hit the floor. He felt blood spurt from his nose and he closed his eyes against the wash of stars and nausea that followed.

Before he could turn over, someone straddled him, grasping his hair and yanking his head back. A sharp blade was pressed into his neck.

"I'm not armed," he mumbled through blood, wincing at the excruciating pain in his face.

"She sent you?" The man growled. "I'll send you back to her in pieces."

Sebastian took a deep breath and then shoved straight up onto his hands and knees. The man faltered and dropped his blade. He made to grab for Sebastian's hair, but Sebastian rolled away and jumped to his feet. He squared off against the man, ready to fight.

"Don't come anywhere near me," Sebastian barked. "Whoever you think I am, you're wrong."

The man retrieved his weapon, not a knife, but a sharp piece of rock. He looked wild-eyed and vicious. Sebastian could almost imagine his dilemma as he considered whether to run or attack.

"I'm trapped down here," Sebastian continued, holding up his hands. "The dark witch has trapped me as well."

"Meghan," the man spit, as if in explanation.

"Meghan?" Sebastian repeated, surprised. According to the Sky Mothers, Meghan head created the dream wood and disappeared into it more than two hundred years before.

The man nodded.

"You're Liam," Sebastian said, vaguely recognizing him from his glimpse into the past. The Liam from his vision had been tan, healthy and robust. This man, pale and rail thin, with yellowing eyes and greasy looking hair, was a wasted version of his former self.

Liam nodded, but did not drop his blade.

"I came here looking for you. Hannah sent me."

"Hannah." Liam whispered the name as if were sacred.

"Yes, she's waiting for you. She believes you're alive."

Liam blinked at him and looked at his hands still holding the rock as if he didn't recognize them.

"Hannah." He said the name again, and this time it seemed to cause him physical pain.

"You've been stuck here all this time?" Sebastian asked.

Liam stared at him.

"How long has it been?" he asked.

"More than a year."

Liam sank to his knees and let the blade drop.

"I thought it might have been longer, decades even."

"Well, I'm happy to be the bearer of good news, then," Sebastian offered, amazed at his ability to feel compassion for the man who just smashed his face two minutes earlier.

"I'm sorry," Liam told him. "I've been waiting for Meghan to come for me. I thought…"

"It's okay."

Sebastian sat on the cave floor. Now that he wasn't in immediate danger, he could rest. He gingerly touched his broken nose.

"Sorry about that," Liam told him.

Sebastian nodded.

"Now you're stuck here too." Liam sighed, scratching at the blonde hair that covered most of his face.

"She wants something that I have outside of here. Maybe that will get us out."

Liam smiled ironically.

"She didn't send you out to get it, now did she?"

"No, but the witches out there aren't stupid. They'll figure out how to bargain with her."

"And this item is something they'll part with to get you back?"

Sebastian smiled.

"Abby will flood the world if they don't."

"Abby's your witch?"

"Well, I don't own her, but yes, she's mine."

Knowing Abby waited for him made each moment both better and worse. He longed to get back to her and also feared not making it out.

"Hannah's mine. Or she was, but at this point…" he gestured helplessly to their surroundings.

"You've given up?"

"No," Liam said defensively. "I tried to kill you, didn't I?"

"How long have you been in here? The cave, I mean?"

Liam offered him a joyless smile.

"There's no time here, not the way we measure it up there, no day and night. Sometimes it gets dark for a few hours and then light again, but with no rhyme or reason. I tried to keep time the first few weeks I was here. It was a wasted effort."

Sebastian grimaced.

"That would drive me insane."

"It does," Liam said. "It will."

CHAPTER 12

"Where is everyone?" Julian asked Bridget, coming upon her in the greenhouse after he found the castle empty.

"Oh." She jumped and dropped a bottle of neutralizer. It smashed on the concrete floor.

"I'm sorry," he said, waving his hand at the spreading liquid. It vanished.

"You nearly scared me out of my britches," she sputtered, holding a hand to her heaving bosom. Her red hair stood on end and Julian sensed he looked as harried as Bridget.

"What is it? What's happened?"

Bridget wrung her hands and shook her head.

"Nothing, nothing at all, just spooked being here all by my lonesome. It's a rare day that I've got the castle all to myself. That's not all true though. Adora is here, after all. She's in the floating garden. I thought the sun and fresh air would do her good."

"Wait, did you just say Adora?"

"Yes, Adora. Oh my, Faustine meant to contact you, did he not?"

Julian shook his head.

"He tried. I had a vision of him reaching out, but it was unclear. You're telling me Adora's alive?"

Bridget nodded.

"Yes, not in the best of shape, but alive and healing every day."

She stopped suddenly. "But what are you doing here? We weren't expecting you home for another few days, at least."

"It's a long story," he murmured absently. Adora's survival felt nothing short of a miracle. Finally, some good news. "Where are Elda and Faustine?" Julian asked. "And Lydie?"

"Faustine had some emergency errand, ran out of here first thing this morning with barely a sip of tea. Elda and Lydie have gone to Florida. I probably wouldn't be so jittery, but I saw something funny in my teacup this morning. A strange little doll seemed to be floating there."

"A doll?" Julian asked, mildly impatient. He trusted Bridget's intuitions, but of all the witches at Ula, she was the most scattered and unsure of herself. It was often hard to distinguish the symbols that came to her.

"Why are Lydie and Elda going to Florida?"

"Apparently Lydie has an aunt who made contact with Elda."

"So that's why Elda asked Lydie to stay."

"Seems that way," Bridget agreed. "But tell me, Julian, has something happened in Australia?"

"Walk with me back to the floating garden. I'll tell you on the way. I have to leave soon. I'm flying back in five hours, which leaves me just enough time to get back to the airport. But I want to see Adora first."

****

Abby walked through the Sky Mothers' compound picking up every book she passed, reading a page, and then returning it. Sebastian had disappeared into the dream wood three days before and Julian could not return with the amulet soon enough. She needed help, but where could she possibly get it? Matilda insisted that they could not penetrate the dream wood and that Meghan had not left behind any clues to the magic that contained it, but Abby doubted that. If she'd learned anything from the Asemaa, it was that someone always recorded the past. Abby had watched Elda, Bridget, and Helena all recording spells and potions in books of shadows. They wanted to remember the precise measurement, incantations and even weather during every spell. That documentation changed the world of magic. Meghan would not have created something as magnificent as the dream wood without some kind of record.

She encountered Kit near the cascading water that had taken Abby's breath away when she first arrived at the Sky Mothers. Kit knelt on a slippery looking rock and carefully collected algae, which she placed in a glass jar.

Kit looked up as Abby approached. She stood and blew into her hands. The slime that had coated her palms disappeared.

"I'm very sorry, Abby. Hannah should never have led Sebastian to the dream wood."

"Thank you," Abby said, honestly. "Can I ask you a question, Kit? Do you know where Meghan stayed when she was part of the Sky Mothers? Which room was hers?"

Kit wrinkled her brow.

"I believe Matilda has her room now. Why do you ask?"

"I just can't believe she didn't explain the dream wood. I'm hoping to find something that can help Sebastian."

Kit nodded.

"I'd do the same. Binda has been here since the start of the Sky Mothers and is adamant that Meghan never recorded it. Apparently, Meghan was terrified that someone wanted Clyde dead. She was very secretive about the magic she performed. If it's out there, I would imagine it's well hidden."

Abby pressed her lips together and scanned the dense forests beyond the coven. It was one thing to search Meghan's room, but if she'd concealed the information with magic, how would she ever find it?

"Have you seen Binda? Maybe I could ask her…"

Kit nodded.

"I believe she's in the garden. The one near the waterfalls."

"Thanks, I'll go look for her."

Kit nodded, but something in her face made Abby pause.

"You don't think she'll talk to me?"

"It's not that. She's just…quiet. I believe she's the kind of witch who will take secrets to her grave."

****

"What is it?" Sebastian asked, following Liam down another small tunnel. It appeared to dead-end, but Liam reached overhead and started to push hard into the rock. "Seems like a wasted effort."

Liam ignored him and continued to push, grunting and breaking out in a shiny sweat. With a final shove, a slab of rock above him dislodged and a sliver of light showed through the crevice. Liam pushed the rock out of the way and then reached his hands through the hole, grasping the ledge and hoisting himself up. Sebastian followed.

As he poked his head through the opening, a cold slimy film seemed to wash over his face.

"Ugh." He dropped back out of the hole.

Liam looked at him through the opening and laughed.

"I forgot how that felt the first time I came through. Don't worry, it's a good thing. Come on up."

Sebastian hoisted himself through a second time, again recoiling as a slippery cold coated his face and body. When he stood in the room, the sensation passed.

"What is this?" he asked, taking in the small, cramped space filled with books. A crude bed made from gnarled tree branches abutted one wall. The cave walls were scrawled with writing in black charcoal.

"I think it belonged to the original hybrid, Clyde."

"Wow," Sebastian touched a pile of rocks suspended over a silver basin filled with water. "It's an air well."

"So, it has a name," Liam commented. "I've been calling it the water maker."

"Same principle."

Sebastian glanced at some of the writing on the walls, much of it the incoherent babbling of a self-serving madman.

"She has imprisoned me to stifle my greatness, but you can't stop a master who is meant to rule the world. Only a small-minded witch would believe that she could stop a great sorcerer. She will rue the day she kissed my infant cheeks," he read out loud.

"There's a lot more." Liam bent down and picked up a stack of dried leaves covered in writing.

A name caught Sebastian's eye and he snatched it from the stack.

Kanti, it said. Not once, but a dozen times at least. Around the name, the man had drawn symbols and written random words like fire, sacrifice and eternity.

Sebastian shook his head as if not quite believing it.

"What's Kanti?" Liam asked. "That word is all over this place."

"I should have known it was all connected. It's always connected," Sebastian grumbled.

Liam watched, waiting for an answer.

"Not what, but who. Kanti is a woman, or was a woman. She's the reason we came to Australia. It's a long story. If we're stuck here, I'll tell you, but right now, let's skip it. Have you ever seen this guy?"

"Clyde? I'd imagine he's dead. We're not witches, after all. He'd be three hundred years old."

"True, and if I wasn't standing here looking at this name, I'd assume that too. But my assumptions often bite me in the ass."

"That's assumptions for you. I don't think he died here in the Forest of Purgatory, though."

"The Forest of Purgatory?"

"I named this place, seemed fitting," Liam told him, smiling ironically.

"Yeah it does," Sebastian admitted.

"That weird feeling when you come up through the hole - I believe it removes the charm that the witch uses to track us. Before I found this room, Meghan could always find me, but not when I'm in here. I can't feel her in here, ever, and I've heard sounds below when she sends her phantoms after me, but they never find me."

"Her phantoms?" Sebastian asked, almost preferring not to know.

"They do her bidding. Black and thick, but not solid. I don't know what they are, but they appear and sort of wash over you and that's it. You wake up in Meghan's hell hall."

Sebastian thought back to the black shadow that had surrounded him in the old house.

"I've met them," he said.

Liam sat heavily on the bed and rested his skeletal face in his hands.

"I can't tell you how happy I am to see you, mate," he admitted.

Sebastian started to ask why, but didn't need to. One look at Liam told him everything he needed to know.

"What do you eat?" Sebastian heard his stomach grumble and imagined the look on Abby's face were she with him. She often commented on his insatiable hunger even in moments of crisis.

"You saw the soggy grass out there?"

"Please, no!" Sebastian grimaced, thinking of the mushy stinking grass.

"That and the fire ants if you crush about fifty trillion of them. Usually give me a wicked stomachache after, though."

"So, she'd let you starve? Did you ever ask her for food?"

Liam shrugged.

"I ate twice, real food, when I pretended to be her son."

"What?"

Liam looked mildly ashamed, but nodded.

"She believes I'm her son. She probably believes you're her son. And that skeleton that lives in the house, I think once upon a time, she believed he was her son. I think she trapped Clyde in here, but somehow, he got away and every time another hybrid is stupid enough to stumble into her spider's web, she wraps them up nice and tight and keeps them for eternity."

"Why did you enter the pond, Liam? I visited the coffin that reveals the past. You went to her intentionally."

"Pretty nasty, huh? Climb into this coffin to see the past. Gave me the willies the first time I was in there."

"Yeah, if I wasn't claustrophobic before, I am now."

"I went to the pond hoping that Meghan would reveal the secret of the dream wood. I wanted Hannah to join me inside, not forever, but just occasionally. I also suspected that the water witch was Meghan and I knew that Binda had spent much of her life trying to find out what happened to her. I figured if I delivered Meghan to Binda, the Sky Mothers would give us their blessing. We wanted to build our own place, but Hannah needed their approval to stay in the coven while living apart. Binda thought me unworthy of Hannah, though. Between you and me, Binda's not exactly fond of the blokes.

"Did you ever get to ask her about the dream wood?"

Liam sighed.

"She speaks in riddles. I think her mind's as mushy as the grass outside. If I asked her questions, she would become furious and insist that I was trying to manipulate her. One day I was Clyde and she doted on me, the next day she would call me a blood traitor and leave me shackled to a tree to get eaten by the ants. I gave up trying to talk to her."

"We've got to get out of here," Sebastian murmured, fearing his own future encounters with the dark witch.

He walked along the perimeter of the room, reading the confused words scrawled on the rock wall.

"Look there, above the table."

Sebastian walked to a crudely made table that looked ready to collapse beneath stacks of rocks carved into various shapes. Some of which appeared to be weapons, much like the one Liam had attacked him with earlier.

Sebastian studied a jumble of images that transitioned through the stages of man as a primitive species, to Homo-Erectus, Homo Sapiens, Neanderthal, and finally to modern man. Except it didn't end there. The next image brought Sebastian closer to the wall. The modern man transformed into a walking wolf with wings. A skin-walker.

"My head feels like it's about to explode," Sebastian said, rubbing his temples. Exhaustion, dehydration, and the overload of information threatened to capsize him.

"I know, seems to me the guy was nuts, but you want to know something really crazy?"

"Hmm?" Sebastian asked, not sure if he did want to know.

"I've seen one of those things. The flying wolf man. I saw one in the dream wood the second time I went in. It was crouched in a giant tree watching me. Scared me half to death. Fortunately, in the dream wood, you can make things disappear, which I did, but I figure the original guy, Clyde, must have created it."

"I've seen one too." Sebastian sighed.

"Yeah, there's some crazy stuff in here."

"I didn't see it the dream wood."

"How's that?" Liam asked, sitting up straighter.

"I've seen one in the world, they exist."

"No! Really?"

Sebastian nodded.

****

Abby took the tiny glass bottle from the pocket of her cloak. She had never used a vanishing serum before. Oliver once told her of magic that could make you disappear, and at the time, she'd brushed it off. Now she intended to put it to use. She had found the book while searching for information about the dream wood and slipped it into her pocket to peruse later. However, after she saw Binda, she felt inspired to put one of the spells to use. The enchantment called 'The Vanishing' contained notes in the margins, the kind of notes that told Abby it was a well-used piece of magic.

She checked to ensure the apothecary was empty before slipping inside and quickly mixing the ingredients in a glass bowl. Fortunately, the Sky Mothers meticulously labeled everything and Abby easily found the ingredients she sought. She had to search for spider eggs, but found those in a glass cooler that blasted her in an icy mist when she opened the door.

Quickly pouring the elixir into an amber bottle, she hurried back to the waterfall to find Binda.

The witch no longer stood in the garden, but Abby glimpsed her disappearing into the woods and raced after her.

She took the potion in a quick gulp and gasped as the fiery liquid scalded her throat and raced, inferno-like, into her stomach. A huge steaming belch erupted from her lips and she clamped a hand over her mouth. Had Binda heard her? Staying perfectly still, she waited for several breaths and then peeked around a tree. Binda's white cloak billowed behind her as she moved steadily through the woods. She did not appear to have slowed her stride.

As Abby followed, keeping her distance to remain undetected, she watched her hands closely. Were they growing lighter? More transparent? Yes, after several minutes, she saw that the leaves had begun to show through her outstretched arms.

Binda stopped at a large dark pond, and Abby ducked behind a tree, though she had likely become invisible.

"Meghan, Meghan," Binda hissed, kneeling over the black water. She leaned close so that her nose nearly touched the glistening surface.

Abby stepped closer, placing each foot as if it were a fragile egg that she must not crack. Binda was an old witch, smart, cunning, and frankly a little scary. Abby did not savor the thought of being discovered spying on her.

"Please Meghan…" she whispered, more loudly. The pond lay silent, but then in its center, Abby saw a ripple. The water undulated. A woman's face appeared just beneath the surface.

Binda moaned and reached for the water, but did not touch it.

"Oh Meghan, my sweet Meghan. I've missed you. Do you know how I've missed you?"

Binda's tone had changed so dramatically that Abby could hardly believe it was the same witch speaking. The hard edge that punctuated Binda's words had been replaced by despair and hopelessness.

The water opened and another voice rose from it. Abby stepped back at the sound and nearly fell over a rotting log.

"Come, at last, have you?" the voice taunted. It was a woman's voice, but mean and slick, like the hiss of a snake, the whisper of a knife slicing through the air. The voice scared Abby and she wanted to grab Binda by the shoulders and pull her away from the pond's edge.

"I've wanted to come a thousand times. And before that, I did come a thousand times. You know that I did, but I had to stop. I couldn't take it anymore, seeing you trapped down there."

The woman beneath the water laughed and the sound echoed through the forest as if they sat in a cavern.

"Hard for you? Hard for you, living free in the world? Don't talk to me of hardships, Binda."

"Please don't be angry with me," Binda started and Abby could see tears splashing from her face into the water.

As the tears touched the surface, the woman in the water contorted her own face into a horrible scowl. The water thrashed and Binda fell back, soaking wet.

She wiped the water away with her cloak.

"I didn't put you in there, Meghan. You did. I won't let you punish me for your mistakes."

"Mistakes," the witch cried out. "And where were you when I needed you most? Building the Sky Mothers. Recruiting new witches, younger witches with pretty blond hair and huge empty heads. You left me to deal with him alone. He killed me, Binda. He destroyed me."

Binda crawled to the edge of the pond on her knees. Her hands shook, but again, she reached toward the surface.

"If I had only known, Meghan. I thought he was trapped. That you would return to me. I didn't know."

"It doesn't matter now. What do you want?"

Binda closed her eyes and Abby felt the outpouring of her sadness so deeply that she wanted to burst into tears.

"There are witches here from Trager City. They speak of an amulet."

The face beneath the water stretched into a huge hideous grin.

"Yes, I know Binda. It is time for Clyde to come home."

"But they won't give you the amulet, Meghan. They mean to destroy it."

The water thrashed and then as quickly grew calm.

"Not if they ever want to see their beloved hybrid again."

CHAPTER 13

"I've been here for a year," Liam reminded Sebastian as he walked the room again.

He touched walls, kicked at the floor and felt along the ceiling.

"If there was a secret passage, I would have found it by now."

"But you said yourself, he got out. And obviously, he created this room to hide from her. It makes sense this would be the way out."

"If we weren't in the center of a mountain, maybe."

"I tried going back through the pond," Sebastian said. "Practically got eaten alive by ants."

"I attempted that too, and if you decide to let the ants eat you and go for it anyway, you'll smash your head into a brick wall that looks like a pond."

"What?"

"You can't get into it. It looks like the pond from below, but it's rock hard. I learned the hard way, five or six times."

"Argh," Sebastian raked his hands through his black curls and tried not to start kicking the walls.

He couldn't imagine being trapped in the dream wood for much longer. He already felt close to his breaking point.

"What if we attacked the witch?" he asked.

Liam offered him a wry smile.

"Tried that too. I've gone after her with rocks, sticks. I've pretended to be her son to get close to her. You name it, I've tried it. One time, I actually got my hands around her throat, but the next instant I was plummeting toward my death."

"But you didn't die?"

"Nope, I woke up on the swamp grass every time."

****

Lydie knocked and then backed away from the door, tempted to duck behind Elda's skirts as if she were a shy little girl instead of a young woman. Elda offered her an encouraging smile, but it did little to calm her pounding heart. She focused on breathing slowly and deeply, not wanting to ruin her first impression by accidentally setting her aunt's house on the fire.

The door opened and a tall woman with long blonde curls answered the door. She wore a fuchsia dress, dangling peacock earrings and a smile that transported Lydie back to her childhood. It was her mother's smile.

"Lydie?" the woman asked, stepping forward as if she meant to hug Lydie, and then offering a tentative hand as if that might be more appropriate.

Without thinking, Lydie flung herself into the woman's arms. She inhaled scents of rosemary and garlic and a tropical smelling lotion, coconut perhaps. Camilla hugged her back, pressing her lips to Lydie's head.

"I can't believe it has been ten years," the woman murmured.

Lydie felt tears streaming down her face. She wanted to stay in her aunt's embrace, partially due to embarrassment at her emotions, but mostly to hold on to this woman who knew her, who loved her.

Camilla hugged her extra tight and then pulled away, looking into her face.

"You look just like her," she said, brushing a tear away from her own face. "For a moment when I opened the door…" her voice caught and she shook her head, laughing and starting to cry harder.

"I'm Elda. It's wonderful to finally meet you," Elda told her, stepping forward and offering her hand.

"Yes, thank you, Elda. Thank you so much for bringing her. Call me Cammi."

Cammi invited them into her home. It reminded Lydie of her childhood home, what she remembered of it. Now her memories were tangled with the dilapidated shack that her family home had turned into in the years after it was abandoned. Cammi's kitchen was bright and sunny and faced a huge vegetable garden with a funny looking scarecrow wearing a top hat. Two cats napped on the blue sectional in her living room.

"Meet Dozer and Nutmeg, Nutty for short."

"We had a cat named Nutmeg," Lydie exclaimed, remembering a fat tabby cat that her mother grew catnip for in the backyard.

"I know you did," Cammi told her. "And the original Nutmeg was a skinny black and white stray that your mother lured back to our house with bits of cheese. Your mom was about ten, and the name became a little tradition for us. This girl here," Camilla said, petting the silky gray cat, "must be the fifth or sixth Nutmeg in our family."

Lydie felt her breath catch in her throat as a million questions tumbled to the front of her mind. This woman, her aunt, had an entire lifetime of her mother to share.

Elda sat next to Lydie on the couch and took her hand.

"Cammi and I decided that I would stay tonight and then head back to Michigan tomorrow. However, you may stay as long as you like," Elda explained.

Lydie stared at Elda, questioning. Did she mean forever? The thought hurt almost as much as the overwhelming joy when Cammi opened the door.

"I thought a week," Elda continued, perhaps sensing Lydie's distress. "But of course, that is your choice and you may come home sooner or stay longer, if you prefer."

Lydie sighed, relieved when Elda spoke of home. She wanted very much to know her aunt, but could not imagine leaving Ula forever.

****

"I have an idea," Sebastian said into the darkness. The candle had burned out hours ago and he'd been listening to the steady snores of Liam from the bed.

Liam grunted.

"Huh?"

"I'm going to jump."

"Jump where?" Liam's voice, thick with sleep, floated to him from the darkness.

It was so dark that Sebastian could not make out his hand in front of his face.

"Off the bridge by the house. It's meant to scare us, to make us think we'll die, but we can't really, right? We're in a dream reality. It's a construct of the imagination."

"The ants feel awfully real."

"So does the grass, and the rock, but the emptiness can't be real. We're in a forest, not on a mountain. How could she create an abyss where solid ground has to be?"

"Sounds like a terrible idea," Liam murmured.

He shifted in the darkness and Sebastian heard him fumbling next to the bed. A flame ignited and Liam held it quickly to a lantern.

"When will you do this?"

"I'm figuring that out. But we need to distract her. I think she knows when we fall and performs magic to keep us trapped here. But if I jumped when she was distracted, I bet I'd land somewhere else-either in the dream wood or back in the forest by the Sky Mothers."

Liam rocked back and forth on the edge of the bed, nodding with his unspoken thoughts.

"You could be right. But how do we distract her?"

"You'll let her capture you, play at being her son, whatever. I'll jump, and then when I have the amulet, I'll send it through the dream wood with Claire. The witch will have to go to the pond to retrieve it. That's when you jump."

Liam frowned and narrowed his eyes.

"This plan sounds a lot more promising for you than me."

"I won't leave you in here. Plus, if I get out, you'll know it worked. It's only a matter of time before you'll have a chance. She wants that amulet. She'll go after it."

"But how can you afford to give it to her?"

Sebastian shrugged.

"I don't know."

****

Abby ran through the woods, narrowly avoiding the stump of a massive tree that had grown over with moss. Her heart pounded in her head and her stomach felt sour like she might be sick. Still, she ran until she reached the compound and then went straight to Helena's yurt. It was empty. She checked the kitchen, the greenhouse, the pool, but did not find her. She returned to her own yurt and paced until her body began to emerge once again as the invisibility potion finally wore off.

She startled Kit walking out of the main entrance of the Sky Mothers compound.

"Whoa, Abby, is everything okay?" she asked, holding up her hands before they collided.

Abby paused, breathing heavily.

"Have you seen Helena or Oliver?"

Kit nodded.

"Yes, they drove into town. Helena wanted to buy a souvenir for someone, Lydie I think."

Abby bit her lip and tried not to scream. Of all the times for Helena and Oliver to disappear.

"Can I help, Abby?"

Abby shook her head.

Kit started to speak and then stopped.

"I almost said it's going to be okay," she admitted. "An old habit. And maybe it will," she went on at the crestfallen look on Abby's face. "But I don't want to pretend the world is something other than it is. Equal measures joy and sorrow, if we're lucky anyway."

Abby felt a sudden desire to confide in Kit or to confront her. Could she possibly know about Binda and the pond in the woods?

"Listen," Kit said. "Maybe I could help you look for stuff about the dream wood. Give you something to focus on?"

Abby nearly said no, but then changed her mind. Perhaps Kit would let something slip, some bit of information about Binda and the witch in the pond.

"I'm sure Matilda wouldn't appreciate us fossicking through her stuff," Kit said. "But we can check out the stone cellars."

"Fossicking?" Abby asked.

Kit smiled.

"Sorry, I forget you're not an Aussie. Rummaging, we best not rummage through her stuff. But most everything gets stored in the stone cellars."

"Is it terrible if I say the stone cellars sound rather ominous?"

Kit laughed.

"Don't worry, they're not spooky."

They walked back toward the gates to the Sky Mothers compound. Kit moved toward a large hump in the earth and peeled back a layer of hanging moss. Abby saw a wooden door set in the hillside. She glanced toward the trees expecting to see Binda emerge at any moment, but no one appeared.

"Reminds me of *The Hobbit*," Abby murmured.

"I read those books," Kit admitted, sliding a heavy skeleton key into the lock. She pushed the door in, and a musty dank smell wafted out.

The space was cramped, a narrow passageway with stone walls that gradually opened into a large chamber. Boxes, storage totes, and old furniture packed the room.

"I'm not sure this is the ideal space for storage," Abby mumbled, touching the damp stone walls.

"It's bewitched. The walls are wet, but the stuff is shielded."

Abby sighed looking at the mounds of books stacked on a three-legged desk.

"How will we ever find anything?" she asked.

As she said it, she remembered a similar comment she'd made months earlier at Sydney and Rod's loft. As if on cue, Kit gave her a wry smile-a smile that mirrored the one Oliver had given her on that prior occasion.

"Right," Abby laughed.

"We're witches."

"I've never been a great summoner," Kit admitted. "But I know a thing or two."

Kit closed her eyes and held her palms close together. A tiny ball of flame erupted between her palms.

"Goddess of fire, bringer of light,
I call forth your gift of sight,
The dream wood's magic, please make known,
Deepest gratitude for all that is shown.
Mote it be."

The fire in Kit's hands leaped away and lit on a cardboard box stacked in a dark corner at the back of the cellar. The fire did not take, but extinguished the moment it touched the box.

"Maybe my summoning skills have improved." Kit laughed.

Abby looked through the box. She found several pieces of clothing, which she assumed were Meghan's. Beneath those, she discovered a framed picture. She lifted it and looked at an image of a small cottage. Two women stood in front of the cabin, their arms clasped around one-another.

"Binda," Abby said, recognizing the older witch on the left, though she looked much younger in the photo.

"And that's Meghan," Kit told her.

"Where is this cabin?" Abby asked.

Kit wrinkled her brow.

"I've seen it, maybe two miles back. A heavy hike if you were a human, but a breeze for us magic folk. Shall we check it out?"

Abby nodded, though she would have preferred to visit the cabin with Helena and Oliver.

"Let me pop back to my room and grab some decent walking shoes."

Abby followed her out, staring at the framed photo. The woman in the picture with Binda smiled as if the witches held the whole world between them. How could such a witch become the creature that Binda had spoken to in the pond?

****

Sebastian did not have a watch and doubted it would work if he did. According to Liam, time operated on another sphere in the Forest of Purgatory. He knew that days had passed. Hadn't they? He wanted to trust his instincts that yes, days had passed, but how could he? Nothing felt real. He couldn't believe that Liam could still have a coherent conversation after a year trapped in the place.

Liam knew how to distract Meghan. During his many plots to kill the dark witch, he'd learned how to get her attention. The most effective included pretending to be her son, Clyde. Sebastian stayed in the cave as Liam walked into the gray light of day.

"Mother?" Liam called out. He took a few steps and sank to his knees. "Mother? It's Clyde. I've come home, please." He moaned and fell forward, his cry a tortured echo through the forest.

When the phantoms appeared from the forest, Sebastian stepped deeper into the cave. They had no form, only an oozing blackness that enveloped Liam and dragged him away. The moment they disappeared from sight, Sebastian sprinted from his hiding place. He knew he had minutes at the most before Meghan would realize that Liam was playing her. The distance seemed longer than he remembered and his feet sunk into the soggy grass in excruciating slowness.

"Please, please," he whispered under his breath, pumping his arms and legs as if his life depended on it, which it did.

In the distance, the ramshackle house came into view. He sprang onto the bridge and leaped off into the emptiness, glimpsing the Forest of Purgatory a final time before he plummeted into nothingness.

CHAPTER 14

It seemed he fell forever. Falling was not the way he imagined it. It was not like flying. Falling happened at an incomprehensible speed with the wind whipping your face, hair, and limbs in such a way that you stopped being a person and turned into a mushy doll pressed and prodded by the air itself. He felt his lips forced open and fought to clamp his teeth shut. Desperately wanting to close his eyes, but terrified that if he lost consciousness, the dark witch would have time to whisk him back to the Forest of Purgatory, he concentrated on the endless empty sky beneath him. There had to be ground, something somewhere, and then he was on it. Nothing had moved into view before him. In one moment, he flailed through endless space and in the next he lay on his stomach, flat on the ground, his face pressed into the grass. Sweet smelling grass that looked and tasted green and fresh. He pushed himself onto his hands and knees and Claire was already there, clutching him around his waist, helping him to his feet.

"It's about time," she whispered. "I thought you'd never come back."

"I have to get out of here, Claire," he told her, spinning in an urgent circle. His stomach lurched when he realized he had landed right next to the pond.

"I know," she told him. "Let's go."

They ran through the woods, away from the pond, and when they stopped at the cliff that rose up to the bridge. They both took off into the air, flying to the cliff edge.

Sebastian paused, feeling the first hesitation at leaving the dream wood. He wanted out, *now*, but knew he would likely never see Claire again.

She gave him a fierce hug and then shoved him hard toward the bridge.

"I'm always with you, Sebastian. Remember."

Before he stepped onto the bridge, she had vanished.

****

Elda had gone to bed, but Lydie and Cammi stayed up far into the night. Cammi told stories, a million stories, about Allison, Lydie's mother.

"I don't understand how I lost you," Lydie murmured during a lull in the conversation.

"Allison and I were so close when we were young, but when your mother turned eleven, she started to change."

Lydie pursed her lips and stared at the tiny red checks on Cammi's tablecloth. She didn't want to hear anything bad about her mother. It was as simple as that.

"I didn't know anything about witches," Cammi continued. "Our parents were not witches. However, our great grandfather was a witch, or had been a witch. The first time my sister lit something on fire, my parents panicked. They thought she was acting out, took her to a child psychologist." Cammi laughed and shook her head, running her fingers through her blond curls until they turned frizzy. "A few weeks after the psychologist, a woman visited our house. Celeste was her name and she came all the way from England to meet my sister. I was so jealous. I'm embarrassed to admit it now, but I threw one your mother's favorite dresses in the garbage. Don't worry, I confessed later, and when we were all grown up I bought her a blouse to make up for it."

Lydie smiled, but didn't interrupt, curious to hear the story of her mother discovering her powers.

"One day, my parents took me for ice cream and told me that Allison was going away for a while with the nice lady to England, to a school of sorts."

"They sent her to a coven?"

Cammi nodded.

"I wouldn't know that for years. Allison came back every two months and then she'd be gone again. I missed her desperately. My best friend had been taken away and I didn't understand why. She moved home for one summer when we were seventeen and then she met Gary, your dad. He was from Michigan, had a little farm, and worked as a holistic doctor. They met at some big party that I later learned was a witch thing, but at the time, I was still in the dark on all that."

"The All Hallow's Ball?"

"Yes, that's the one," Cammi agreed. "On Halloween night. Anyway, she moved to Michigan and we saw each other a few times a year, but life had set us on our separate paths. Your birth brought us back together. Though I had no idea how brief our reunion would be. After your parents were attacked, your mother confided in me. She told me everything, and at first, I thought she was nuts. I kept thinking, who do I call, who can help her? She's clearly having delusions, it must be postpartum psychosis."

Lydie grabbed another cookie and stuffed it in her mouth. It felt so good to hear the story of her past, but it hurt too, oh how it hurt.

"Then Gary came home and Cammi admitted she told me. I expected him to pull me aside and say, 'Don't worry, I'm getting her help.' Instead, he brought a bucket of water into the living room and proceeded to create a cyclone six inches from my face. Then he turned the water to ice, and without touching the ice, he carved it into a sculpture of your mother. I nearly fell over then and there, but your mom got me a cup of tea. I was supposed to be there taking care of her, new baby and all, but our roles had reversed. When I calmed down, she lit the fire in the hearth with a thought and then lit every candle in the room and snuffed them out and lit them again without moving from the couch."

"I still don't understand why I never heard from you," Lydie said.

Cammi frowned and placed her hands flat on the table.

"I thought you had died. Your mother told me about the Vepars. When they were attacked and killed, the police said you surely had died as well and they simply hadn't found your body." Cammi started to cry and pulled a napkin from the center of the table to wipe her running nose. "It broke me. I spent a year in a horrible depression, Both of our parents were gone and now my only sister and my only niece had been murdered. I felt so alone in the world. I sold my house and moved to California. Then about five years ago, I came back. I missed Florida. While I was going through my stuff in storage a year ago, I came across a letter your mother had written me after the first attack. She spoke about a coven that was helping to shelter them. I didn't know if the coven still existed or if they'd ever receive my letter, but I had to try. I addressed it to your old home in the hope that they would somehow intercept it. I didn't expect to hear that you had lived. I can barely tell you what that felt like, the most amazing joy. A miracle. I simply hoped to discover what had happened. I felt enough time had passed that I was ready to know, but then Elda contacted me and said that you had survived…" Cammi began to cry again and this time Lydie scooted her chair to her aunt's side. She wrapped her arms around her and they sat that way for a long time.

****

Sebastian raced across the bridge and into the forest. He stopped and looked back at the bridge, thinking of Liam. What had become of Liam? Had the witch realized that Sebastian had escaped? Would she hurt Liam for his part in their plan?

A figure stepped in front of him as he wove through the trees back toward the Sky Mothers. He stopped and squinted, trying to make them out.

"Julian?" he asked hesitantly. The person was too large to be Abby.

Binda moved from the shadows into the light. Her face looked pinched and angry.

"How did you get out?" she hissed.

Sebastian didn't respond, but turned and ran. He barely took three steps and his legs froze. He pitched forward and landed hard on his hands. In an instant, he lost feeling in his hands and arms and then his whole body grew numb. His head flopped onto the forest floor.

Binda rolled him easily onto his back.

He tried to yell, but his lips and tongue no longer worked. Only his eyes functioned, darting wildly around, with no hope in sight.

He watched her, terrified. Could Binda return him to the Forest of Purgatory?

****

Faustine paused at the warped tree that revealed the symbol of the fate triad. It looked different. The symbol had faded, sap filling the crevice and hardening into an amber sheath. Stranger still, tiny green buds stood along the branches of the withered tree. Faustine had never seen a bud on the tree. The forest beyond the tree had also changed. The ferns looked less vibrant, less unnatural, as if the magic that had seeped into them had disappeared.

As he approached the red willow, he paused again, watching and waiting. The willow's scarlet branches had lost some of their color. Many of them had fallen to the earth and sat in heaps rotting on the forest floor. Had the Lourdes somehow abandoned her lair? He walked closer, reaching into his cloak for the powder that Julian had given him. He did not expect to find a Vepar awaiting him, but wanted to be ready. He also did not expect to find the Lourdes. He could not sense her at all.

He stopped on the mushy red earth that surrounded the willow. At the hole that descended into her lair, a powerful aroma of death hit him full in the face. He immediately pressed a hand over his mouth and nose, his eyes watering. Had she left some animal, or worse, a human in her lair to decay?

He walked down the roots slowly, pressing his hands into the dirt walls, and training his ears for any sound. Silence greeted him.

The Lourdes lay slumped over her table. Her face was turned away from him, but he could see and hear the flies buzzing over her rotting body. The Lourdes was dead.

****

Binda did not carry him, but levitated his useless body and pushed him ahead of her. They did not return to the Sky Mothers. Instead, she turned away from the ocean and walked him deeper into the woods. After a half hour, they came to a small dark cottage. She opened the door and drifted him inside.

He had control of only his eyes and he took in every detail. The low plank ceiling stood only a few feet above Binda's head. In the corner, a bed piled with quilts abutted the wall beneath a dark window. Maps and papers cluttered a long wooden drafting table. A single well-worn chair sat next to a wood burning stove.

Binda directed him to the bed, she pulled back the blankets and rested his body on the mattress. It felt lumpy and old, but better than the vertigo he'd felt while floating.

She pulled the blankets back over him, despite the heat, and he couldn't help feeling he was being tucked in by an insane grandmother. He would have laughed if he had any control of his vocal chords.

"You'll be safe here until the amulet has been taken into the dream wood. Then I will set you free. Of course, you won't remember any of this, but that is for the best."

He wanted to ask why. A thousand questions rose to his frozen lips and were left unspoken. In the world of witches, questions did not have to be asked to be heard, and he knew that Binda heard, if not sensed, all that he wanted to know.

She poured a glass of water from the sink and sat heavily in the single chair. She looked ancient. The tough, solid witch he'd met when he first arrived at the Sky Mothers was replaced by a paper cutout of her former self-flimsy and empty. As she sipped her water, she watched him.

"Burning questions, you have, Sebastian. Not knowing is the worst thing of all. Once upon a time, I thought death was worse because then you must accept that someone is gone. Someone that occupied a whole portion of your life will never fill that space again. And they're irreplaceable. That's what no one tells you. People move through life with many partners. They marry and divorce, they change friends and roommates. But when you are truly connected to another, their loss destroys you. Even if you physically survive, the whole of you has been portioned off, cut away. Now you are a half-life. But not knowing is even worse than that. You limp around, obsessed. You are less than a half-life because the part of you that remains is haunted by not knowing, waiting, hoping and dreading."

Sebastian listened closely. Binda intended to wipe his memory and having had firsthand experience, he had no doubt that she could do it. How could he make himself remember? At some point, the magic that paralyzed him would wear off. Could he fight her? Somehow slip past her?

"When Meghan disappeared into the dream wood, it was like any other day. It rained that morning. The humid rain of summer, of the monsoon season. We ate papaya and oysters for breakfast. Meghan, troubled by guilt, had created a book of poetry for Clyde. She looked forward to giving him the gift and I looked forward to the smile she would wear when she returned from visiting him."

Binda stood and refilled her glass.

"I'm sure you're parched," she told Sebastian, moving to his bedside and tilting the water to his lips.

He could not drink, but the cool liquid slipped down his throat and took the gritty, dusty feeling with it.

She returned to her chair.

"I waited until hours after sunset and then I walked to the bridge. I called out her name. I believed she had merely stayed on with him for comfort. Her choice to confine him to the dream wood had been a hard one, but in his best interest, of course. Clyde was willful, deceptive. She didn't see it, dared not recognize him fully, but I did. He was only seventeen then, but already he'd wreaked havoc on their world. He murdered her other son, his own brother. A vicious act born of jealousy and hatred. I saw it the moment I met him, I felt it in his fingertips, the blood he'd shed. His brother was not the only life he'd taken, but beautiful Meghan in all her purity and kindness could not see the monster that she so desperately protected. I went home that night and slept soundly in our bed by the sea. I woke with the dawn, prepared a mango and some tea and returned to the bridge. We would greet the morning together, but she did not come. I stayed that day and into the night. I climbed a tree and sought the stars for guidance, but they held no great vision for me. It was on the second morning that the ball of dread formed in my belly. It lives there to this day like I swallowed a stone and it has grown and warped and filled me in the worst possible way."

Sebastian's right ear itched. He wanted to reach his hand to scratch it, but of course, his arm did not move. His fingers, however, did. A tiny movement, barely perceptible, but he knew. The magic had begun to wear off.

"She never came out of the dream wood," Binda continued, and her eyes had the glassy look of having left the present for another time, a sadder time.

Sebastian wiggled his toes. After another moment, he lifted his tongue within his mouth and fought the urge to lick his dry lips.

"You can't imagine the questions. They begin as logical things and turn sinister. She had an accident, she needed time to strengthen the magic, Clyde needed her help. Later, I believed he'd killed her, and after that, I feared she'd taken him and fled to another place altogether. Perhaps she no longer wanted to be a part of the Sky Mothers. What had been our dream had possibly been mine alone. Those are the worst types of realizations, that this beautiful, magnificent world you've constructed is built on a foundation of mistruths. Meghan needed me when she arrived with Clyde. She was alone in the world, on the run. Perhaps she never loved me at all, only clung to me in order to escape the witches who hunted her child."

Binda shifted and Sebastian stilled, not wanting to alert her that he had begun to regain control of his body.

CHAPTER 15

Faustine walked through the burrow slowly. He allowed his mind to seek the book without looking too closely. A trunk in the corner of the room drew his attention. The trunk was open and the book lay on top as if she had left it there intentionally. The trunk contained other items, a jumble of letters wrapped in twine, a journal, more ancient looking books, some of them green with a layer of mold. Hunched down, he started to sift through the contents when he heard the snapping of a branch overhead. He stuffed the book, letters, and journal beneath his cloak and pressed back against the wall. In the part of the woods where the Lourdes lived, animals did not wander. They had learned decades ago to stay away from the dark witch who lived in the ground.

The crunching grew louder and closer. Faustine opened his mind, but only a blurry shadow arrived. He could get no real sense of the person above him. A hiker perhaps.

Faustine pressed farther into the dirt alcove until he had no space left. He whispered an incantation of invisibility and focused his energy on blending into his surroundings. He took the book and letters from within his shirt and turned to the wall behind him. He stared hard at the wall and without crumbling, the dirt shifted. He reached for Elda in his mind and the moment he connected to her, he sent a vision of shoving the papers into the opening. He felt her questioning thoughts trying to stay with him, but he immediately cut her off. He would need all his energy to conceal himself from the presence approaching. He moved to the other side of the space, distancing himself from the trunk and again focusing on invisibility.

Heavy footfalls pounded on the roots that descended into the cavern.

****

Kit moved toward the little cottage, pausing to peer into one of the windows. Abby surveyed the yard beyond the cottage noticing that it did not feel abandoned.

Kit made a little choking sound and quickly stepped away from the window. Abby knew from her expression that she'd seen something disturbing.

"What? Is there someone in there?"

Kit put a hand on her forearm to stop her going forward.

"I need a minute to think, okay?"

She started to pull away, but Kit gripped her harder and Abby knew she would have to call on her element to break Kit's hold.

"Tell me," Abby snapped, her voice rising.

"Shhh…" Kit whispered, holding her other hand over Abby's mouth. "Binda is in the cabin and so is…Sebastian."

Abby felt her heart lurch in her chest. It was enough to break Kit's grip. She ran toward the window, but a wall of fire blazed before her and she nearly collided with it. She stopped just in time and recoiled from the heat. She spun around.

"What do you think you're doing?" she spat.

Kit strode to her and held up a hand.

"Abby, please, just listen to me. Something is not right and Binda is edgy, we don't want to spook her."

"She has Sebastian in there! And you're worried about spooking her."

"Please," Kit pleaded. "She must have a reason. If we panic, we're lost."

"There are two of us," Abby insisted. "Start a fire or I'll make a rainstorm and we'll flush her out."

"You want to make a rainstorm in the cabin? Because I sure as hell don't intend to light it on fire."

Abby started to speak and then something hard hit her from behind and she sprawled on the ground.

"What the?" Kit spun around. "Hannah!"

"I heard you arguing. She wants to light someone on fire in the cabin," Hannah muttered, stepping out of the trees.

Abby tried to stand up, but Hannah waved a hand at her.

"No," she barked. "You stay on the ground."

"Hannah, you don't understand," Kit started, but it was too late. The forest, previously filled with sunlight, turned black as pitch.

Abby could see nothing. She crawled on hands and knees in the direction she believed the cabin to be. The wind started to pick up. The trees began to thrash and wail. Leaves and twigs pummeled Abby's back and stuck in her hair. Binda knew she'd been discovered.

****

The moment Sebastian heard the voice, he knew his chance to escape had come.

"No," the word, yelled, drifted through the open window and Binda sprang to her feet. She began to whisper in a language he did not recognize and as she raised her arms the world beyond the cabin went dark.

Sebastian could see Binda in the dim light of the wood burning stove and he knew that her focus had shifted. The howling of the wind shielded the sound of the window as he thrust it up. He dove out and landed hard on his right side. The bright day had been transformed into a screeching wail of wind and trees and darkness. He crouched and ran for the denser forest, knowing that Binda could release the storm at any moment and he needed to hide.

His foot struck something hard and someone yelped beneath him.

"Abby?" he exclaimed, dropping to his knees.

She sat up and though he couldn't see her, he felt her wrap her arms around his waist.

"Yes, yes, it's me. You made it out. I was so worried, Sebastian."

"Shhh…" he grasped her head and kissed her on the mouth. Putting his lips close to her ear, he whispered, "We need to get into the woods."

Holding hands, they stood and hurried for the forest, hoping that they moved away from the cabin rather than toward it. Sebastian knew that Abby could have illuminated their path, but the light would have also given away their location.

A sudden shriek from the cabin told Sebastian that Binda had realized he escaped.

****

"Did you have any sense of who it was?" Elda asked Faustine that evening at Ula.

They had both arrived home several hours before and Faustine filled Elda in on the discovery of the Lourdes's body as well as the stranger who nearly met him in the lair.

"It had to have been a Vepar," Faustine said, hoisting the trunk onto the desk and opening it carefully. "I couldn't get a sense of him though. He stopped when he heard a screech from the woods and I knew the sound, a skin-walker."

"You don't think the skin-walker was after him? Maybe he was trying to hide?"

"No, I felt a blast of frustration, almost like he was pissed at the skin-walker for making the sound."

"Well, thank the Goddess you're okay. When you sent me that vision, I was on the airplane. I was practically walking up the walls by the time we landed."

"I'm sorry about that. I should have sent another to let you know I was safe. It took all of my focus to stay invisible when I left the lair with this." He tapped the trunk.

Elda leaned forward and peered at the book. She touched it gingerly, concerned about damaging the ancient pages.

"Was she murdered?"

"She was in the later stages of decomposition," Faustine told her, grimacing at the memory. "But sitting at her table. It did not appear that any sort of struggle occurred."

"A natural death, then?"

"I doubt it," Faustine admitted. "The timing feels too convenient with all that has occurred. But maybe not a violent death, just an intentional one."

"She was never easy to deceive."

"No, but the last time I visited her, she spoke of a desire for death. Perhaps she simply allowed it."

****

After several minutes of hiking blindly through the woods, Abby and Sebastian left the darkness that Binda had created and returned to the light.

Abby stopped and hugged him, burying her face in his chest.

"I was terrified when you didn't come back out of the dream wood. I thought…" she stopped and sagged against him. As the relief settled in, the tension of the previous days began to disappear, and with it came a heaviness. She wanted to lie down and sleep for days.

He held her close and breathed into the top of her head.

"I would never have abandoned you, Abby. Even when I knew I was trapped, I also knew that I would get out, somehow I would get out."

"How did you escape? What happened?"

"Wait." He held a finger to her lips and she heard it too. A vehicle coming down the road toward the Sky Mothers' Coven.

"Is it Binda?" he asked her.

"It's Oliver and Helena, I know it," she cheered

They ran through the woods, breaking onto the dirt road just as Oliver came around the corner. Sebastian flung himself in front of the Rover, waving his arms and yelling "stop."

Oliver slammed on the brakes and he and Helena jumped out.

"You're free!" Helena beamed, running to Sebastian and hugging him.

"What's happened?" Oliver asked, recognizing the panic in both Abby and Sebastian's faces.

"Best if we talk and drive," Sebastian said, glancing into the woods behind him. "The other way, though. We'd better not go back to the Sky Mother's just yet."

As they drove, Sebastian told them about his experience in the Forest of Purgatory.

****

Fuming, Julian stood in the wind tunnel at the Sky Mothers. When he had returned to Australia, Abby and the others had been at the airport to meet him. They told him all that had transpired with the Forest of Purgatory, Meghan, and Binda. Now he fought to control the magic that longed to explode from his flailing hands. How could Binda have betrayed them all? How dare Matilda defend her now?

"It is unacceptable," he spat, for the third or fourth time. "I'm of a mind to leave this instant, take the amulet and my witches back to Ula and write off the Sky Mothers completely."

"Julian, please," Matilda pleaded. "You cannot possibly understand how angry I am with Binda. All of us are angry, and you are right to have your misgivings, however-"

"Misgivings?" Julian roared. "Your elder witch has been lying since the moment we arrived. She had vital information that she intentionally withheld. She kidnapped Sebastian! And all of that after the disgrace you call Hannah lured Sebastian into the woods and conspired to send him into a dangerous, possibly deadly world of magic where other hybrids had vanished before."

Abby, Sebastian, Oliver, and Helena stood in the doorway behind Julian. They had intended to put their opinions forth as well, but Julian left little space for additional comments.

"All that you say is true, Julian," Matilda said, holding her hands out and trying to calm him.

He backed away from her and shook his head, disgusted.

"Please, let us make this right. We want the truth as much as you, Julian. Help us discover what that is."

Sebastian stepped forward.

"She's right, Julian. We can't leave without knowing everything."

Julian shot him a furious look, but did not refuse the suggestion outright. He paced away from Matilda, his fists balled at his sides.

Helena held Abby's shoulders firmly in her hands.

"Hannah is in her room," Matilda promised. "I've put the lock charms on her door and she will not leave until I release her."

"And Binda?" Julian spat.

"She's here. She came back on her own, Julian. She feels terrible and she wants to explain."

Helena released Abby and walked forward. She placed a soothing hand on Julian's back and Abby saw his shoulders release a hint of their tension.

"Matilda, you understand of course, why we are concerned. But we appreciate the graciousness with which you opened your home to us. We would appreciate the opportunity to speak in-depth with Binda. We need some assurances though."

Helena opened the beaded bag at her wrist and pulled out a small amber colored bottle.

"She needs to take a Serum of Infallibility."

"Truth serum," Oliver whispered to Abby and Sebastian.

Matilda took the bottle and nodded.

"Of course."

CHAPTER 16

Binda sat in the room that Sebastian had visited the first day at Sky Mothers, the space where she had examined him and deemed him a hybrid. She held her shoulders stiffly and watched the ocean through one of the open doorways. Her face looked drawn and old.

Matilda handed her the serum without a word and gestured to the other chairs arranged in the room. Julian, Abby, Sebastian, Oliver, and Helena took seats. Kit walked in and sat close to Oliver.

Binda opened the serum and drank it expressionlessly.

After several minutes, she spoke.

"I am sorry. I know how I must seem to you, old and hard and angry, but I have not always been this way. My actions are inexcusable and my apology is but a breath in a wind of deception. I was once a witch of great integrity. I took pride in that integrity. Pride, like deception, is toxic. I chose to lie rather than smudge my pure name in this coven. I could not bear for any of my witches to see me as less."

She looked at Kit and smiled sadly. Kit nodded at her as if to convey that she still had faith in the elder Sky Mother.

"I can hardly believe it has been three hundred years, but it has, of course, it has. You'd think I would have let go a long time ago. I should have, but love lives on. I met Meghan in 1702. I was a tribeswoman then, but I had discovered my powers as a young woman and I lived alone in the wilds. I found the Mother Tree one day as I searched for a place to begin my coven. I had dreamed the Sky Mothers dream and knew that I would create a coven of women. Meghan appeared like a vision from my dream, a white woman. I'd never seen anything like her. We did not speak the same language, but we were witches after all. We communicated with more than words. She came from the New World."

Binda closed her eyes and a tiny smile curved her lips.

"Some memories do not fade. I remember Meghan, I remember she wore trousers and smoked from a pipe carved from bone. I knew she was a witch before I saw her. I had sensed her. I had dreamed her. I took her with me into the bush. She and Clyde and I lived in a stone hut, but she immediately set to creating the dream wood. I built the Sky Mothers and she built the dream wood."

"How did they get here though?" Julian asked. "Americans were not traveling to Australia in the early 1700s."

Binda nodded.

"A portal. A jump through space. Meghan called it the tunnel of darkness. She did not know where they would end up. They fled in the night and abandoned nearly all of their belongings."

"And Clyde was Meghan's son?" Helena asked, clarifying. "Was he a child?"

"He was her son, yes, but he was not a child. He was seventeen, he was a man."

"Why did Meghan flee the New World with Clyde?" Julian asked.

Binda frowned and looked at Matilda. Matilda brought her hands together and a glass of water appeared between her palms. She walked it to Binda. Binda took a long drink and thanked her.

"She would not tell me," Binda admitted. "I loved her so much. I wanted her to stay, so I didn't ask questions. In the beginning, I believed those who hunted her did so because they feared her power. Later, she told me that Clyde had committed murder against his own kin. It was not men that stalked Meghan and Clyde, but witches. Eventually, I learned the truth. Clyde had murdered his brother Eugene, a witch. Eugene was part of a coven known as The Serpent House and they wanted justice for his death. Meghan fled to protect him."

"Did he have a father?" Sebastian asked.

"Dead. Dead since the brothers were young. Meghan did her best, but one child was a witch and the other was a human. It was not an easy life for any of them."

"Let me stop you for a moment, Binda," Julian interjected. "Did you know that Clyde was connected to us? That he was part of this curse?"

"Of course not." Binda sighed. "I was very curious about Sebastian because he is a hybrid and only hybrids can enter the dream wood. However, I never had any intention of sending him in there. It was only after I learned of the amulet that I made the connection. You see, Meghan told me about the amulet. It was one of several items that disappeared from Eugene's coven after his murder."

"The amulet belonged to Eugene's coven? So, Clyde stole it?" Oliver asked.

"That was my impression, yes."

"Why does she want it back?" Julian asked.

Binda shrugged.

"She said that he would come, but she often says things, crazy things that don't make sense. He was only a man. How could he possibly live? He must have died centuries ago."

"Why would Meghan protect him?" Sebastian asked. "I mean, he killed his own brother!"

"He was her child. How could she not?"

Abby understood. Before her pregnancy, she would have had the same question, but now, she couldn't imagine any deed, however dark, that could cause her to abandon her child.

"Where was Clyde while the two of you created the Sky Mothers?" Sebastian asked.

Binda's face darkened.

"Lost in his own dark dreams. We built him a separate hut. He filled it with books and coins and valuable things. He was a thief and a gambler, but Meghan loved him and I loved Meghan. They had magic books. Meghan knew spells. She had spent time in a coven, she was practiced in the ways of magic. I was an earth witch. I could build, but Meghan was the creator. She could take a handful of dust and hand you a wooden horse that would grow into a beast that could be ridden through the forest. The dream wood was not merely a feat of expert magic. Meghan was a special witch, a uniquely powerful witch. Clyde loved the dream wood. He would follow her across that bridge, grinning. In the evening she would return, but he would stay for days, weeks. We finished the Sky Mothers compound. It was much less grand in those days. Two more witches joined us. Clyde rarely left the dream wood, but he had begun to create things that concerned Meghan. You see, the dream wood manifests the hybrid's desires. Meghan would stumble upon strange creatures in the dream wood, frightening beasts and evidence that Clyde was plotting something."

"Plotting what?" Julian demanded.

Binda shrugged.

"I underestimated him. He was young, foolish, and power hungry. I saw a man who was crippled by his longings, his lust for all that he did not possess. I didn't probe. I was busy with the Sky Mothers. But Meghan told me that she had created another level in the dream wood. If she had to, she could keep him there. It was a mirror image of the dream wood, but once inside, he couldn't get back out."

"It's not a mirror image," Sebastian murmured. "It's a nightmare."

"She didn't create that. Clyde found a way to manipulate it. He must have because he trapped her and escaped himself."

"Why did she want to trap him to begin with?" Helena asked.

"As I said, he had plotted something dark. I don't know what, but it scared her. He was happy in the dream wood. She didn't want to hurt him, but she had to ensure his safety, and perhaps the safety of others."

"How did he escape?" Julian asked.

Binda closed her eyes.

"I don't know. For a long time, I did not know that he had escaped. For years, more than a hundred years, I thought maybe they had both died in the dream wood. I knew nothing."

"And then you found the pond?" Abby asked, referring to the pond where Binda had been speaking to the witch beneath the surface, to Meghan.

"Yes. I would walk the forest for hours in those days. I felt dead inside. I wanted so much to find a way into the dream wood, but I'd given up. Then one day, I stopped at that pond and she appeared. I could not reach her and she could not leave. She was angry. She is angry."

"And insane," Sebastian added.

Binda glared at him.

"She sacrificed her life for her child, and for what? To spend eternity suffering for her kindness, for her love."

"You can speak with her, Binda?" Matilda asked, pressing her lips into a thin, concerned line.

Binda nodded.

"I visited her today. It was the first time in years."

"Why do you stay away?" Kit broke in.

Binda closed her eyes as if hearing the question caused her physical pain.

"I am helpless. I couldn't take it anymore. Her rage, her accusations. The witch I knew, the witch I loved, is gone."

"What can you tell us about Kanti?" Julian asked, steering the conversation back to the curse.

"I've never heard of him," Binda admitted.

"Her," Abby cut in.

"Who is she? Part of the coven that Meghan and Clyde fled?"

"Clyde wrote about her. He created a room in a cave in the Forest of Purgatory. Meghan couldn't reach him there. He filled the walls with his writing, his plans, maybe. He wrote about Kanti. He intended to abduct her," Sebastian explained.

"And eventually he did," Julian added. "But that happened in northern Michigan. So how did he get from here to there?"

"Probably the same way they came here originally," Binda offered. "Meghan never showed me the portal. I'm not sure she even remembered where it was, but Clyde had a special mind. He remembered everything. He could speak your exact words back to you months after you'd said them. He remembered where certain trees, rocks, and plants could be found. He didn't just read books. He memorized them. He knew the page numbers of facts that he quoted. Meghan thought he was a genius."

"But not you?" Julian asked.

Binda stared him hard in the eyes.

"I thought he was evil."

****

"Sorry about all this," Kit told them. They had returned to the yurts overlooking the ocean. Julian wanted to speak alone after their conversation with Binda, but he trusted Kit and wanted her insight.

"It's not your fault," Oliver reminded her, but they did not touch. He kept his distance and Abby was not sure if it was Kit or Oliver who wanted space.

"I have the amulet," Julian began. "However, I fear it's a fake."

Abby dropped the cup she'd been holding and her tea spilled across the table. She looked at Sebastian. Helena clapped her hands and the spilled tea disappeared.

"How could that be?" Sebastian asked. "I wore it, there was something alive inside that thing."

Julian nodded.

"You're right, there was. I felt it too. We all saw it. The original amulet was alive. But this amulet…" He took a black pouch from his bag and laid it on the table. "Is most certainly not."

Oliver peeled back the edges of the fabric and they stared at the golden snake devouring its own tale. The red stone gleamed in the center. It looked identical to the original and yet…it didn't. The original amulet had a presence, a power that emanated from its very core. This amulet looked like a beautiful trinket for sale in a jewelry store.

Abby reached out hesitantly. She brushed her fingers along the stone quickly. She felt nothing. Sebastian too reached for the amulet. He picked it up, hefted the weight in his hand and then held it against his chest.

He shook his head.

"You're right."

Helena looked stricken and turned from the table.

"I'll make some lavender tea," she told them. "And Abby, you're behind in your supplements. I will arrange a tonic for you." She busied herself at the counter and Abby could see her shoulders pinched with tension.

"How could the original amulet have been taken?" Kit asked. "Has it been unprotected?" She voiced the question in a neutral tone, no note of accusation. Although she was a Sky Mother, she was not invested in Binda's plight.

"The space that holds your Mother Tree, we have something similar at Ula. It is a room for magical objects. Only a friend could enter and they would have to be in the castle, which is a challenging feat in and of itself."

"Then you must conclude it was one of your own?" Kit asked, maintaining steady eye contact with Julian. Abby felt Sebastian bristle beside her. As the only non-witch, he expected to be accused.

Julian did not immediately answer.

"Ula has been breached before. And we also must consider the issue of the amulet and the spirit within it. She is powerful and aided with possession. I cannot say that she did not find a way to creep from that chamber and slip into the body of one of our witches to steal the amulet. In that regard, the witch would not be at fault, she would have virtually no recollection of the experience. I am concerned because Adora was at Ula when I returned."

"Adora?" Helena asked, hurrying over with her tray of tea.

"Yes, she escaped from the Vepar's lair. Bridget and Elda have largely mended her, but she is weak. How do we know that the Vepar's did not release her so that she would return to Ula and steal the amulet?" he thought aloud.

"Would she do that? You trust her, don't you?" Oliver asked.

"I trust her completely, but as I said, she has been compromised. Under possession, it would not be Adora who stole the amulet, but Kanti."

"Could this get any more complicated?" Sebastian grunted. "I'm sorry, Helena, the tea looks great, but I want a beer."

He strode to the refrigerator and pulled open the door.

"Make that two," Oliver called.

"You won't find any in there," Kit told him. "But I happen to make my own amber fluid. I'll go grab a few."

"That'd be great, thank you, Kit," Sebastian told her. He took a seat next to Abby.

Oliver watched Kit walk down the hill and shook his head.

"That woman trains spiders, takes care of the kangaroos, does all the deep-sea fishing, tends to the poisonous plants, speaks to the fire, and now she also makes beer."

"Better marry her." Sebastian elbowed him.

Oliver rolled his eyes.

"She'd sooner kill me than marry me."

"What makes you say that, honey?" Helena asked. "She has kind eyes when she looks at you."

"Okay, enough about my love life," Oliver grumbled. "Back to the amulet and the nightmare that has become our lives."

"Obviously, we already had a dilemma. Meghan wants the amulet, but we're not sure why. Sebastian has set up a plan with the hybrid Liam to escape during delivery of the amulet. We want to fulfill that promise and help Liam get out. If this were the real amulet, we'd be in trouble, but since it's a fake, we can safely send it in. However, once it's out of our hands, we can't use it to track who put it in Ula and someone must have put it there."

"Is it terrible to say that I could care less if Liam gets out. I mean his girlfriend is a pill. We'd probably be doing him a favor if we left him inside," Oliver offered.

Abby smiled, but shook her head.

"She's just desperate. I get it. I'd make everyone's life hell if Sebastian were trapped in there for a year."

Sebastian wrapped his arm around her and kissed her temple.

"Agreed. I'm not fond of Hannah, but I like Liam and he deserves his freedom. We have to send the amulet in. There must be other ways of tracking who stole the original, right?" he asked the question of Julian, but Helena answered.

"The Crystal of Sight. If Faustine wears that crystal, he can see into everyone's pasts, even under possession, I would assume."

"Smart thinking, Helena. That's what we'll do," said Julian. "Sebastian, are you up for crossing the bridge with the amulet? You said you could give it to your guide in the dream wood and she could deliver it?"

He nodded.

"I think so."

He had not told the other witches that his guide was Claire. He hated the thought of sending her to the water witch alone, but he savored the chance to see her a final time.

"What next?" Abby asked, sipping Helena's tonic and grimacing.

"We have to meet with Jack," Sebastian reminded her. "That meeting is set for April. I figured Julian and I would go."

Abby nodded.

She had forgotten about Jack, the man in Texas that the reporter Stephen had met with shortly before his death. Lorna had told her and Oliver about the man and how to reach him.

"Jack can shed some light on Kanti, perhaps, but it's clear to me that Clyde is another player in this curse."

Abby squeezed her hands into fists, digging her fingernails into her palms. It hurt and it felt good. The continuing chaos made her feel out of control, lost, and she wanted to scream, "make it stop."

Oliver shifted closer to her as if he sensed her agitation. He passed her a small pale pink stone, rose quartz. She took it and pressed it against her heart. After several seconds, she felt some of her anger dissipate.

"So, we get more information from Jack, but could he possibly know about Clyde?"

"Hard to say," Julian admitted. "Which is why we need to track what happened to Clyde after he returned to America. And I'd like to know what occurred before he left. Ideally, we get in touch with a witch from the Serpent House."

"Could that coven still exist?" Oliver asked. "I mean, we've been around Trager for years. Dafne grew up there. Wouldn't we have known about a coven?"

"Not necessarily," Julian said. "But in all likelihood yes. I find it hard to believe Dafne and her Trager witches wouldn't have been contacted if there was a local coven. I'd say they broke apart before Dafne's time. The question is when, and why?"

CHAPTER 17

Sebastian hugged Abby and she clutched him as if he might never return. "Five minutes, tops," he promised.

She backed away and stood with Helena, Julian, and Oliver. Oliver gave him a thumbs-up and Julian offered a tense smile.

"Not a minute more, Sebastian," Helena called.

He waved and turned, trotting across the bridge. His stomach felt knotted and queasy. He could not shake the image of the water witch waiting for him on the other side. However, when he stepped from the bridge, the forest he'd originally encountered appeared. That forest gave way to other worlds, a dozen or more, but he did not look at them.

"Claire?" he whispered, searching the trees. "Claire?"

He took another step away from the bridge and then another, ready to spring back at any moment if Meghan appeared.

Someone grabbed him from behind and he lurched away, twisting around to face his assailant.

"Whoa there, cowboy," Claire laughed. "It was a hug, not an attack."

"Good grief, Claire," he cried, shaking his head. "You scared me half to death."

"Well, better half than the whole way."

"Very funny."

"I was worried about you," she said, taking a step forward and offering her hand.

He took it and pulled her into a hug.

"With good reason, but there's no time to get into all that now. I need a favor."

"Of course, big brother. Hand it over."

"You know about the amulet?"

She grinned and cocked her head to the side.

"Haven't you listened to a word I've said? I know all kinds of stuff."

"And you can take it to her? The water witch?"

"Yep, she has no power over me, though she's going to be irate when she sees it's a fake."

"Yeah, which is why I need you to stall her as long as possible. There's another guy down there, Liam, and he needs time to escape."

"Shall I dazzle her with my knowledge of root vegetables?"

"You can tell her anything you want, so long as it buys us some time."

"Oh, she'll listen, all right. If she thinks I'm holding her prized possession, what choice does she have?"

"Good point."

"You've got about a minute and thirty seconds left," she said, smiling in that funny Claire way, sad and happy and mischievous.

Sebastian closed his eyes.

"I wish this existed at home in Trager. I wish I could see you every day."

Claire held his hand and kissed it.

"I'm there, Sebastian. I'm always there."

****

After Sebastian had escaped the Forest of Purgatory, Meghan punished Liam. She went into his head and played again and again the worst memories of his life. She created new, horrible memories of Hannah being tortured, of his family in Brisbane getting slaughtered in the night. When he woke in a wet heap of sweat and tears, he pressed his face into the mushy stinking ground and held the earth as if he clutched his mother and not the soggy wet grass of the Forest of Purgatory.

He didn't know how much time had passed, but he knew that Sebastian's friends would deliver the amulet at any moment. He couldn't consider the possibility that it had already happened. If Meghan had the amulet, Liam would never escape. He would never have an opportunity to jump from the bridge. He would be destined to die in the dream wood.

Eventually, thirst and hunger got the best of him. He stood on shaky legs and stumbled to the cave. He crawled into Clyde's room, drank quickly from the basin, and ate a handful of dried bark before racing back to the forest. He watched the floating pond for hours. The cycles of night and day, which sometimes lasted mere minutes before transitioning, shifted before him. When he saw the witch slithering up the tree and into the pond, he was close to nodding off. He sat at the base of a tree, hidden in shadows. Her movement jolted him awake. As she moved through the water, he sprang to his feet and ran for the old house.

****

"If our plan worked, Liam should be coming across the bridge any time," Sebastian murmured.

Hannah, Matilda, and Kit had joined the group in the woods. Hannah paced back and forth in front of the bridge, her long hair swishing as she walked. She looked rabid with strange expressions of joy quickly followed by terror.

"Quite the poker face," Oliver muttered.

Helena elbowed him, but Kit smiled.

More time passed and the general euphoria in the group began to shift. Sebastian had left the amulet with Claire more than twenty minutes earlier. If Liam had escaped, it shouldn't have taken so long.

"He's not coming," Hannah suddenly shrieked. "She killed him. She was so angry that you escaped that she killed him." She directed her venomous words at Sebastian and started to step in his direction. Abby, Juliana, and Oliver immediately blocked her way.

"Hannah, don't be a mongrel," Kit told her.

Hannah glared at Kit, but turned back toward the bridge. She walked slowly at first, more of an angry stomp, and then suddenly she was running.

Abby followed Hannah's gaze.

A man walked across the bridge. He was tall and skeletal, with sunken eyes and matted blonde hair. His clothes hung like dirty rags from his meager frame.

Still, Hannah jumped into his arms and he caught her easily. They both cried and hugged and collapsed on the ground.

"You're alive, you're alive, you're alive," Hannah cried.

Liam said nothing, but Abby could hear his quiet sobs as he pressed his face into Hannah's neck.

Matilda and Kit walked to them. Kit helped Liam to his feet and he hugged her hard, continuing to cry. He grabbed Matilda next and she rubbed his back and murmured soothing things as Hannah watched them, her face splotchy and wet with tears.

When Liam spotted Sebastian, he broke away and ran to him. He grabbed him and lifted him from the ground, nearly buckling beneath his weight.

"You saved me, mate. You saved my life."

****

For five days, Lydie and her Aunt Cammi talked ceaselessly. They hiked the Everglades and went to Disney World. Lydie had never been and Cammi insisted it was a rite of passage for all kids, especially magic ones. As their time together wound to an end and Lydie stood in the little guest bedroom packing her bag, her head spun from all the stories Cammi had shared. Lydie's memories of her mother had always felt a little fuzzy and far away, but Cammi had brought the color back to those wonderful years.

She held up a black and white sweatshirt with a classic Mickey Mouse grinning back at her. Cammi had insisted on souvenirs and even though she generally was not one to wear cartoon animals of any kind, she intended to sleep in the sweatshirt every night until it no longer smelled like Cammi's detergent.

"Mind if I come in?" Cammi asked from the doorway.

Lydie smiled and waved her in.

"Just getting my stuff organized."

"These five days passed like an hour," Cammi said, perching on the edge Lydie's bed and picking up one of her t-shirts. "What's Pink Sabbath?"

"A witch band, all girls. They cover a lot of Black Sabbath, pretty wicked stuff."

"Wow, a witch band?"

"Yeah, they played at an All Hallow's Ball I went to a couple years ago."

"Do they have concerts and tours?"

"Yeah, not at Ula though," Lydie smiled wryly. "My coven is old school. More old school than old school, in fact."

"Do you like that?"

Lydie averted her eyes, concentrating extra hard on folding her jeans. "Sometimes."

"And other times you wish for a normal life?"

Lydie nodded.

"When your mother told me about Ula, she said it was like living in a museum."

"Yeah, I was born there, but Elda told me after six months, my parents wanted to move out."

"I wish they would have stayed," Cammi said, rotating the little silver rings she wore on her fingers.

"Me too," Lydie muttered. She had never felt anger at her parents for leaving Ula until that moment. It flared up from nowhere and the pretty yellow curtains burst into flame.

"Oh," Cammi yelped and fell from the bed, hitting her tailbone hard on the floor.

Lydie rushed to the curtains and waved her hands over the material. The fire vanished. She smoothed her fingers along the singed fabric and it was restored.

"I'm so sorry, are you okay?" she asked her aunt, helping her back to her feet.

"You are your mother's child," she declared, rubbing her backside.

"I can help with that too." Lydie smiled. She rummaged through her bag and pulled out a small bottle of gray salve. "Helena, one of the," she paused on the word witch, "ladies at Ula makes a spooktactular pain salve. Works instantly."

Cammi took it gratefully.

"I really am sorry about the curtains, but I fixed them, okay?"

Cammi nodded.

"I don't care about the curtains and I don't care that you occasionally light random things on fire. I am so grateful to have had these last five days with you and I want there to be more. Okay?"

Lydie stepped into Cammi's outstretched arms.

"Me too."

****

Their final night at the Sky Mothers was a joyous one. Despite Binda's betrayal, they celebrated Liam's return with a raucous dinner and bonfire on the beach. The witches prepared an enormous feast, but Liam, after nearly a year of surviving on bark and ants, could barely stomach more than a few spoonfuls of broth and a slice of bread. Still, he commented on every dish, how each recipe smelled and looked. He thanked the witches again and again for their hospitality. Most of all, he stared at Hannah and she looked back at him. They were lovers reunited and their bliss created a sense of good fortune that left everyone a little romantic and weepy.

As the fire waned, the witches drifted away. Hannah and Liam were first to disappear, and then Kit and Oliver followed. Abby had nodded off and Sebastian carried her back to their yurt. Only Julian, Matilda, and Helena remained.

"I hope that you will all return," Matilda said, looking earnestly at Helena and Julian. "And that with time, you will forgive us."

"You are already forgiven," Julian assured her. "And now that we know how closely we are linked, I am sure that we will be back."

"And perhaps you can visit us at Ula as well," Helena added.

Ula's name, the jewel of the sea, had been given to it centuries earlier, but for Helena it still held true. She loved her coven and each time she visited another, she understood how lucky she was to call Ula home.

****

Victor locked the door behind him. He walked to the bureau and pulled the velvet box from his chest pocket. He looked at the amulet wistfully. He longed to put it on, felt the eagerness coursing through his bones, his blood. Just looking at the snake and her red heart made his pulse quicken and a line of sweat pop along his hairline. He glanced up and caught himself in the mirror. His long hair hung limp and his eyes held the wild sheen of a meth addict seeking his fix. Victor had seen enough of them to know the look. He had even wondered a few times - do they ever look in the mirror? Do they ever look up and not recognize the desperate animal standing before them? Is that look ever a moment of truth where they put down the needle, step away from the darkness, and call their mom?

He touched the golden snake, felt it slither and shimmer beneath his fingertips. Ecstasy more powerful than an orgasm coursed through him. He shuddered.

"Not now," he said. "I can't do this right now."

He slid the necklace back into the box and closed the lid, slammed it shut really. Sebastian had failed. Dafne had failed, they all had failed, but he, Victor, had not. He would carry it through.

No one understood the power encased in that small velvet box.

CHAPTER 18

Abby dropped her bags inside the door and closed her eyes. The familiar smell of their home greeted her. She leaned her head against the wall and surrendered to the sweet relief of returning home. When they had set off for Australia, it felt like an adventure and a vacation. Then it had turned on them. Their escape became another layer of the prison created by the curse. Perhaps she should have expected as much. Coincidences were unheard of in the world of witches. Every meeting, place, and encounter held value in the larger story.

"Home," Sebastian murmured behind her. He set his bags down and pulled her away from the wall.

They stood in the foyer, intertwined, and Abby felt every muscle in her body relax.

"Do we have to go to Ula tomorrow?" she mumbled into Sebastian's chest.

The decision had been made that all the witches would gather at Ula the following day to decipher the whereabouts of the amulet.

Sebastian sighed.

"No, we can pretend we mixed up the dates and go next week instead."

Abby laughed.

"I'll say I lost my car keys and we've both been stricken with the flu."

"And the furnace is out again so we have to stay and fix it…"

"And my feet are swollen from the pregnancy so I can't wear shoes."

Sebastian smoothed her hair away from her face.

"Really though, if you don't want to, we can put it off for a few days."

She shook her head.

"I want to walk in this door and really feel at ease. Right now, it's so good to be home, but in the back of my mind, there's this huge shadow. The curse, the amulet and now Clyde. Not to mention this baby's growing every day. I don't want her coming into a world of chaos. Plus, the wedding has been planned. Bridget's been working for weeks."

Sebastian laughed.

"Wedding trumps curse?"

"I wish." Abby sighed. "I'm afraid the curse has taken over our lives. I'm ready to bury it once and for all."

****

Faustine entered the library. He looked tired. Abby knew that they all looked tired because they were tired.

"You all know why we're here. The original amulet was stolen," he told them curtly. "Julian and Matilda examined the false necklace in Australia. The stone was recent. It had been treated with a chemical that has only existed during this century. The gold was new as well. It certainly was not the same amulet that originally came into the castle."

Elda followed behind him and Abby could see deep grooves in her face as if the last month had aged her another century.

"Someone took the amulet from our dungeons. It is inconceivable to me that we do this, but…"

"We must," Faustine finished. "Each of us will go to the tower. I will connect with you telepathically and examine your memories with the Crystal of Sight."

"A witch lie detector?" Sebastian asked, wryly.

Oliver grinned. "Detective Faustine on the job."

Faustine offered him a dry look.

"I know how it seems, and of course we don't suspect any of you, but perhaps, one of you was..." Elda started.

"Possessed?" Lydie finished,

Abby hadn't heard her come in. She sat in a paisley chair, looking older than Abby remembered.

She crossed her long tan legs at the ankle and a henna pattern wound up one of her shins. Her wild blonde curls were twisted high on her head and Abby thought she saw a hint of dark makeup around her eyes.

"We must be open to all the possibilities," Elda murmured, not in agreement exactly, but acknowledging Lydie's words.

"Are you perfecting your phantom approach?" Oliver teased, twittering his fingers at Lydie. Her chair shook and Lydie looked hard at Oliver.

"I would return that magic, but I don't want to light you on fire, Oliver dear."

"Are these the terrible thirteens we're experiencing?" Oliver joked.

"Oh no, we missed your birthday." Abby fretted. "I'm sorry Lydie."

Lydie shrugged.

"My aunt made chocolate cake."

"Maybe we could have a little celebration at our house?" Abby looked at Sebastian.

"Of course."

"Sure," Lydie said, noncommittally. She stood and walked from the room.

"I think she's a bit salty about the Australia trip," Oliver said.

"I'd say," Sebastian agreed.

"No," Elda disagreed. "She's changing. It's a difficult time for any young woman, and Lydie is special. She met her aunt while you were away. It was a big deal and something I'm sure she'll want to share when the time is right."

"How can we help?" Abby asked.

Elda smiled and took her hand, squeezing.

"You have plenty enough to do, dear. Showing up when she needs you, listening if she wants to talk, that's how you can help."

****

One by one, they visited Faustine's tower and one by one, they were cleared of stealing the amulet. Abby had not believed that any of them would be implicated, and yet, her own hands shook when she sat down opposite Faustine and looked into the shining crystal hanging over his third eye.

When Faustine told her she could leave, she paused, unsure how to ask the questions rolling through her mind.

"It wasn't me, right?"

Faustine cocked an eyebrow and watched her closely.

"Did you think it was you?"

"Well, no, but, I mean, I wouldn't remember, right?"

"It wasn't you, Abby."

She left the tower and tried not to cry with relief. What would she have done if she had stolen the amulet? How could she look any of them in the eye after such a betrayal? It wouldn't have been her fault, of course, and they would all reassure her of that, but still.

After Faustine completed a scan of all the witches of Ula, including Adora, he concluded that none of them had taken the amulet.

"Which leaves Galla of Sorciére and the Chicago witches," Julian mentioned later at dinner. Bridget had made homemade pizzas, which Abby ate with relish. She hadn't had pizza in months.

"Will you ask them to come to Ula?" Sebastian asked Faustine.

"Oliver has volunteered to visit Chicago. He will not be able to glean as much information with the crystal as I can, but I believe he will get a solid impression of the witches. They are suspicious of covens and I prefer not to put them on the defensive. It is best if we seek them out in their space."

Abby glanced at Oliver who gave her a smile and a shrug.

"I've had a hankering for some time in the big city."

"And for Ezra," Lydie snapped, picking at her food.

"Whoa there little gator," Oliver joked, leaning over to tickle her.

Lydie scooted her chair away and shot him a dark look.

He widened his eyes at Abby and made a hurt face.

"Sebastian and I are taking a trip to Lansing to see my mom tomorrow, Lydie, but we'll be back in the evening. Would you like to come stay with us for a few days?"

Lydie glanced up at her and then over at Elda.

Elda smiled and nodded.

"Maybe," Lydie said, but continued pushing her pizza around her plate without taking a bite.

****

"Are you sure we shouldn't put the wedding off? I mean, what's another month or two?" Abby asked Helena as they prepared to leave Ula.

Helena had packed a tote of vitamins, supplements and pregnancy potions for Abby to take back to their home in Trager. There were satchels of herbs to aid in Abby's sleep, bath tonics, and lotions for skin elasticity.

"Marriage is sacred," Helena reminded her. "Those binds offer their own special power and we need to call upon that now. I don't mean to scare you, but you've observed what occurred with Dafne and the Lourdes of Warning. The curse seeks to separate and destroy. We must do our best to shield you and Sebastian and your child. The wedding will be another layer of protection."

Abby held up a pair of dried chicken's feet wrapped in twine.

Helena laughed.

"I'm superstitious, honey. Don't worry; no chickens were harmed in the making of that charm. I've had those feet for a long time. My mother gave them to me when I was a girl. They came from our lucky hen."

"What do you suppose I do with them?"

"Put them under your pillow."

Abby grimaced.

"I'm only kidding," Helena laughed. "Bury them in a pot on your porch. My mother did that and swore that those little feet protected us from ill will."

Abby looked at them a bit more closely.

"Okay, but they better not kill my tulips."

CHAPTER 19

Abby took a deep breath and stepped out of her car. She and Sebastian were parked outside of her mother's house and he had been giving her a pep talk in preparation for what lay ahead. She had not seen her mother since they performed the ritual in the fire. Julian believed that they relieved her of some dark energy, but Abby had no idea what to expect.

She walked to the garage door and glanced back at Sebastian who gave her a thumbs-up. It had been locked the last time she visited. The knob turned and she pushed open the door, expecting to see boxes everywhere, but the garage sat empty. At the door to the house, she knocked loudly and then cracked it open.

"Mom, it's me, Abby," she called, slipping into the kitchen.

She surveyed the space in wonder. Clean, even spotless, surfaces greeted her. The bags of trash next to the door were gone. She saw a small candle burning in the center of the kitchen table. It smelled like cinnamon.

"Mom?" she called again.

She felt a strange combination of hope and fear. The dismantling of her mother in the previous months had felt like a terminal illness that rapidly took hold with no possibility of reversal. When Elda and Helena had suggested treating Becky with magic, Abby had agreed out of desperation and guilt, but very little of her believed in a positive outcome. Her mother had always been sort of unhinged. How could magic fix that?

"Oh!" Abby's mother jumped, startled as she bustled into the kitchen carrying a basket of laundry.

She wore one of Abby's old MSU sweatshirts and a pair of pleated mom jeans. On her feet, Abby saw fluffy leopard slippers. Her hair was brushed into a tight ponytail and her face looked raw and pink, like she had just washed it.

"Abigail, you practically gave me a heart attack," she gasped, setting the laundry on the table. "To what do I owe the pleasure of your unannounced visit?"

"Mom, you look great," Abby told her honestly.

She looked like the mom that Abby remembered from her childhood. The bags under her eyes and the puffiness of her face had dissipated. She looked tired, but healthy.

Becky pawed at her hair self-consciously, but offered Abby a smile.

"I feel better, to tell you the truth. Ever since that spa weekend, I don't know." She looked flustered and Abby wondered what her mother remembered of the weekend.

"I'm so happy that you feel better, Mom."

Abby strode across the room and hugged her. She breathed in the familiar scent of her Dove soap and the unfamiliar scent of Chanel perfume, the perfume that Sydney used to wear.

"Abby." Her mother pulled away and looked down at her body. "You've gotten fat!"

Abby burst out laughing.

"Mom, I've gotten pregnant, not fat."

Becky's eyes opened wide and she stared at Abby's stomach for an instant before returning her gaze to her face.

Her expression was unreadable and Abby fought the urge to apologize for something, though she did not know what.

Becky sat down roughly in a chair.

"Mom?" Abby asked.

Becky looked up at her, troubled.

"Pregnant? You're in graduate school. What about college?"

Abby almost laughed. She had told her parents that she had moved to the Upper Peninsula to get her master's degree. She didn't think she had ever specified a major or a career intention. Her mother knew that she had not moved to go to college, but suddenly Abby wondered if the previous several months had vanished from Becky's mind completely. Had she forgotten about Grandma Arlene's special box? Had she forgotten that Abby was no longer an ordinary young woman?

"Mom, what do you remember about the last few months?"

Becky frowned and Abby saw the effort as she searched her mind.

"You left and then Sydney died." Becky gestured with her hand as if that small movement encapsulated everything she hadn't said, but of course, it didn't.

"Do you remember meeting Sebastian?"

"Sebastian was the name of the boy who used to visit Sydney. There was a boy and a girl, and their parents too. They died, all of them, except the boy," Becky murmured, remembering. "How sad. I remember when Sydney called to tell me, she just cried and cried."

Abby listened intently. Her mother had never told her that story. Her mother had never told her much of anything.

"They were friends of your grandmother Arlene originally."

"Same Sebastian, mom. He and I are getting married."

Becky stared hard at the table in front of her.

"Yes, I think I do remember," she said suddenly. "Very pretty blue eyes."

"That's him. He's in the car right now."

"Here?" Becky looked up sharply. "Well at least let me get this laundry to the basement before you invite him in."

Becky's tone sounded irritated, but also satisfied as if it were only appropriate that Abby should bring her fiancé home.

"Let me help," Abby said picking up the basket.

"Oh no, you don't. I miscarried twice before I had you, and I won't be the reason for some great tragedy befalling you. Lord knows I've suffered enough as your mother."

She swept the basket from the table and hurried for the stairs.

Now, this was her mother. Abby felt oddly hopeful. She realized that a part of her fear about healing her mother included finding a Stepford-Wife style mother wearing an apron covered in little cherries while she baked cookies in pink high heels. Instead, the magic had seemed to return Becky to her former self, maybe a little softer around the edges too.

Abby opened the door into the garage and found Sebastian waiting just inside.

"I wasn't spying, I swear," he said holding up his hands. "I just wanted to make sure you were okay."

She kissed his cheek and nodded.

"Everything is good, better than good."

"Really?" he looked skeptical as he followed her inside.

During their last visit, the house had been trashed and Abby's mother had acted nuts.

"What happened to Cody, I wonder?" Abby whispered as Sebastian surveyed the kitchen, referring to the strange young guy that Becky had invited to share her home.

"Is this the same house?"

"One and the same."

"Hello there!" Becky called, coming up the basement stairs.

Abby was delighted to see that Becky hadn't stripped off her mom clothes in lieu of a ball gown in the basement.

"Hi, Mrs. Daniels. Really nice to see you again."

Becky studied him as if trying to remember.

"Would you like coffee? Or I have tea. Only the herbal kind for you, missy," she directed her comment at Abby.

"Herbal would be great," Sebastian told her. Abby knew he was a coffee man through and through, though at Helena's urging, Sebastian now made copious amounts of raspberry leaf tea. Abby was growing sick of the stuff.

Becky boiled water and ushered them into chairs. Abby watched her in quiet awe and felt the hard lump of trepidation finally beginning to dissolve. This was her mother. The woman she had spent the first eighteen years of her life with. This woman was not perfect-who was, after all? But she was her mother.

"Are you buried in snow up there?" Becky asked. "In the UP?"

"Actually, we bought a house in Trager City," Sebastian told her before Abby could stop him.

Becky paused with her back to them and Abby held her breath.

"Okay, I think I remember you said that, Abigail. Hmmm, I don't know what's gotten into me. Lately my mind…"

She returned with their teas. Abby recognized one of the old mugs. The other two were new and shiny with glittery gold foil butterflies on the side. They were pretty.

"These are beautiful, Mom. Where did you get them?"

Becky touched one of the mugs and frowned.

"The QVC?" she said, but she clearly did not remember.

"Delicious," Sebastian lied. Sebastian hated jasmine tea, but he drank it, smiling. Abby squeezed his knee appreciatively.

"Mom, we're getting married in a few weeks," Abby blurted.

She had been contemplating how to tell her mother, how to gently deliver the news. The problem was that Becky loved weddings. Abby knew her mother had always envisioned a big fluffy wedding filled with calla lilies and lace for her only child's big day. Abby, unfortunately, was not the bridal type. The thought of a large wedding made her skin crawl. She had intended for a soft delivery of the news, but nerves got the best of her.

Becky's eyes opened wide.

"Three weeks? Impossible! There's no time." Becky stood up, looked wildly around and started for the living room.

"Mom," Abby patted Becky's chair.

Becky narrowed her eyes and glanced at the chair.

"You're going to elope? You're getting married in a courthouse? You will strip me of the honor of watching my only daughter walk down the aisle?" She burst into tears.

Abby stood and hurried to her mother.

"No, no, we're not eloping. We just want a small wedding, okay Mom? Small. It will still be a wedding with a dress and flowers and all the fun stuff, and we have the most beautiful location already picked out."

Abby paused, unsure how to go forward. She had expected a crazy version of her mother who at least remembered the magical aspect of Abby's new life. This version seemed to barely remember the day of the week. Cloaking and concealment spells would hide the more magical aspects of Ula and the island, but the wedding would be different. There would be no additional family members, no planning for Becky to do at all.

"There's an amazing place where we spend a lot of time." Sebastian broke in. He gave Abby a little nod as if to signal that he had this. "It's called Ula. Have you heard of it?"

Becky cocked her head to the side and then her shoulders sagged as if remembering.

"Yes, perhaps."

She wandered into the living room and settled into a chair in the darkness. The shades were drawn and the room smelled of lemon furniture polish. Abby and Sebastian followed her. The boxes, leftovers, and jumble of furniture were gone.

"Mrs. Daniels, I know this is a lot to take in and I can see that you're disappointed. What can we do? How can we support you right now?"

Abby smiled at the earnestness in Sebastian's voice. She thought vaguely he should have been a therapist.

Becky looked at him with cloudy, sad eyes.

"I had forgotten. Forgotten it all, I guess. My mother and the bonfire and the monster in the woods."

"What?" Abby asked, trying to make sense of her mother's words. "The monster in the woods?"

"It was a long time ago, Abigail. I...I never told anyone. After a few days, I didn't even believe it myself."

Becky paused and smoothed her hands down the front of her shirt. She looked around the room as if she barely recognized it.

"It's strange here without your father. It's so empty, not that he filled much space. Your grandmother Arlene once told me that I could fit all your father's opinions in a teaspoon."

Abby wanted to direct her mother back to the monster, but recognized the tangent unfolding. She could feel Sebastian beside her. He wanted Abby to be quiet so that Becky could tell the story in her own time.

"It was Sydney's fault," Becky hissed in a girlish voice that Abby had never heard. A shudder moved over Becky's features, and for an instant, Abby thought she could see her as a girl, scared, and filled with resentment.

"Sydney ran into the woods that day. We were camping. My parents and Sydney loved to camp. Maybe I did until that trip. After that, I never wanted to go again. She ran into the woods and I chased her, but then she must have doubled back. I lost her. I found this tree, this terrible, amazing tree. It was bright red. A bright red weeping willow."

Abby gasped and put a hand to her mouth to keep from blurting out the name of the witch who lived beneath that tree.

Becky looked at her, thinking that the response referred to the insanity of a red weeping willow.

"I know, it was unreal. Maybe it really was unreal."

"It was real," Sebastian told her. He watched her intently.

Becky looked back at him and her eyes widened in surprise as if finally registering that he too knew that the tree existed. He was not merely humoring her.

"I saw the monster then. Sagging skin and a horrible twisted body like a dead thing."

Becky closed her eyes. When she opened them, she turned to Abby.

"I went back. The next night, I woke to her calling for my mother. She called my mother Ra. My mother went to her and I followed. I was so scared. I've never been so scared. The monster wanted something, but my mother wouldn't give it to her. She walked away, she left me there."

Becky started to cry and then sob. Her shoulders shook and she hung her head as if ashamed that her mother had abandoned her in those dark woods.

"She called to me and I tried to resist. I wanted to yell out to my mother. I wanted to run away, but I couldn't. My body wouldn't listen. I crawled out from behind my tree and across the dewy ferns. She reached for me and took my hair in her hands. I thought she would eat me. I kept waiting, but she didn't. She told me things. She told me horrible things," she paused and looked at Abby. "About you."

Abby rocked back, surprised.

"About me? But, I wasn't even born yet, right? You were a child?"

"She called you by name. She spoke of a curse."

Abby felt as if the air had left her lungs. Sebastian sensed her distress and moved close to her, pressing his hand firmly into the small of her back, steadying her.

Becky stood and went to the kitchen, filling a glass of water. She took a long drink and then splashed more on her face.

"I'm not sure where this is all coming from."

"Keep going," Sebastian urged.

"You believe me?" she asked, and her voice sounded so small and so scared. Abby stood and wrapped her mother in a hug. Her stiff, cold mother, who usually loathed hugs, leaned into her. Abby felt her body softening, and Abby drew on her element to fill her mother with warmth and tenderness.

"Yes, Mom. Yes, we believe you."

"She told me that you would become just like her, that I was powerless to stop it, that you would abandon me for the dark shadows that live in your blood, our blood. She told me that your own child…" Becky pulled away and looked at Abby with such fear that Abby struggled to stay close, to not pull away. "That your child would be the ultimate sacrifice, your child would end the curse, and the witch who created it would rise again."

Sebastian moved into the kitchen. His eyes were dark and angry, but he took Becky's hand and turned her to face him.

"That's not going to happen. The witch who told you those things was evil. She was sick and deranged and now she's dead."

"But it's happened, so much of it has happened," Becky shrieked. "You are Abby, just as she said. She knew your name, your fate. You left me, you're one of them, and now, now…" she gestured helplessly at Abby's rounded belly.

"Mom." Abby gripped Becky's shoulders. "That witch was afflicted. It is true that she saw things, but she didn't know what the future held. She was angry and filled with hate. She wanted to poison you against your own child. Maybe she even did, a little."

"No, no, I didn't remember Abigail. Until, not until the spa. Why?" She narrowed her eyes at Abby. "You did something? It wasn't a spa."

Becky turned and fled through the garage door and onto the lawn. Abby and Sebastian chased after her, but Becky didn't stop. She jumped into her car and locked the door before Sebastian could stop her. Becky started the car and reversed down the driveway. Tears covered her face and she looked terrified.

Abby closed her eyes and summoned her power. She went into the engine. She knew little about cars, less about engines, but focused on the battery. In her mind, the water in the battery evaporated. Becky backed the car into the street and it stalled. The car drifted. Becky looked at them, shocked. She tried to start the car again, but it didn't make a sound. Abby watched her mother try again, and then defeated, she rested her head on the steering wheel.

Sebastian pushed the car back into the driveway. After several long minutes, during which Abby and Sebastian could hear Becky sobbing against the wheel, Becky climbed out. Her face was puffy and her eyes were swollen. She did not speak to them, but walked, resigned, back into the house.

For a moment, Abby wanted Helena or Elda to come and soothe her mother. She felt inadequate as a witch. She had powers and potions at her disposal, but standing in her childhood home, she felt helpless.

She looked to Sebastian, expecting her own distress to be mirrored back to her, but instead he looked calm and ready. He guided Becky into the living room and settled her into a chair. He brought her a cup of tea and tucked a blanket across her lap. Becky let him. Though she shot furtive glances at Abby.

Abby went to the sink and ran her hands beneath the cold water. Eyes closed, she allowed the water to climb up her wrists. The energy filled her like a cool, invigorating mist.

"How do I help my mother," she whispered under her breath.

She didn't expect an answer. Abby had learned to detach from her emotions when she needed answers. *Get out of your head, out of your story and into the essence of all things, the energy of the universe. That's where truth lives*, Elda had once told her.

Abby realized that she had to tell her mother everything.

She almost crushed the thought. How could she possibly tell her everything? Could her fragile, moody mother handle such a blow to her concept of reality?

CHAPTER 20

Abby took a deep breath. She sat on a leather footstool and faced her mother.

"Mom, I'm going to tell you some things. I would really appreciate it if you'd wait until I'm done talking to ask me any questions."

Becky had closed her eyes and her lips were set in a grim line. She nodded.

"Last summer, I left Lansing because I was really unhappy. I didn't love Nick, I loathed my job, and everything around me had begun to feel suffocating. I packed a bag with a few things and drove to Aunt Sydney's house. I knew that Sydney and Rod were spending a couple of weeks in the Cayman Islands and I wanted to clear my head."

Sebastian returned with a mug of tea for Abby and then sat on the couch. He nodded, encouraging her to go on.

"I met Sebastian at Aunt Sydney's."

"Julia," Becky murmured.

Abby saw Sebastian's face perk up at the mention of his mother's name, but he didn't interrupt.

"The day after I arrived at Sydney's house, I was walking in the woods and I found a dead body."

Becky's eyes shot open and she looked at Abby, startled.

Abby held up her hand, signaling that she was fine.

"It was terrible. I missed you so much. That was probably the moment I most wanted to race home and pretend I never left. The girl, Devin Blake, was close to my age. Sebastian and I started to investigate her death and we were attacked by the people that killed her. The thing is, they weren't people. They're called Vepars. They're like demons in human bodies."

Becky stared at Abby with horror and disbelief.

"We escaped. Sebastian's little sister Claire had also been killed by Vepars, two years before."

"Claire?" Becky asked.

"You knew her?" Sebastian cut in, he couldn't help himself.

"I met her once. You didn't visit Sydney that weekend. Claire and your mother came alone. It was a girls' weekend. She showed me her collection of paint-brushes. They all had names."

Sebastian laughed.

"Groucho was her favorite."

Becky smiled.

"Claire had a journal that described a secret island in Lake Superior." Abby continued. We went there and found the Coven of Ula."

"Ula…" Becky breathed. "I heard my mother speaking of it once, whispering to my father."

"The people who live in the Coven of Ula are…"

"Witches," Becky finished for her.

Abby watched her mother closely, trying to decide if she should continue.

"How do you know that, Mom?"

"Because my mother was a witch. Sydney used to tell me. She was proud, but I knew it was a curse. I'd seen the witch beneath the willow tree."

"She's different, Mom. Something horrible happened to her and it drove her insane."

"We're all a little mad," Becky said, with a small smile, as if remembering another time. "Your Grandma Arlene used to say that a lot."

"At Ula, I found out that I am one of them. I'm a witch."

Becky bit her lip and pressed the palms of her hands into her eyes. She shook her head from side to side.

"It's all coming true."

"It's not, Mom. The witch who told you those horrible things was trying to hurt you. It's not coming true."

"My mother is dead. Sydney is dead. Sebastian's parents, and sister are dead. Don't you see a pattern, here? Being one of them doesn't make you invincible. It's a death sentence!" Becky's voice had grown shrill and Abby scooted closer to her.

"Please, listen to me and trust me. I have the power to manipulate water. I am so strong. My blood heals other witches and people. It's not a curse, it's a gift. Sebastian is not a witch, but he's magical too. He's called a hybrid."

"A hybrid?" Becky looked at him with new and distrustful eyes.

"Kind of like a mutt," he joked, but she didn't smile.

"It's true that there is a curse in our blood. It was created three hundred years ago by a woman named Kanti. We're going to break the curse, mom. Once we've done that, we'll be safe."

"Does the curse destroy all the Vepars?"

"Well, no," Abby admitted.

"Then, how could you possibly be safe?"

****

"A dog!" Lydie shrieked and ran for the beautiful Siberian husky that jumped out of the boat after Helena.

Lydie raced down the dock and, without pausing, she and the dog threw themselves at one another. They both rolled off the dock and splashed into the water.

Helena and Julian laughed as Lydie cried out at the cold. She and the dripping husky splashed through the water and back to the shore.

"She's gorgeous, Helena," Elda said, walking down the stone steps in front of the castle.

"Aepa," Helena told her.

"You named her after your old coven," Elda murmured. "A beautiful tribute."

"Yes, and she's air all the way. She was chasing butterflies when I spotted her at the humane society."

"Lydie seems to like her," Julian added, walking up the steps.

Aepa chased Lydie along the lagoon edge.

"I would bring home a dog every day if we could keep Lydie feeling that way," Helena sighed.

Elda nodded.

"She has changed."

"You're right," Julian interrupted abruptly. "When I last knew her, she was a vengeful toddler who lit my coat on fire when I told her to stop swimming and come to dinner. We all change. That's the point. What are we here for, if not an evolution? Whose life was a success that came into this world and left unchanged? I challenge you to show me a single entity that has."

Elda pushed her shoulders back and nodded.

"You're right, of course, you're right. How can we mourn the growing of a child into a woman?"

"Because we're women," Helena murmured, continuing to watch Lydie. "We are the keepers of the past. Without our love for every facet of our lives, who would remember and tell the stories? I agree with you, Julian, everyone will and must change. But I also hold tight to that feisty little girl who refused to wear dresses and insisted we cut her hair short so she didn't light it on fire when she practiced magic."

Elda hooked an arm through each of theirs.

"That is why I so love you both. The transformer and the keeper."

"And the preserver," Julian said, nudging Elda.

"Yes, I am that."

"What is Lydie?" Helena asked, enjoying their little game.

"She is the destroyer," said Julian.

"The destroyer?" Elda asked, frowning.

"Sure, not intentionally, though sometimes. As she evolves, everything around her must be destroyed and rebuilt to accommodate what she represents - youth, rebellion, vibrancy."

"I prefer to think of her as the creator, then," Helena cut in.

"Two sides of the same coin."

****

Ezra arrived at the loft glistening and red-faced.

"Power yoga," she told Oliver when she strode past him into the kitchen. "You'd think a witch would breeze through it, but I swear that instructor is part devil."

Oliver smiled wryly.

"If it weren't possible, I might laugh."

She grinned and filled a glass with water. Drinking in long, loud gulps.

"Damn that's good."

She looked around the vacant loft.

"Where is everyone?"

"Doing their good deeds for the day. Kendra is at hospice. Dante and Marcus were off to revive some ailing bean sprouts. And Victor said he had top-secret work that he refused to disclose."

"Typical Victor," she said.

"Really?" Oliver asked, treading carefully. "Does he usually break away from the group?"

Ezra took another drink and shook her head.

"Not to isolate himself, but when he's on to something new he hides it and then does a big reveal. When he created the city grid, he filled the loft with exploding tinsel balloons to surprise us."

Oliver smiled, but something gnawed at him.

"Has everything been cool with Victor? He seemed a little distant when I first got here."

Oliver watched Ezra carefully. He didn't want to alert her to his suspicions. Victor, after all, was the center of her coven, whether they called it a coven or not.

"That's a question for him, I'd say."

"I'm not asking him, I'm asking you."

"Why, Oliver? Why are you asking me? Why are you here at all? Bored of stuffy old Ula, looking for some fun? The Australia adventure didn't satisfy your need to step out of your comfort zone?"

Oliver stood and reached for Ezra's hand. He wasn't thinking. He pulled her toward him and leaned his face down. He kissed her.

She shoved him away and stared into his bewildered face.

"If you think making out is going to soften me into divulging my secrets, you've watched a few too many romantic comedies."

She didn't blush, but Oliver felt his own face growing hot.

"I'm sorry, that was stupid of me. And I didn't do it to soften you, well not in that way anyhow."

Ezra sighed and ran her hands through her short hair. The last time he's seen her, it had been turquoise. She had since dyed it silver with streaks of purple and black.

He had shown up the night before unannounced. He wanted the element of surprise. He had brought a stack of irrelevant Asemaa documents as his guise, telling Victor that he hoped he could look at them and see if anything jumped out.

"Oliver, I like you, but now is not the time for this. I can't trust your motives and you don't need one more thing to figure out. And let's not forget your feelings for Abby."

Oliver shook his head and started to argue.

She held up a hand to stop him.

"You're an honest guy, to your core. It's endearing and I haven't met a lot of men in my lifetime that are, so don't tarnish that by lying to me, or worse, lying to yourself. I understand unrequited love. I've been on both the giving and receiving end of that nasty little heartache, and these days I don't delude myself-ever. You should give yourself that same courtesy."

Oliver searched for a joke, but came up empty. He sat roughly back on the barstool and smiled grimly.

"You're like a backhanded therapist."

She cocked an eyebrow.

"I'm way worse than that."

****

"Gwen," Abby called, waving as the woman walked through the door. She was surprised to see another of the Asemaa with her: Lorna.

"Look at you," Gwen gushed, hugging Abby and then pulling her away to look at her belly. "That baby's growing!"

Abby blushed and touched her stomach.

She had worn a large sweater, but at nearly five months, the baby had started to reveal herself.

"Yes, Sebastian has started calling her Super Baby."

"No doubt she'll live up to the name," Lorna said, offering Abby a tight smile and nod.

"He's over by the window," Abby told them, pointing toward Sebastian. He occupied an elevated table in one of the busy cafe's window alcoves.

"I've heard this place has delicious sandwiches," Gwen offered, following Abby to their seats.

Lorna introduced herself to Sebastian and then leaned back in her chair, watching the door and the restaurant interior simultaneously.

"I'm happy to see the two of you together," Abby started. "Has everything been okay?"

"Right as rain." Gwen beamed. "Lorna's been staying with Ebony and me for two weeks. It's been like old times."

Lorna arched an eyebrow at Gwen but didn't comment.

"Well, slightly more stressful than life before, but still, it's progress, I think."

"Nothing weird has happened, then?" Sebastian asked.

"Should it have?" Lorna snapped, shifting her attention to Sebastian.

Gwen gave her a warning look.

"Lorna, I think you'd better go with the chamomile tea. Skip the coffee this morning."

Lorna rolled her eyes.

"Nothing strange has happened, no. In fact, life has been really calm and sweet lately," Gwen added. "Have things calmed down for you guys as well?" Gwen looked hopeful.

"I'd like to say yes," Sebastian sighed. "Unfortunately, we're still dealing with some pretty intense stuff."

"Does that make it easier for you?" Lorna asked, swiveling her gaze back to Sebastian. "Calling it intense stuff? Instead of demons and murderers?"

Abby clutched Sebastian's hand beneath the table, knowing that his anger would quickly rise at Lorna's comments.

"Are words important to you Lorna? Do you prefer to give Vepars more power? To instill more fear within yourself?" he asked evenly.

Lorna glared at him, but said nothing.

"I'm sorry," Gwen apologized for her angry friend. "I was excited to see you both. I didn't expect…"

She gestured helplessly toward Lorna.

"We're not your enemies, Lorna," Abby told her, annoyed. "In fact, we never invited you into this to begin with. You did it all by yourself, didn't you? It made you feel special. Isn't that what you said? Well, mission accomplished. So, let me be honest. We are living in a nightmare that you can't even imagine and I'm not interested in placating you through my lunch, so if you're not going to relax, then let's end this right now and I'll schedule another time to see Gwen alone."

Lorna pursed her lips and looked ready to walk out.

"Lorna, please," Gwen said, reaching for her friend's hand. "Remember Sydney."

Lorna looked at her lap and Abby watched her eyes soften and fill with tears. She brushed them away and nodded.

"I'm sorry, you're right. It's not your fault. I've just been so angry ever since Sydney died, and then Stephen… The world has stopped making sense."

"I get it, Lorna. I really do. We all want the same thing."

Lorna nodded and glanced out the window.

"Have you spoken with Jack yet? The man from Texas?" Gwen asked.

"I'm flying out to meet him in two days," Sebastian admitted. "But we're here because we hoped to ask you about something else. Have you ever heard of a coven called the Serpent House?"

Gwen furrowed her brow.

"It doesn't ring a bell."

"Snake Island," Lorna interrupted.

Gwen turned to her.

"Snake Island?"

Lorna nodded, looking strangely excited.

"Yes, don't you remember? Sydney told us about it. It's an abandoned island off the shore of Trager City. Supposedly a coven existed there centuries ago."

"Oh wait," Gwen nodded. "I do remember, but it wasn't in any of our documents. Sydney read about it in a history book for Trager. She said we should get a map and take her boat out there sometime as a little Asemaa field trip. Nothing ever came of it, though."

"You never went?" Sebastian asked, curious.

"No, she mentioned it right before one of our lulls in the Asemaa. We had a gap of a couple months before meeting again and we had all forgotten about it."

"Until now," Lorna said.

CHAPTER 21

"I've never been here," Sebastian told Abby as she pushed open the door to Rod's loft.

It looked exactly as it had the last time she visited, but everything felt different. On her previous venture to the loft, she believed Sebastian had died. Now she had him by her side. It hurt to see Sydney and Rod's life halted in its midst. The pictures and the clothes and the little bits of them spread over surfaces and along the walls. But having Sebastian walk through it with her softened the sharpness of her feelings.

"Classic Sydney and Rod," Sebastian laughed, tapping his finger on a framed picture of the couple in New Orleans. The photographer had captured Rod kissing Sydney's neck as she grinned into the camera. Heavy with brightly colored beads, a sea of smiling strangers behind them, they existed in their own little world.

"Do you think they're together now?" Abby asked, studying the picture.

"Yes, I do. Claire didn't say much about life on the other side, but she said my parents are there and that loneliness doesn't exist. I believe that Sydney and Rod are together right now, sitting at the edge of eternity, sipping margaritas and cheering us on."

Abby smiled and touched Sydney's grinning face in the photo. Her blue eyes shone and her smile stretched so wide that her cheeks probably ached the next day.

"I hope so," Abby said. She took a deep breath and turned away from the wall of pictures. It would have been easy to get lost wandering down memory lane.

"Bookshelf," Sebastian said, hunching over a long shelf beneath a window that faced downtown Trager. "Mostly steamy romance and murder mysteries."

Abby went to Sydney and Rod's room. She glanced at the bed and felt a little nudge of guilt in the pit of her belly. The last time she had been at the apartment, she had slept in that bed with Oliver. Nothing had happened, of course, but she had not told Sebastian. She wanted to believe he would think nothing of it, but she doubted he would be so understanding. Not that he'd be outright angry. Sebastian hid his feelings well, but it was the kind of information that caused more questions than answers.

Abby scanned the shelf. Sydney had travel books for Greece, Australia, and South America. She passed over books on pool cleaning and maintenance, wine tasting and herbal health. The name Trager caught her eye and she read the title: *How to Survive Trager City in the Winter*. The cover depicted a man wearing long johns and a cowboy hat, holding two huge cans of beer as he attempted to navigate a snowy hill. She smiled and shook her head. The author was likely one of Sydney's friends. The title next to it looked more promising: *Trager City: Past, Present, and Future*.

"Any luck?" Sebastian asked.

"Yeah, maybe."

She flipped to the section about the past and scanned the headings.

"Here we go," she said, stopping at a section called Myth and Lore of Trager City. She read aloud:

"Trager City may seem like an ordinary northern Michigan town to the tourists who pop in for a campfire and a swim in the lake. However, the old-timers in the area boast a much more sordid past. From witches to vampires, the city has been housing supernatural creatures for centuries-or so the legends say. One source tells us that once upon a time, our picturesque town was overrun with witches. Fortunately, they kept to themselves on a little-known island approximately five miles off shore. Locals call it Snake Island and perhaps that name was born from its ancient inhabitants: a coven of witches who referred to their home as Serpent House. These days, the island lives up to its name-overrun with snakes of all kinds. Few travelers venture beyond its shores."

"The next paragraph talks about BigFoot," Abby said, scanning to see if she crossed anything else of value.

"So it's true, then," Sebastian murmured, reading over Abby's shoulder. "I'm amazed that we've never heard of it."

"I love that you said it's true despite being nestled between a paragraph about BigFoot and another about the Wolfman."

Sebastian laughed.

"Yeah, but there's a reason people say there's a kernel of truth in every myth."

"What people say that?"

He grinned and tugged a strand of her hair.

"Me," he laughed.

"Well, I'll accept that so long as it doesn't apply to the Wolfman."

****

Lydie passed the library and paused. She heard Faustine and Julian talking about Australia. Helena had given her a brief overview of what had transpired there, and Oliver promised to fill her in on the whole tale, but he left for Chicago before he had the chance. The witches had finally returned from Australia, but she felt as alone as she had before they left. In fact, meeting her aunt had amplified her feelings of loneliness. At Ula, who did she have to remember her mother with? The witches barely spoke of Max and Dafne, two of their own who had died within the last several months.

"The Lourdes is truly dead, then?" Julian asked.

Elda had confided to Lydie that the Lourdes had died, but again, withheld the details.

"Yes. We have her trunk in the oratory, but I haven't had the heart to go through it," Faustine replied.

"But you discovered the book that Dafne received from the L'Obscurite?"

"Yes, and I've read it in its entirety. Disturbing-if I had to sum it up in a word."

Lydie heard a door open and hurried down the hall. She didn't want to be found eavesdropping. She slipped to the stairway and descended quickly, listening for any voices below. She passed Dafne's door and touched the handle, feeling her breath get stuck beneath her ribs and hover there, on the verge of explosion. She wanted to go inside, but didn't. Instead, she continued to the oratory.

"Knock, knock," she said, pushing the door in cautiously.

Elda spent a great deal of time in the space, poring over books of shadows, and Lydie didn't want to startle her. She also wanted the space to herself.

When no one answered, she opened the door wide and darted inside, closing it firmly behind her. She saw the trunk immediately and strode to it, undoing the clasp and flipping up the lid. The inside smelled musty and sour. Lydie wrinkled her nose and stared at the contents. Letters wrapped in twine sat on the top of the stack and she snatched them out and tucked them into her cloak. Lydie closed the trunk and retreated to her room. She knew that Faustine and Elda would be upset that she took the letters, but she was sick of feeling left out. Now she would be the one with information.

****

That evening, Ezra promised to take Oliver to the best sushi restaurant in the city. As they prepared to leave, Kendra walked in the door holding an unwieldy box that she carried effortlessly.

"Where are you guys off to?" she asked, sliding the box on the counter.

"Sushi Om," Ezra told her, buckling the high black boots that she wore over yellow fishnet tights. Above that, she had chosen a pair of paint-smeared terrycloth shorts and a tight black tank top. Oliver had decided that her fashion sense was truly one of a kind.

"Ooh, sounds good. Is Victor here?" Kendra looked around the loft, but the answer was written on her face. "Out again?"

Oliver could see that Kendra was disappointed and trying to hide it.

"Come with us," Oliver insisted. "Ezra said that Dante and Marcus might meet us too."

"Yeah, I think I will," Kendra replied, darting a last glance at Victor's empty bedroom.

She changed quickly and they left the loft on foot. The walk took a little less than fifteen minutes and they settled into a small booth at the back of the crowded restaurant.

When Ezra excused herself to the bathroom, Oliver took his chance with Kendra.

"Any idea what Victor has been working on? Ezra said he's been really busy with some secret project."

Kendra froze and her eyes shifted quickly toward the door. A human would never have noticed, but Oliver was not a human and he had been watching. Whatever Victor was up to, it had Kendra spooked.

She shrugged and ran her fingers through her long blond hair.

"Beats me. He likes to fly under the radar when he's working on something new."

Oliver nodded. He was not telepathic, but before he left Ula, Faustine had given him instructions and sent him with the Crystal of Sight. He slipped the crystal into his palm and leaned his head into his hand, resting the crystal near his third eye. He closed his eyes as if his head ached.

A blast of images cascaded through his mind and he tried to scan them.

He saw one, so briefly that he barely caught it. Victor stood at his dresser holding a black velvet box. He turned a guilty and then angry gaze on Kendra when she walked into his room uninvited, but then the image was gone.

"Headache?" Kendra asked.

Keeping the crystal concealed, Oliver slid his hand beneath the table.

"Yeah, getting better though."

"Here," she dug in her purse and pulled out a roll-on oil. "Rub a bit on your temples. Your headache will be a thing of the past."

He grinned and took the bottle, swiping his temples and holding it to his nose.

"Spearmint?"

"Among other things. So how are the wedding arrangements going?" Kendra asked. "I chatted with Abby to see if we could do anything, but apparently Bridget and Helena are quite the little wedding planners."

Oliver laughed.

"Yeah, don't dare take away their beloved wedding. They're like cackling hens right now, constantly changing the color of the candles and the arrangement of flowers."

"Sounds miserable." Ezra laughed, returning to the table. "Now I understand why you escaped to Chicago."

"Oh, come one." Kendra smiled, wistfully. "Weddings are beautiful. I've always loved them, the ceremonies especially. I'm not sure that two people are ever more committed to a higher love than on that day."

"Are you a hopeless romantic, Kendra?" Oliver teased.

"I prefer to think that I'm just a romantic, not a hopeless one."

"Hopeless if your partner is Victor," Ezra told her, winking.

Kendra smiled, but Oliver saw a sadness in her eyes at Ezra's words.

****

Elda moved in her astral body to the Cave of Elders. Though the cave was empty, she could send a message through the smoke in hopes of making contact with a coven that knew of the Serpent House. She did not have to build a fire. As she stood in the space and made her intention known, the fire sparked and grew.

"Earth, Air, Fire, and Water
Sisters and Brothers Hear My Call
It is Air that I Seek
Knowledge of a Time Now Passed
Souls of the Serpent House
Can You Hear My Call
Souls of the Serpent House
Can You Hear My Call
Souls of the Serpent House, reach out to me
Mote it be
Mote it be."

She could have returned to Ula. If a witch responded to her request, she would feel the tug in her astral body and return to the cave, but she chose instead to wait. The cave soothed her. She drifted in the smoke and firelight, the burden of her physical life slipped to the periphery of her consciousness. In her astral body, she touched the world of formlessness. It was a sweet, easy space, and sometimes it made her long for the end of life in her physical body.

Several hours passed before another witch joined her in the cave. The woman wore a flowing black cloak. Her white hair stood in stark contrast to the black hood.

Elda moved toward her and extended her hands. They did not touch, but their energies collided and then broke apart.

"You seek a soul of the Serpent House?" the witch asked, watching Elda with curious gray eyes.

"I do."

"She is not well. Astral travel is unavailable to her."

Elda nodded.

"I understand. She is of your coven?"

"Yes, though we are more a family than a coven. You can find us in Montana. Our farm is called the Winds of Change, near Butte."

"Can we come to you? And speak with this witch?"

"She would like that, yes. She is not long for this world and wants to be of service to you. She remembers the Serpent House in great detail. It was her first coven. She still harbors pain from its destruction."

"It was destroyed?" Elda asked.

"I am Ellen. The witch you seek is Nora. She will be expecting you."

When Elda returned to her physical body, she was alone in the dungeons. The stone slab in the underground room aided in astral travel, but Elda rarely went there. It reminded her too much of Max. As she sat in the velvet chair on the raised slab, she could hear his voice echoing through the chamber as he lectured Lydie in that gentle way of his. Max and Dafne, two integral members of Ula, had passed. She wondered how many more might die before the curse would be broken.

CHAPTER 22

Oliver volunteered to help Ezra at the medical clinic that the guerrilla witches ran in Chicago. In truth, he felt out of his element. Witches, like people, had specific skills and abilities. Oliver hunted Vepars. Healing had never come easily to him.

Ezra lifted a small girl onto an examination table.

"How ya doing sweetie? Eye still hurt?"

"Nope," the little girl told her. "See?"

The little girl held her eye open really wide and pushed her face close to Ezra's.

Ezra laughed.

"Looks like somebody gave you a whole new set of peepers," Ezra exclaimed. "But just to be safe, take this tincture home. Have your momma put one drop in every night for the next two weeks."

The little girl took the tiny blue bottle.

"Can I have a sucker?"

Ezra shook her head.

"You know I don't pedal those drugs in here, but I can do one better." Ezra pulled a huge bowl of fruit from beneath the table. "Take as much as you want."

The little girl snatched two apples and an orange and hopped down from the table.

"Bye, Rachel," Ezra called as the girl ran for the door.

Oliver had been carefully unpacking boxes of sterile gloves and arranging them in a cupboard. He could have unpacked them in about two minutes, but the clinic was bustling with people, none of them witches, so he had to keep things conventional. Plus, he got to watch Ezra out of the corner of his eye while he worked, which he rather enjoyed. He found himself thinking of Ezra more and more. When he was at the loft, he looked up hopefully each time the door opened and felt a little sigh of disappointment if Dante or Marcus walked through instead.

"What happened to her eye?" Oliver asked when Ezra glanced at him.

"Pink eye, pretty common. She has five siblings, and a whole gaggle of neighbor kids who get dropped in her little apartment as a pseudo less-than-legal-daycare. I treat her for all manner of ailments, her whole family too." Ezra shrugged as if to say, "such is life."

The double glass doors at the front of the building flew open and a tall wiry man shoved a gurney into the room.

"It's an O.D.," a short Indian woman, with wild dark hair shouted.

She ran across the room and began to assemble an IV.

Ezra dropped the cloth she'd been using to wipe the bed in front of her and sprinted to the stretcher.

"Room One," she told the man pushing the gurney.

The clinic didn't have rooms, but a series of stalls separated by hanging white curtains. Each space held a hospital bed, a small table, and a swivel chair. Ezra kicked the chair and sent it wheeling across the room.

"He's in cardiac arrest," Ezra told the small Indian women who'd arrived with the IV. "We need to intubate. Where's Jules?"

Oliver had met Jules that morning. Dr. Andrea Jules, a tall, stick thin woman with ebony skin and giant cat eyes glasses, had given him a firm handshake and a quick once over before returning to setting a man's broken arm.

"I'm here," Jules yelled, running toward them and fumbling with a cup of coffee.

"Ouch, shit," she yelped as it scalded her hand.

Oliver flicked his fingers toward her and the cup steadied. He slipped across the room and took it quickly from her grasp.

Ezra pulled the sheet around the patient and Oliver watched the clinic, chaos a moment earlier, return to its pre-emergency calm.

After the doctor and nurses emerged from the room, Ezra stayed behind. Oliver slipped behind the curtain.

Ezra glanced at him.

A man with cropped black hair lay on the bed. Tattoos covered both his arms and most of his neck. Ezra leaned over him, pressing her hands against his torso.

"Just giving his lungs a little extra help," Ezra told him.

"Did you give him anything?" Oliver whispered, referring to a potion or tincture that contained a bit more than herbs.

Ezra shook her head. "I rarely need to. The staff here are miracle workers in their own right. If he starts to slip, I'll help out, but I prefer not to use magic unless necessary."

"Why?"

Ezra cocked her head as if she hadn't ever really thought about it.

"I guess I don't want to take it for granted. Before I became a witch, I watched a lot of people die. It's part of life after all, but now, I rarely have to watch anyone die. I can save most of them. It's such an amazing gift, but it also feels like a huge responsibility. There are days that I am not here.

Usually, those are the days that we lose patients. I can't save everyone and it would be naive and arrogant of me to pretend that I can. Humans die, witches die. None of us are getting out of here alive. I treat magic with reverence and respect."

"I definitely see your point. Makes me feel like a jerk for using magic to wash my clothes."

Ezra grinned.

"Always the joker. Believe me, I use magic for all manner of trivial things, but when it comes to bringing magic to non-witches, I tread carefully."

****

Jack opened the door into his small, musty apartment. The air hung thick with cigarette smoke. Sebastian grimaced, but Julian waved a hand near Sebastian's face and the air cleared.

Sebastian had flown to Texas with Julian that morning, reluctant to leave Abby behind, but slightly reassured by her insistence that she intended to take naps for most of the day and catch up on laundry.

Jack leaned heavily on a walker. Two bright blue eyes shone from his tanned, wrinkled face. He smiled and gestured them inside.

"Don't mind the mess, boys. My daughter comes by on Sunday to clean up after her old man."

"No worries," Sebastian told him. Despite Jack's disclaimer, the apartment was neat and clean. A single ashtray contained a pile of cigarette butts, otherwise, the surfaces were empty of dishes and debris. Sebastian and Julian took a seat on a long brown couch, draped with a blue and red afghan.

"Thank you for meeting us," Julian told him, holding out a small package wrapped in brown paper.

Jack took it.

"What's this, then?"

"Cookies, courtesy of our dear friend Bridget," Julian shrugged. "Apparently it's not polite to make house calls without dessert of some kind."

"My kind of woman," Jack laughed, ripping off the paper. "Oatmeal, chocolate chip, and molasses. Well, your friend has outdone herself. You'll offer my kind regards."

"Of course," Julian agreed.

"I must tell you, after I dug up that amulet, I became a bit obsessed. Back in those days, I was a workin' man with money on my mind. Then I went on that little dig and came back different, haunted."

"Who was the man that organized the dig?" Julian asked.

"A man by the name of Ira. Course I didn't know Ira from any other Tom or Harry. My friend Troy called me up and said there was money to be had and off I went. I lived in Michigan in those days, Grand Rapids area. I packed up my shovels and drove north and met the boys out in the woods. Ira had a map, real clear-like. He knew exactly where to dig for those bones. Of course, I realized later he tricked us good. He knew darn well there was no treasure with those bones." He shook his head as if still amazed by the betrayal.

"What did he look like?" Sebastian asked, wanting to ensure they were talking about the same man.

"Tall, real skinny with short little arms. Weird looking, and weird acting, too. He was not a friendly fella, and Troy swore later that the man had smiled at him with sharp teeth like a vampire might have." Jack shuddered and picked up another cookie, taking a bite and chewing slowly. "Sugar helps, you know? Makes the memories a little easier to look at."

"You uncovered the bones, and then what?"

"I jumped in the hole, swearing like a sailor. 'Where's all the damn gold?' I said. But that man Ira just kept pointing to the amulet. He handed me a black cloth and asked me to wrap it up. Somethin' strange happened right about then, we all got a little fuzzy headed. You see, I'm not the kinda man that takes a beating lying down, but I took that cloth, folded the amulet inside, and handed it over. He told us we had to bury the bones in a different location, at the base of a big oak tree, and we did, with barely a grunt among us. I don't remember much after that, but when we woke in the morning, Ira was long gone. He muddled our brains. Don't know how, but he did."

"Yes, I'm sure he did," Julian agreed. "I still don't understand how Stephen found you, though. We were told that you recognized the name Kanti, but obviously Ira didn't give you that name."

Jack started to struggle up from his chair and Sebastian stopped him.

"What can I get you?"

Jack gestured to a small dining table stacked with books. "There's a folder there on the top, green one."

Sebastian went to the folder and glanced at the books. Many had subjects about Native American history while others appeared to cover the occult and the supernatural.

"I couldn't sleep for months after that dig. I began to dream of a Native American girl, and I knew who she was, the owner of those bones. I started to do research and in those days we didn't have the interweb so I did a lot of travelin' and talking. You might say this was a strange thing to do, but I couldn't let it rest. Lost my wife fer it. She couldn't take the obsession no more. Took our two kids and found herself a dentist to marry. But that's neither here nor there. My big break came one day in Trager City. They was holdin' a Native American festival with dancing and singing and a pow wow. I got to askin' questions and a man said to me, 'You mean Kanti?' I didn't know that name, but let me tell you it struck me like a tuning fork finding home. I took that man for a beer that turned into about six beers."

Sebastian handed him the green folder and Jack picked up a pair of reading glasses, sliding them on as he flipped through pages. He pulled out a sheet of paper covered in tightly written, nearly illegible, words.

"I wrote it all down, had to. I wanted to mull it over when my belly wasn't full of beer. This man described Kanti as a 'gifted child in an Algonquian Tribe. Daughter of Nadie and Ahanu.' He said 'she had the sight.' She could see visions in the fire, speak to it, sing to it. The tribe would later come to believe that Kanti was taken for her specialness, but when she first disappeared, they believed an animal attacked her. A boy in the tribe saw her get abducted. He described a huge hairy beast. He believed it was a man, but he also called it an animal. They thought they were looking for a bear or perhaps a very large wolf. However, it made little sense that such an animal could take her so quietly. In the forest, they found the remains of a camp near their own. Remnants of a white man and a giant man remained. They began to search for her. It was a frustrating and fruitless search. They would hear tidbits about the girl. They would follow a trail of sightings only to discover that the white man, the girl, and his giant had left days earlier. Her tribe heard that she had escaped from the man and fled. But she did not merely run away. She turned the tables. She killed the giant in a brutal way. She and the white man vanished without a trace. They never received another sighting, another clue as to her whereabouts. They learned of a child, but they never found the child. Kanti's mother mourned her for the rest of her life. The entire tribe mourned her. She became a mythical figure. Kanti the Destroyer. The children told stories of the great woman, stolen from her tribe, who gave birth to a half-man half-bear that would someday rule the world through magic fire. Beware of Kanti if you play with fire, if you stray into the woods, if you disrespect your mother and father. She will punish you. The phantom of the great beast she killed will steal you from your bed at night, it will drag you into the forest where she waits to punish you for your crimes."

Jack stopped reading and slipped his glasses off.

"Man," Sebastian leaned back and let out a long sigh.

"Who was the person that gave you this information?"

"Called himself Grandfather, didn't give me another name. He carried the traditions, I believe, told stories to the young ones in the Native American culture."

"And the white man and Kanti both just vanished? She and this man? There was no story of one killing the other? Of a body? Anything?"

"Well," Jack paused. "I heard a handful of strange tales over the years.

One man said that the white man had been a murderer and a thief. They called him the Snake Tamer. This man told me that the Snake Tamer could live forever, but he exchanged the lives of others for his immortality."

Sebastian frowned, thinking of the bit of history that he and Abby had read just the day before about Snake Island.

"I started having nightmares the night we dug up the body. Horrible dreams of being buried alive and trying to claw my way out, dreams of being burned. We woke that girl. And you know what? I started thinking those dreams were her memories."

Julian shot Sebastian a look out of the corner of his eye and he knew why - Abby was having very similar dreams.

"I heard another story too." Jack pulled out a faded napkin from his folder. "A woman told me this one, an old brittle thing with one glass eye and teeth full of gold. She looked like something out of one of my own Gramma's story-books. I was sittin' having a cup of coffee, mindin' my own, and she slid onto the stool right next to me. She said, 'listen stranger, I hear you're lookin' for a little Indian girl went missin' a few centuries back?' I turned and looked at her like an alien had just waltzed in and struck up a conversation with me. How on earth could she know what I was lookin' fer? Ya know? Anyway, she told me that the girl cursed her own child and if I wasn't careful, that poisoned blood would find a way into my family and it'd eat us all alive."

Jack slid the napkin back into his folder and glanced at a picture on his side table. It showed a young girl, around ten years old, practicing hula-hoop in the sprinklers.

"My granddaughter, Amy," he said proudly when he noticed them looking.

"You believe the white man that kidnapped her, murdered her, and buried her in the woods where you recovered her bones?" Julian asked.

"I believe he did far worse than that," Jack answered. "No justice in this sick world." He shook his head sadly.

"Oh, she's getting her justice all right," Sebastian muttered.

"How so?"

Julian gave him a warning look, but Jack had moved to the front of his chair and his eyes gleamed.

"There is a curse?" he prodded.

"Maybe you did wake her," Julian murmured, thinking. "Dafne did not know of her, nor did the Lourdes as far as we can tell. Only Abby has had contact with her."

"And Victor," Sebastian added.

"Yes, and why Victor?"

"Who's Victor and Abby?" Jack asked.

"It's a long story."

Jack sat back in his worn recliner and folded his hands in his lap.

"I've got nothing but time these days. Clear your heads, boys, tell me a story."

Julian looked reluctant, but Sebastian felt the old man deserved a story in exchange for the information he'd given them.

"Sure, why not."

They began to talk, each telling bits of what they knew and the other filling in the gaps, carefully omitting the word 'witches.'

"We believe the curse began with Kanti. We don't know how she did it, but the curse appears approximately every one hundred years, and we assume the time-frame triggers it," Julian explained.

"Or some other catalyst," Sebastian added. "Such as the woman," he nearly said witch and caught himself, "falling in love."

"Both the woman and her lover are effected. The lover is drawn to do terrible things in pursuit of power."

"Such as killing family and friends."

"The curse seems to have a timeframe. A few months of chaos and then the darkness subsides."

"And there's quiet for another hundred years."

"What does she gain? Kanti? What is the point of the curse?" Sebastian asked out loud. He had asked the question in his head a hundred times, but still had no answer.

"Maybe I have an answer for you," Jack said, looking thoughtful. "I worked for about ten years as a crisis counselor. Hard work, and if you do it long enough you grow bitter, jaded with life. Fortunately, I saw that happenin' and pursued my calling as a fly fisherman. I learned something in those years, though. Trauma has a life all its own. It needs a beginning, a middle, and an end. Most people, when they get hurt or abused, get stuck in the middle. Their beginning was the abuse, their middle was the shock, the denial, the trying to understand. Their ending, for the ones that get it, is acceptance. The only people I met who were ever okay looked upon that trauma with wide-open eyes. They said, 'it happened, it was wrong, but now it's over.' They said it until they accepted that it was a part of their story and it was okay that it had happened. That was the ending, their acceptance, their willingness to look at it without spending their whole lives asking why. Why is a great jumping-off point, but you gotta land sometime. You gotta get two solid feet back on the ground and start walking into the future. A lot of people who get traumatized float and flail. They want an answer that this world will never give them. I think this Kanti might be flailing. She was a special kind of someone. Maybe special enough that she can hold onto a grudge so hard that it keeps her in the world. People who have been abused often become abusers. Kanti gets to relive her own suffering every time the curse swings back around. It keeps her tethered to her experience, it brings others into the experience with her so that she's not alone."

"You're telling me she created a centuries-long curse because she was traumatized and never got over it," Sebastian asked, unconvinced.

"Sure," Jack said mildly. "Do you know what trauma looks like in the normal world? A child gets abused, he abuses his children, they abuse theirs. Generations, centuries of pain, all paying it forward. They're stuck. They never get the closure they need so they have to revisit the experience again and again. Now take that trauma, which in a normal person can span centuries, and put it into the body of a magic child. A child who is forced to create another child. I believe in the power of our intentions. I've seen things with my own two eyes that don't abide by the laws of our world."

Julian took a big breath and let it out slowly.

"You know Jack, I think you may be right."

CHAPTER 23

"It's best if I go to Montana as well," Elda told Faustine.

They shared tea and biscuits in the breakfast room and discussed Elda's conversation with the witch Ellen.

"Yes, I agree. Julian is abrasive. We don't want to upset her. Julian and Sebastian are meeting with the man in Texas today. Shall we see if Julian wants to join you in Montana?"

"Yes, I think so. Helena and Bridget are busy with the wedding preparations, and I believe Helena is finally getting Lydie excited as well so this is an ideal time to slip away."

"Adora is improving. Bridget told me she took eggs and toast to her room this morning and that the sores in her mouth are all but gone."

Elda sighed and smiled.

"That warms my heart. I feared for her, Faustine. That perhaps we would lose her too."

"Not if I have any say in it," Faustine told her. "We've had too much death at Ula. A balance must be restored."

"I feel as if we're close, so close."

"As do I."

****

He wore her down. Oliver knew if he hung around long enough, Ezra would eventually open up to him.

One night as they walked along the Chicago River, he reached for her hand. At first she stiffened, and he knew she considered pulling her hand out of his, but in the end, she held on.

"I miss my brother most of all," he admitted.

They had been talking about what they most missed from their pre-witch lives.

"You don't see him at all?"

"No, he got married, had a set of twin boys. I hunt Vepars. I'm not interested in watching them die because of me. I learned really quickly at Ula that the life of a witch can be pretty perilous, especially for the human families of witches."

"Elda and Faustine don't seem like the doomsday types. What made you believe that?"

"Elda and Faustine weren't my teachers. Julian and Dafne were. They both lost the people they loved to Vepars. They had no reservations in stressing to me the realities of life as a witch. If a Vepar believes they can get to you through your family, they will. I cut ties with my family within two months of entering the coven. I pretended to join a religious cult. I told them I was moving to India and they would never see me again."

"And you stuck to that?" Ezra asked, surprised.

"Yeah, they've never seen me again. I've seen them, of course. I can't help it. I want to know my nephews. Sometimes I want to hug my brother so much it hurts. I miss my parents too. I watch my mom go to the country club to play tennis. My dad sits on the back deck and watches birds. I can imagine walking through the front door. I've come close a few times, but for their sakes, I don't."

Ezra gave his hand a long squeeze.

"What about you, what do you miss?"

Ezra ran a hand through her short spiky hair. He'd found her making coffee in the kitchen loft that morning with white hair streaked pink and yellow.

"I miss my dog Elanor."

Oliver snorted.

Ezra elbowed him and laughed. "I loved my dog, thank you very much."

"A dog named Elanor no less." he joked.

"My grandma's name was Elanor and my dad insisted on it. I could have vetoed him, but I loved Grandma too, so I figured, why not? My dad died before I became a witch. My evil step-monster kept Elanor."

"Where was your mom?"

Ezra rubbed her neck and shoulder.

"In rehab, on drugs, in rehab. I don't know. She was off and on with heroin before I even came into the world. My dad was pretty much a shell of grief until he met Mary. She hated me in the fashion of step-parents the world over. I had a brother who died of a heroin overdose when I was eight."

"I'm sorry," Oliver told her, stopping. "Here, let me."

He turned her to face the water and massaged her neck and shoulders. Earth elements had a special talent for massage, manipulating the physical. He felt Ezra lean into his touch.

"My dad died of a heart attack. The truth is that he had been a heroin user too. When my mom got pregnant with me, he checked into rehab, got clean, and never looked back, but once an addict, always an addict. He would be the first to tell you that. He stopped doing heroin, but took up whiskey, cigarettes, weed, gambling, TV, sugar. He picked up a million new addictions to kick the worst one of all."

"Damn," Oliver murmured, at a loss for words.

"You don't need to," Ezra told him, before he could go on. "Believe me, I get it. I'm surrounded by tragedy every day. Words of comfort don't actually exist. It's enough to have someone that listens, even better if they don't offer some false sentiment about how they're in a better place, which I believe, by the way. I'm a witch. I know that our souls transcend, that there is freedom after the bondage of this life, but the human still lives in me too, and she curses the gods that created love."

"Love? Rather than mortality?"

"Who would care that we live and die if it weren't for love? I don't see death as the issue, but our desperate love for the person slipping through our fingers. We want so much to keep them, hold on so tight, but still, they go."

Oliver felt in the earth around them with his energy. When he found the rock he searched for, he held out his hand, drawing it forth. The rock rose up, hovering in front of Ezra. She stopped an inch before it smacked into her face.

"Very suave." She laughed, reaching up to touch the crude heart-shaped rock.

"Best I could do on the fly."

Ezra smoothed her fingers along the rough edges.

"This is a much more appropriate depiction of love," she said. "Rough, gritty, a little ugly even. Those smooth glossy red hearts that I see everywhere around Valentine's Day make me want to gag."

"Mental note taken," Oliver told her, pulling on her hand until she stopped.

He brought her close.

She was short, the top of her head fit easily beneath his chin. Instead of looking up at him, she stared straight ahead at his chest. He gently pressed his fingers under her chin until her soft brown eyes stared into his.

"Oliver, we've had this conversation."

He kissed her anyway, knowing that she might reject him a second time. It would hurt a bit, but it was worth it, on the slim chance that she kissed him back.

At first, she didn't. She stood perfectly still as his lips pressed against hers and then slowly, reluctantly, she parted her lips and kissed him.

****

"We've got this place all to ourselves," Abby told Baboon, scratching his neck as he stretched out on the couch beside her. She had looked forward to the day alone, but suddenly felt overwhelmed. The wedding was fast approaching and the curse still hung over them like a dark stormy cloud, threatening to not only ruin their wedding day, but their entire lives.

She knew that Oliver had gone to Chicago to try and get a sense of whether Victor or Kendra had stolen the amulet. It made her uneasy and she fought the desire to call Oliver and get a progress update. She wanted to believe that Victor could not have stolen the amulet. However, she found it impossible to believe that Kendra would have taken the necklace. Kendra wasn't invested the way Victor was. He had a blood link to Kanti, as Abby herself did. Victor had also approached Abby at the All Hallow's Ball. He initiated their contact at the urging of Kanti, and had been dreaming of her for years. Could she have gotten to him, somehow?

"Bath time?" she asked Baboon, who responded in typical cat fashion with silence.

She stopped in the nursery and touched the mobile of white paper birds, watching them sway lazily in the morning sun. She and Sebastian had searched the house when they returned to Australia to make sure nothing was amiss. It was not vandals that Abby worried about, but the spirit of Kanti who'd come into their home previously.

Abby ran the bath scalding hot and poured bath salts and lavender oil into the water. She watched the oils swirl and dance. Holding her hand above the surface, she invited the water to her. A stream rose out of the bathtub and bathed her hands and wrists in steaming warmth. As she watched, the oils started to form a strange shape. She leaned closer and then quickly jerked upright as a face appeared in the water. Kanti's dark, pleading eyes stared back at her and her mouth opened in a huge, terrified scream. Abby stumbled back and her hips bumped the vanity. She started to flee, but the face had vanished. A ripple of water was the only evidence that the face had ever existed.

Abby watched the water for several minutes and then leaned over the tub and pulled the plug. Did she want Kanti to reappear? A part of her did. A part of her wanted the woman, the girl, to speak to her.

"Tell me what you want," she whispered, as the bath drained, leaving an oily sheen on the porcelain bottom.

Sun streamed through the window and lit their bedroom. Abby gazed at Lake Michigan, trying to puzzle together what the dreams and the visions meant. The latest Kanti dreams had left her feeling scared and hurt for the young Native American woman. She had been tortured and now she wanted, what? Justice? Revenge?

"I don't know," Abby whispered. She sat on the edge of the bed and then lay back. It was so soft. Indulgent, Sebastian called it. She closed her eyes and Kanti stole into her dreams.

Kanti lay on the floor of the cabin, her pregnant belly rose and fell in rapid bursts. She tried to slow her breath, conserve it, as the fire consumed the cabin. The flames rose up the wall, destroying everything in their path. Smoke had begun to fill the single room. Bound at hands and feet, she could not escape. Would he finally kill her this time? Or was it merely another in his sick games where he brought her to the edge of death and then ripped her back, stealing even the hope of that release.

Abby gasped and sat up in bed. Her heart pounded and her mouth felt paper dry as if she'd been screaming. The sun had lowered in the sky and the light in the room had the orange glow of the impending sunset. Her bedside clock read 7:04 p.m. Sebastian would return anytime. His flight was supposed to arrive in Trager at six thirty pm.

Abby shuffled out of bed and glanced in the mirror. A pale, troubled face looked back at her. She pulled her hair into a messy bun and slipped on a clean t-shirt and linen pants, discarding her sweaty clothes in the hamper.

In the kitchen, she set about warming up leftover turkey chili for her and Sebastian. He would be hungry after his flight and she wanted something to busy her shaking hands.

She thought about the dream and recalled the sheer panic that Kanti felt as the cabin filled with fire. The dream reminded her of the experiences both Kendra and Julian had described during the bone magic in Chicago months earlier. In fact, the previous dreams of being buried alive and burned also mimicked sensations the witches recalled after Dante performed the magic.

"Whoa, she's a water goddess and she cooks? I better marry that girl!"

Abby dropped the metal spoon in her hand and it clattered against the tile floor.

"You scared me!" she declared, placing a hand over her heart.

Sebastian retrieved her spoon and kissed her, giving her a long hug.

"I'm sorry, beautiful. I brought you something. Do you forgive me?" He gave her a pleading look, jutting out his lower lip and whipping a small brown paper bag from his coat.

She smiled.

"So long as you have chocolate in that bag."

"Have you developed mind-reading abilities?" he asked, as she pulled open the paper and discovered a package of dark chocolate storks.

"Storks!" she opened them and took a bite, passing one to Sebastian. The chocolate tasted dark and sweet with a hint of nutmeg. She sat at the counter and closed her eyes.

"The airport in Texas had a baby store. Those seemed fitting."

"Mmmm, thank you," she murmured. "Tell me about Jack."

Sebastian scooped them each a bowl of chili and took a seat next to her.

"He was an interesting guy. He's been tracking Kanti since he dug up her bones fifty years ago."

"And he's actually had luck?"

"Some," Sebastian explained. "He discovered that she was part of an Algonquian tribe, and just as your dreams have revealed, she was taken by a huge man wearing furs. That man apparently worked for Clyde, at least we assume it was Clyde. Jack only knew him as the 'white man.' Jack had his own theory about the curse."

"He knew about the curse?" Abby asked, surprised. "Ouch!" she yelped. "Burned my tongue." She pointed at her chili.

He handed her a glass of water.

"Sort of. A strange woman approached him at a diner. She told him that Kanti cursed her own child and if he wasn't careful, the bad blood would somehow get into his family."

Abby frowned.

"That's weird."

"Yeah, though he didn't think it was that strange. Anyway, he believes Kanti cursed her child as a result of her own trauma, maybe even accidentally, and she continues to relive the trauma each time the curse resurfaces."

Abby thought about her dream and nodded. The level of fear alone would create a powerful energy around the baby that she was carrying. Abby had learned so much about how a child's development was influenced by the experiences in utero. If Kanti spent her entire pregnancy in a state of terror, how would that manifest in a child, especially when the mother was magic?

CHAPTER 24

The sprawling Montana farm occupied a mountain valley, lush with wildflowers. Beautiful silver and chestnut horses grazed in the paddock and small children chased a group of hens through an open barn door.

"It reminds me of America when I first came here," Elda murmured to Julian as he parked the car in the circular dirt driveway.

"Yes, a sweeter time. Though we both fled some pretty terrible experiences so I'm sure we were biased."

Elda nodded, but did not speak.

Both she and Julian had come to America and Ula after their own homes were destroyed. Though Vepars were their enemies in those days, the bigger enemies were civil war, famine, and desperation.

Several white farmhouses were scattered across the property surrounded by barns, stables, and gardens.

A woman walked from the main farmhouse door. The screen swung shut behind her and she waved a hand.

Elda recognized her from the cave of elders, though she had replaced her black cloak with worn jeans and a man's button-down shirt. Her white hair hung in a braid over her shoulder.

"Ellen," Elda said kindly, taking the other witch's hands in her own. They were soft and warm and Elda felt a tug at her heart. She could smell cinnamon and apples, and a bit of flour dotted the woman's right cheek.

"Lovely to meet you in the physical world, Elda," Ellen told her.

"Julian," Julian offered, extending his hand. The woman took it, but rather than let go, she held his hand and took Elda's as well, leading them toward the house.

"Nora's having an especially lucid day. It's a good time for a visit."

Ellen led them through the foyer and down a hallway. She knocked twice and then pushed into a large sunlit room that overlooked a garden of sunflowers. A witch sat in a wheelchair next to the window. She wore a long gray robe. Her thin dark hair was streaked silver and white.

She turned as the door opened and watched them through startlingly clear amber eyes.

"I think I've waited my whole life for you to show up," she told them in a soft voice that likely had once been strong and booming. Even in her wheelchair, aged and shrinking, she had a presence.

Ellen gestured toward two wicker chairs and a small table set with coffee and apple muffins.

"If you need anything, don't hesitate. Just touch that little jade frog and I'll come a'running."

Elda smiled at the little green frog perched on the windowsill.

"Thank you, Ellen," Nora told her.

Ellen nodded and backed out of the room, closing the door behind her.

"I'm not sure where to begin," Elda told her, settling into a chair.

"I would like to begin, if you don't mind?" Nora said, shifting her wheelchair to face them full on. "Does Clyde live?"

Elda glanced at Julian, surprised.

"I would imagine not," Julian told her. "He was a man, after all, a hybrid yes, but he was born more than three hundred years ago."

Nora shook her head and took in a swift, frustrated breath.

"Then already you underestimate him."

"That's why we're here, Nora. We've only just learned of him. We need your help."

Nora watched them closely. She held a beautiful pink rosary that she braided through her fingers.

"I'm disappointed, I must admit. When Ellen came to me with witches seeking information on the Serpent House, I knew that Clyde lay at the heart of those inquiries. He destroyed it, after all."

"He destroyed your coven?" Julian asked, surprised.

Nora nodded and returned her gaze to the window. A small girl with dark pigtails walked among the rows of sunflowers.

"Rosemary," Nora told them. "My kin, she shares my spirit, you know? We are co-conspirators always tricking the goats."

Nora rapped on the glass and Rosemary look up. She offered a huge smile, short one front tooth, and held up a hen feather.

"I saw this life when I was just a girl. But I believed this family would belong to myself and Eugene. He was my great love. Even after all these years, decades, centuries, I still remember the first moment I saw him."

Julian had learned of Eugene from Binda in Australia. Eugene was the brother that Clyde murdered.

"I was sixteen, new to my powers, but not to the world of magic. I was born in Serpent House. My great-grandfather built it. We were a small coven, eight total, with several witches who lived on the mainland and joined us from time to time. Meghan was one of those witches. She brought Eugene to the coven when he was nineteen. He had been exhibiting powers for several years, but she wanted to teach him on her own without the influence of a coven. She felt it was time for him to learn the ways of our magical world. I remember running down the grand staircase. I had frozen the water in my glass and I was proud to bursting. I raced into my grandfather's study and there he stood with Eugene."

Nora paused and lifted a glass of water to her lips. She took a sip and then watched the water until it froze.

"It still amazes me." She smiled. "He stood next to my grandfather, shoulder to shoulder, reading a map of some sort. His dark hair fell into his eyes and when he looked up, my heart stopped. The ice melted. The second our eyes met, that ice returned to water. He melted me."

Nora's words had grown slower, more drawn out and Elda wondered if she might be slipping away.

Julian too noticed the digression and stood quickly.

"Here Nora, hold this. It will help."

He handed her a large purple stone.

"Fluorite," she said. "Yes, very helpful, I think."

She lifted it to her forehead and held it there.

"It was like I woke up when I met Eugene," Nora told them, her golden eyes troubled and sad. "He had long, silky black hair pulled in a neat ponytail, and a smile that just about ripped me in two. I was young and idealistic. And the moment I saw him, I knew. He looked at me and it was like we'd always known each other. We were nearly inseparable after that day. Eugene was a special kind of witch. Strong, but soft and humble. He didn't have an ounce of malice or hatred in his being. Sometimes I think that's what killed him. Even in the end, he had faith in his brother. He believed that Clyde, at his core, was a good man. He used to tell me that Clyde had been dealt a hand that any man would struggle to cope with. A magical older brother with the world at his fingertips, when he himself was ill and picked on, an outcast. Clyde was not handsome or funny or kind. Eugene was all of those things and so much more. Meghan adored Eugene. I think our relationship hurt her. She didn't want to lose her spectacular child."

"Tell us about Clyde," Julian urged.

"Clyde was a sickly and sullen child. Nose always stuffed in a book, red eyes, and pale puffy skin. The kids at school poked fun at him. Eugene told me they called him Small Pox, the usual kid stuff. For a boy who looked ill, it was not a surprise. The challenge was that his mother was a witch and his father was a man. It was Meghan who wanted to live normally, but when Eugene started exhibiting powers, magic became a much larger part of their lives. Meghan was entranced by her magical son, doted on him, and Clyde was always second, always less. Meghan and Eugene went on adventures and Clyde stayed behind. Clyde became obsessed with magic and power. He hoarded and stole books and texts from the church, from Indian tribes. He badgered Eugen constantly for information about Serpent House, about witches, and also about Vepars."

"Where was their father in all of this?" Elda asked.

"Drunk, according to Eugene. Meghan tried to help him, performed every piece of magic she could to cure him of the disease, but he was a broken man. He had never been much of a father. He disappeared for weeks at a time and Meghan would search for him. One day, while she and Eugene were away at Serpent House, Clyde went looking for him. He found him dead in the woods."

"From alcohol?"

"Perhaps," Nora said. "Eugene thought so, but I had met Clyde and I had my misgivings. He had such darkness in him, hatred even. I wondered if he had a hand in his father's death."

"And then he murdered Eugene?" Julian asked.

Nora pursed her lips and looked again at the sunflowers beyond her window.

"We were due to be married that autumn. Our whole lives stretched out like a glorious dream that you never have to wake up from. A celebration was planned at Serpent House. It was my eighteenth birthday. Eugene never arrived. Meghan appeared around midnight, frantic. Eugene had left early that morning to purchase a gift for me, but did not return. When she learned he had never arrived at Serpent House, terror took over."

"Why such an extreme reaction?"

"Because Meghan knew. I was so young and naive that I didn't recognize it at the time. The face of a mother who has lost a child. It had not been confirmed, but she felt it. She knew in her heart he had passed. We went to the shore, all the witches of Serpent House. We combed the town and then the woods. My grandfather found him, staked to the ground, tortured." Her voice broke and she held the rosary to her lips.

****

Oliver knew it was the wrong time to ask his questions. He and Ezra lay in her bed at the loft. She had curled away from him, but he wrapped his body around hers and kissed her shoulder.

"How did you end up here, Ezra? With the Guerrilla Witches?"

Oliver felt Ezra shrug beneath him.

"Victor found me."

"How, though? I mean, at Ula we follow bloodlines."

"He told me that he had a feeling when he saw me. He sensed that I was a witch. He didn't come right out and ask me. He tested me."

"How?"

"Isn't this time for sleep or a shower? Are you always this inquisitive after sex?"

"Absolutely." He nuzzled the back of her neck and she laughed, twisting away from him.

"You're tickling me," she said. "And my knee-jerk reaction to tickling is to immobilize you."

He grinned.

"Okay, no more tickling, I promise. How did he test you?"

Ezra turned to look at him, studying his face.

Oliver thought she would refuse to answer and demand to know why he had so many questions.

"I was an emergency room nurse and Victor brought in a lost cause. She was young, only fifteen, and had overdosed on heroin. The drug that I hate most in this world. In human hands she was dead."

"But you saved her."

"I saved her."

"And afterward he approached you and said he was a witch too?"

"Sort of. He said he had friends that were special. And did I want to meet them?"

"That was Kendra and the others?"

"Actually no, they were witches from down south. They didn't even tell me their names. Victor joined them at this huge abandoned warehouse in West Town. They were doing crazy stuff. Flying, making things explode with their minds, causing thunderstorms inside the building. I watched Victor drill a hole through three floors above us with his mind, rocked my world. I didn't know what witches were, but I knew I was one of them. It was the first time I ever felt included, known."

"And you've been with him ever since?"

"Yep, I was the first of the Guerrillas. Victor and I envisioned the group together one night, high on espresso and our own magic. I was so excited for the future, the world we could create."

"You sound disappointed in that dream? Has it not lived up to your expectations?"

"There are a lot of distractions in this life. Witches don't always get to do good all the time. Many of the problems that face humans, face us too."

"Did Victor find the other Guerrilla Witches too?"

"Yep."

"And he found them the same way? A sense?"

"Pretty much. Why don't you trust him, Oliver?"

"It's not that I don't trust him," Oliver told her, telling a small lie. In truth, he didn't trust Victor. Ever since he took Abby into the Vepar's lair, he'd questioned Victor's intentions.

"Don't bullshit me," Ezra said, sitting up and swinging her legs over the bed. She slid her shorts up and buttoned them, grabbing her crumpled sweatshirt from the floor. She slipped it on, braless, and turned to face him.

Oliver sat up and sighed.

"Okay sure, I don't trust him. I have questions about him, but that's not why I'm here with you. I want to be with you, Ezra. I've wanted to know you since the first time we met."

"What if I were sitting here grilling you about Abby? How forthcoming would you be, Oliver? Or about Helena? Or Faustine?"

"I have nothing to hide regarding any of them. And I'm not defensive about it either. I'm curious why you are?"

Ezra put on her boots, zipping them quickly and angrily.

"I need some air," she told him.

After she left, he lay in bed for another few minutes, contemplating his next move. He could follow her, but Ezra did not seem like the type of woman who wanted a man to rescue her. He felt, instead, that he was getting closer to what lay at the heart of her defensiveness. He had to prove himself trustworthy. He couldn't run away when she started to flinch from him.

****

Lydie unwrapped the twine and reclined on her bed. Garfield curled up next to her feet and tried to distract her with long kitty stretches and copious purring.

"I promise, I'll give you a good long petting after I read these. Deal?"

The cat surveyed her with curiosity and then indifference when she did not begin to pet him.

She opened the first letter and realized they were love letters between the Lourdes, or Milda, and Alva, then known as Ira.

She read the first one and set it aside, disappointed.

It was unlikely she would stumble upon anything of value in a bunch of sappy love letters. Sure, they made for interesting reading, particularly because she knew the futures that had waited for those two troubled souls. In the letter, Milda spoke of her daughter, Delphia. She described how her hair looked like fresh honey and when she laughed the flowers bloomed brighter. Lydie had not known the Lourdes, but her story was a cautionary tale at Ula and evidence of how even a powerful witch and seer could be tricked by dark magic.

Lydie read the letters quickly, skipping the mushy parts and making faces of disgust when she read Ira's poetry of devotion.

"Two-faced liar," she whispered under her breath, startling Garfield who gave her a reproachful look before returning to his nap.

As she opened the next one, a little sheet of paper fell from within the stack.

She smoothed the paper on her lap.

It was not a letter, but a series of names with dates next to each and the same notation: dead. Lydie read the names, recognizing several from the night that Victor had explained Abby's and his ancestry and their ultimate connections to Dafne. According to the note, every single female descendant was dead except for the Lourdes, Abby's mother, and Abby. The Lourdes had scrawled something on the bottom of the page. "I will be next and then Abby's mother and Abby with child last of all. Kanti must kill us all."

CHAPTER 25

"I'm so sorry," Elda told Nora, after she revealed Eugene's murder. Nora nodded.

"I've had a long time to accept it. Not that acceptance is the right word. The sheer devastation has dulled. I can speak of it now. For years…" She shook her head. "That was only the beginning, of course. When we returned to Serpent House, our home was on fire."

"Clyde?"

"Yes, though we hadn't made the connection. We were all in grief and shock. My grandfather and some of the older witches went on the offense and they knew it was Clyde within a day or two, but I could barely get out of bed. My mother made arrangements for us to rent a house on the mainland. Some of the other witches stayed with relatives. By the time my grandfather realized who was at fault, Clyde and Meghan had fled."

"Why did Meghan take Clyde? She must have been so angry with him?" Julian wondered out loud.

"Back then, I felt the same way. I hated Meghan for shielding Clyde. I thought she was an abomination. Of course, we're given opportunities in this life to see the other side of the story. After I had children, I understood. A part of me still wanted to hate her, but you never love anyone so much as your children, and the truth is that no matter the monstrosities they commit, you continue to love them. You can't help it. It is greater than you. Do you have children, Elda?"

"No," Elda said, shaking her head and trying not to reveal the sadness in her heart.

Nora gave her a smile and a nod.

"Meghan took him and ran. My coven hunted for them. My grandfather reached out to every witch he knew. He wanted justice for Eugene."

"But that was not all?" Julian asked.

"No, Clyde stole things from our coven. Ancient magical items of great value. We believe he staged the fire to cover his tracks, but our home had spells that protected it from a complete burning. He did damage, surely, but the house did not crumble."

"What did he take?" Elda asked.

Nora sighed. She leaned forward, with effort, and reached for the jade frog. She stroked it gently and the green shimmered beneath her touch.

Ellen walked in a moment later.

"Everything okay?" she asked. She walked to Nora and replaced her water glass with a fresh one and handed her a dish of peeled apples.

"Ellen, my dear, could you bring me my scrapbook?"

"Of course," Ellen told her, leaning down and planting a kiss on top of her head. "More coffee?" she asked Julian and Elda.

"No, thank you," Elda told her.

Ellen left but returned quickly with a large square album. She placed it in Nora's lap. After she left, Nora wheeled closer to Elda and Julian. She flipped through the pages and stopped on a large black and white photograph of a painting.

"We had a painter in our coven. Louis, he came from Paris. A very talented witch. He painted many portraits of Serpent House, but most of them were destroyed in the fire. We managed to save this one. The original hangs upstairs. You can see it if you like, but this is a photo of that painting."

Elda and Julian leaned over the picture. Nora did not have to point out the item she intended to show them. Julian spotted it immediately.

"The amulet," he said, placing his finger on the necklace. It hung around a young woman's slender neck. She wore a dress, buttoned high, and the jeweled snake rested on the pale fabric over her chest.

"You've seen it?"

"Yes, unfortunately, we have."

"My mother is wearing it in this portrait. My father hated it. It had come to us by accident. A ship wrecked a hundred miles from our island. One morning, my grandfather found a wooden box half buried on our beach. Inside, he found this amulet, a stash of precious gems and books from Egypt. He started to research the ouroboros. He discovered that men in Egypt believed these symbols granted their owner everlasting life. Within the alchemy of this snake, magic had already been bestowed. My mother found it mysterious and romantic, but my father believed it held dark spirits. My grandfather, ever the scientist, wanted to understand its magical properties. None of us had ever met a witch from Egypt and we were all curious. Eugene began to study the amulet with my grandfather. That is how Clyde learned of it."

"And Clyde became obsessed?" Julian asked.

Nora nodded.

"Eugene confided in my grandfather that Clyde was stealing his notes on the ouroboros. He asked many questions of Eugene. He wanted to know about immortality. Could a man become immortal? Obviously, Eugene did not have answers, but he grew concerned about Clyde's mental health. He wondered if his brother was going insane."

"What did your grandfather believe?"

"Initially, he thought Eugene may have been right and Clyde merely suffered a weak mind, but later, after he met him, he felt differently. He told Eugene that Clyde was filled with hatred and lust. He encouraged Eugene to seal his vow with the Serpent House and cut ties with his brother. My grandfather knew that Clyde was dangerous."

"And Meghan did not recognize the darkness in her child?"

"Clyde manipulated her. He knew she suffered enormous guilt for the pain her non-magical child had endured. She could never do enough to make it right. She preferred Eugene and Clyde knew. She couldn't help it. She loved Clyde too and wanted desperately to prove as much. He made sure to give her plenty of opportunities. He still maintained a weak personality when Meghan was around. I saw it with my own eyes. In the presence of others, he was arrogant, boastful, cruel even, but for Meghan, he was petulant and slow. You see, Clyde had Meghan's power. She did things for him, gave him things. She needed to make up for the deficit, so she spoiled him with her magic."

"And now she's trapped in purgatory for it," Julian murmured.

"She's what? Do you mean to tell me that Meghan lives?" Nora asked, sitting straighter in her chair.

"Yes, I did not see her with my own eyes, but she is imprisoned in a world that she created in Australia. She built it to confine Clyde, but somehow he escaped and trapped her instead."

Nora scowled.

"Sometimes, I still believe that it was all her fault. She was a powerful witch, an unnatural witch. Eugene told me stories, amazing stories. I cannot believe that she lives. You know what that means, though, don't you?"

Julian shook his head.

"That Clyde lives as well."

****

Lydie strode into the kitchen where Helena and Bridget stood over a wedding cake magazine.

"I think the yellow flowers, surely. Abby and Sebastian have a love meant for the sunshine," Bridget enthused.

"I was thinking an ashy pink color, Bridge. I mean let's be real here, their courtship has been a dance between dark and light. Don't we want to honor that?"

"I found something," Lydie said, holding the paper up in triumph.

"Or maybe this satiny pearl color? It's void of color, yes, but there will be so many other flowers…"

"Hello? I said I found something important! Or have I become invisible now too?"

Helena and Bridget both looked up, surprised.

Helena dropped the magazine and hurried to Lydie.

"Oh Lydie, I'm sorry. We've just been so caught up in the wedding plans that…"

"That you forgot there was a curse that might destroy all of our lives at any moment? That we're the only ones that can stop it, but hey, let's worry about wedding cake instead," Lydie fumed and turned on her heel.

The kitchen door slammed and she stalked down the hallway.

"Lydie," Helena called, following her. "Honey, stop, please."

Lydie stopped.

She wanted to keep walking. But she simply could not blow off Helena. Helena was the most loving, gentle person she had ever known. Even in her moments of greatest frustration, she never blamed Helena.

"I'm sorry," Helena whispered, touching her shoulder from behind. "I am so very sorry. Can we take a walk? Go to the floating garden? I want to hear what you've discovered and perhaps I could tell you more about Australia."

Lydie nodded, feeling some of her anger dissipate at Helena's touch.

They left the castle and walked to the floating garden. As always, it was in full bloom. The flowers, fragrant and dazzling, shifted toward them as they left the stone stairway.

Lydie thrust the paper into Helena's hands and walked to the lemon tree that her mother had planted. The tree only stood a few feet high, but it burst with lemons. Lydie tugged one off and held it to her nose, inhaling the scent.

She watched Helena as her eyes scanned the page, her brow furrowed. She chewed her lower lip, and Lydie could see as she read the names, her eyes darted again and again to the conclusion that the Lourdes had scrawled across the bottom. "She must kill us all."

"I think it means that the only way to end the curse is to kill everyone in her family," Lydie announced. "Everyone that descended from her."

"All of these names are women," Helena murmured, still going back and forth to dates and names. "If that's true, it would mean every single female descendant of Kanti and Clyde are dead except for Abby and her mother."

"I know." Lydie's moment of self-satisfaction at finding the note had departed. Fear had replaced her pride and she suddenly wanted to be back in Florida where curses and Vepars and spirits of the dead did not exist. It was a paradoxical feeling for her. She had never been anything but a witch and didn't know another life. Could she ever truly leave it behind?

"We need to show this to Faustine," Helena started.

"Wait." Lydie said. "I need to know what happened in Australia."

****

Oliver intercepted Ezra on her way back to the loft. She had changed into running clothes and wore gray pants, drenched with sweat, and a loose-fitting black-t-shirt cut wide and jagged around her collarbones. She nearly walked passed him, but stopped when he held up two cups of coffee.

"Coffee?" He shook a paper bag. "And croissants."

Wiping an arm across her sweaty face, she lifted one of the coffees from the cardboard container and took a scalding sip.

"Mmmm, thanks."

She didn't walk into the building, but instead ducked behind a trash can and emerged less than a minute later dry and fully clothed in jean shorts cut just above her knee and a long-sleeved t-shirt.

"That's a trick I have yet to learn," he told her, surveying her outfit.

"I'm on the go a lot, it's worthwhile for me to conjure clothes on the fly. I originally did it to help homeless people, but realized I could benefit as well."

"You'll have to teach me."

She nodded and took another sip of her coffee.

"You're right, I'm defensive," she started. "And the truth is that I haven't been here for a while, relating to someone intimately, if you will." She laughed. "Listen to me, I sound like I've spent too much time with a shrink."

"Have you?"

She cocked an eyebrow at him.

"In another life, sure. How do you think I became so well adjusted?"

He laughed and handed her a croissant.

"I live with Victor and the other Guerrilla witches, but I'm on my own, we all are. There's an understanding in our kind of community. We don't tell, judge, spread misinformation. I don't have dinner with Victor every night. Sometimes I don't see him for days. He may take off without telling anyone where he's going. I do it too, and it's important to me to feel safe with my friends. I need to trust them for this carefully constructed world we've created to work. You dig?"

"Yeah, I do."

He got it, but he didn't at the same time. He didn't live in that world. He trusted his coven completely. He had trusted Dafne even as she sewed the seeds of her own destruction.

"But silence is a choice too, Ezra. You're a witch, a witch who's devoted her life to helping others. Would you allow Victor to undermine that because you don't want to rock the boat?"

"I've been rocking the boat my entire life, Oliver," she snapped. "This isn't a matter of trying to play it safe. I'm doing my best here. But yes, sure, Victor has been different lately. He's been vacant, physically and mentally."

"Have you asked him why?"

Ezra shrugged.

"No. I've asked Kendra and she thinks he's become a bit obsessed with the curse on Abby and Sebastian. She thinks he wants to save the day and find out how to break it."

"But you don't think so?"

Ezra sighed and shoved the rest of the croissant in her mouth as if it might save her from saying what was on her mind.

"I've been around a lot of darkness in my life. It's a courtship, a dance and when the devil ensnares you, it's hard to break away."

****

"It's Victor," Oliver told Faustine.

He stood on the curb watching car brake lights shining from the slick Chicago pavement. It wasn't raining so much as misting. Chicago's rush hour traffic made him long for northern Michigan. He had told Ezra that he needed to check in with Ula and ducked out of the loft to make the call. He and Faustine had pre-planned the contact so that Faustine could take a boat to the mainland where he had cell service.

"Are you sure?" Faustine asked, sounding unsurprised.

"Well, I haven't laid eyes on it, but yes. I saw a memory of Kendra's that revealed something that I believe was the amulet. And Ezra says he's been acting strangely."

"Okay," Faustine said. "Don't confront him. I'm formulating a plan. Elda and Julian have flown to Montana to speak to a witch from Serpent House and they will return tonight."

"The wedding is next week," Oliver reminded him.

"Exactly, we'll have all of the witches here, Victor included."

"You plan to confront him at Abby's wedding?"

"Of course not," Faustine said, a note of irritation in his voice. "But it is an ideal opportunity after the wedding is over."

"I see." Oliver heard a car honk and watched a woman stick her hand out her car window and flip her middle finger at a truck driver. "I'll be back tomorrow as well and I told Lydie we could stay with Abby and Sebastian for a couple of days."

"Good, Lydie's found something concerning and we should discuss it."

"What's that?" Oliver asked, glancing back toward the building. He didn't want Ezra to overhear his conversation.

"We'll talk about it tomorrow."

Sky Mothers

CHAPTER 26

Abby opened the door to Lydie and Oliver, their arms filled with magazines.

"Are we scrapbooking?" She laughed, inviting them in.

"I wish," Oliver grumbled. "Helena and Bridget have marked about fifty million pages and we have to send her your feedback on flowers, decorations, and seating by tomorrow."

"Good grief. Is there a magic spell that can make those decisions for me?"

"Yes," Lydie announced triumphantly. "I found one before I left. We have more important things to talk about."

Lydie showed Abby how to do the spell. It was quick and easy and involved lighting a candle, whispering a desire for the magazine to reveal only that which she would love in her wedding and then setting the magazine on fire. The fire would burn everything except the pages she would have picked anyway. After five minutes, they had a stack of eight pages.

"Wow, good thinking, Lydie," Oliver told her, holding up his hand for a high five.

"What did I miss?" Sebastian asked, shouldering open the door and carrying an enormous bag of kitty food.

"Dinner?" Oliver asked.

"You're more than welcome to it," he said, hoisting the bag into Oliver's arms.

Oliver looked at the label.

"Nope, chicken livers are not my style."

"We're having lasagna," Abby said, cutting open the bag and filling Baboon's bowl. "And you missed the wedding stuff, which we can show you if you'd like, or we can get down to business?"

"Wedding stuff later. I want to hear what Elda and Julian found out in Montana."

"They got a pretty deep backstory on Clyde. However, it didn't tell us much about the curse. One thing is certain, he was a bad dude and obsessed with immortality. Between what this witch Nora said and what Faustine read in the Yarrow book that Dafne got from the L'Obscurite, it seems pretty clear that he was performing some very dark magic in an attempt to live forever."

"There was something else too," Lydie broke in, avoiding Oliver's gaze. "I found a piece of paper in the Lourdes's stuff that listed dates and names for all of the women who descended from Kanti and you and your mom are the only ones left alive."

Abby stared back at her, trying to make sense out of what she was saying.

"That can't be, can it? I mean there must be dozens of women."

"Thirty-six."

"Thirty-six!" Sebastian exclaimed.

"Unless she missed someone, which she could have," Oliver broke in. "But the names match what Victor discovered when he was tracing the bloodlines."

Abby sat heavily on a stool.

"What does it mean? How could they all be dead?"

"It gets worse," Lydie said, and this time she looked to Oliver to break the news.

"There were two names on that list that were a bit shocking. Your mother and sister, Sebastian."

"I'm sorry, what?" Sebastian looked at them in disbelief.

"But that would mean." He looked at Abby, shaking his head as if denying the possibility.

"It's not a close relationship, but Alva, Tobias, and Sebastian all descended from Kanti and Clyde originally as well. I don't know how she did it, but the Lourdes tracked the entire family tree. Kanti's child was named Kimi, which was later shortened to Kim. Kim had two children a boy and a girl. The girl is where Abby descends from and Sebastian, Tobias, and Alva come from the boy's family."

Sebastian put his head in his hands.

Abby leaned toward him and rubbed his back.

"Are you saying my mother was murdered?" he mumbled.

"Not necessarily," Lydie started.

"So, what then? All the women that descend from them are just randomly dead? It's a coincidence?"

"Probably not," Lydie admitted, looking defeated.

"Faustine believes there's something happening to the women in your family right now because the curse is cycling back around for the third time. Three is a powerful number. The Lourdes wrote something disturbing at the bottom of the family tree. It said, 'we all must die,' referring to herself and the women in your family. Faustine thinks that Kanti wants to end the curse, or at least she wants to be free of whatever is tethering her spirit to the world," Oliver explained.

"And if we die, she's free?"

Sebastian slammed his hand down on the table.

"No, no, we're done talking about this. I'm sorry, but I just..." He left the room and they listened to his footfalls on the stairs.

"I'm sorry," Lydie sputtered. "It was too much, maybe Helena should have told you."

Abby took Lydie's hand.

"It's not your fault, Lydie, and Sebastian isn't mad at you. He's scared and with good reason."

Oliver let out a long breath and stared at the ceiling.

"It's not going to happen, okay? Julian has already gone to your mother. He added protective spells to her house and he's built a shield around her. It would take a highly skilled witch to break down the spell and the moment someone tried, he'd be alerted."

"He's five hours away!"

"Not anymore, he's not. He put a two-way mirror in her house. And we have one for you as well."

"Like we used for the All Hallow's Ball?"

"Yep. For emergencies only."

"Sebastian's going to love that. Any more news? I almost hate to ask," she grumbled.

"Victor stole the amulet," Oliver added.

"No. Are you sure?"

"I'm almost one-hundred percent positive."

Abby grimaced.

"I need a cookie, anyone else?"

"Better grab the whole plate," Lydie told her, plopping on the next stool over.

Oliver slid the plate of cookies across the counter, taking a chocolate chip from the top.

"Any other devastating news?" Abby asked, nibbling at the edge of her own cookie, though suddenly she had no appetite at all.

"Julian has a theory. He thinks Clyde followed Yarrow's instructions and found immortality," Oliver explained.

"Which involves what exactly?"

"Well, a whole bunch of stuff, but Yarrow devotes an entire section of the book to procreation. He says nothing will ensure immortality as well as descendants. If Clyde performed the magic Yarrow laid out, then he bound himself through blood to the child that he and Kanti created. Their bind would travel through every additional child, which would basically buy him more time. Clyde had to steal Kanti's power to perform these spells, so in all likelihood, she is trapped here because he is still alive."

"After three hundred years?"

"Probably not in his original form, but yes."

"So, every one of his descendants must die in order for him to die?"

"Julian doesn't think so. He thinks only the women must die, probably because the original child was a girl so the bind and the curse are carried through their DNA."

"This is starting to feel like it's over my head. You're saying the curse and both Kanti and Clyde are destroyed if my mother, my child, and I die?"

"That's Julian's theory, yes."

CHAPTER 27

"I just can't believe it could be Victor," Abby told Oliver, the following afternoon. She had spent the night awake, thinking about all that she'd learned from Oliver and Lydie the day before. Sebastian had tossed, restless as well, both of them unable to shake the disturbing news.

Abby and Oliver sat on the porch, basking in the afternoon sun. Sebastian had taken Lydie to town to get groceries for dinner.

Abby had settled her changing body on a round wicker bed that Sebastian had bought for their porch. Piled with pillows, and shielded by a flowing white canopy, she felt like a goddess lounging on a Greek island. A pregnant, hot, heavily emotional goddess.

Oliver looked up from the yoga mat that he had stretched on the deck. He had been carefully working the soles of his feet together, but his knees stuck high in the air.

"Butterfly," he told her. "I swear it's not made for men."

"Or women," she agreed, eying the lines of concentration on his face.

"I know you trust Victor, but the truth is he came into your life under rather strange circumstances, and look at the timing. He literally appeared the night that Sebastian disappeared and this whole nightmare began."

"Yeah, but Dafne was the reason Sebastian disappeared. Victor didn't have anything to do with that."

"You're probably right, but I'm not talking about particulars. This is a much larger story. He was drawn to find you at the beginning of this curse unfolding. He knew your Aunt Sydney. If Kanti was directing him to you, why didn't he seek you out a year ago, ten years ago? She wanted him to make contact right when the curse was triggered. Maybe to have a man on the inside?"

Abby sat up and wriggled into the same butterfly position that Sebastian was attempting.

"Let's talk about something else, this curse is wearing me out today." She sighed. "Tell me about you and Ezra." Abby grinned. "You're becoming quite the ladies' man."

Oliver rolled his eyes.

"I like Ezra," he said, finally settling into the posture and leaning back on a pile of cushions.

"Oh, come on. Pretend I'm your best mate and spill your guts about your new love."

"Aren't there soap operas to fulfill these kinds of cravings?"

"None that cast witches."

He laughed and then grimaced at his carefully held groin muscles.

"Love is a strong word."

Abby frowned. Overhead, low flying white clouds reflected the surface of the Lake. It was one of those perfect spring days with a warm breeze that hinted at summer.

"It's not love, then?"

Oliver looked at Abby and she felt a moment of sadness as the energy moved through him.

"Maybe. I don't know. Love feels out of reach with Ezra. She's shielded like Fort Knox. I fell in love a couple times before I was a witch and it always felt light and easy and exciting. There's nothing light and easy about Ezra. She is deliberate, calculating even."

"Calculating?" Abby asked, surprised.

"Not in the way it sounds, but yeah. Every word and action has a purpose, which is great; I admire her tenacity and drive. But sometimes, I'm not sure how to be with her. She doesn't get my jokes."

Abby laughed and threw a pillow at him.

"What?" he asked, pretending to be offended.

"But obviously there's something. Right?"

"When did you fall in love with Sebastian?"

Abby watched Oliver and considered his question. When had she fallen in love with Sebastian?

"I feel like our love existed before we met." She paused, expecting Oliver to heckle her, but he remained silent. "It was the awareness that the love was waiting that propelled me away from a life that I felt unhappy in. It was more than that, of course, but the love was part of it. When I first met Sebastian, I didn't know what to think of him. He was handsome and kind, funny, but he was distant. I think he and Ezra share a few traits, actually. Survivors of trauma don't open up easily. But then we were thrown into pandemonium. We only had each other. The Vepar attack and discovering Ula-those experiences accelerated our connection. I guess the moment I knew I was in love with him was when I lost him. When I realized that he had vanished from Sorciére, I thought the love of my life was gone. I don't think I'd given it a label before that."

"So, you think I should take Ezra Vepar hunting?" Oliver joked.

"I think you're already in it, no need to find more trouble. If you're meant to become more than you are, you'll see it soon enough."

"I want someone in my life. I want this," he gestured to the house behind them. "A partner, a home, a love that's worth dying for."

Abby bit her lip and felt the warm rush of tears over her cheeks. She cried regularly, often at strange moments, but Oliver's words had struck a chord. Sebastian was a love worth dying for and so was their child. She too wanted those things for Oliver.

"She'll be your date for the wedding?"

He rolled his eyes and laughed.

"I didn't know it was a date kind of thing. Plus, she's the DJ. Who wants a date that can't dance?"

Abby grinned and leaned back on her pillows. It was mid-April and an unseasonably warm day. Sixty-five degrees and sunny. She forgot in winter how much she missed the sun.

"She's a witch. I'm sure she can abandon her post to dance with you."

Oliver cocked an eyebrow at her.

"Are you trying to play matchmaker, Abby?"

"We got ice cream!" Lydie announced, walking onto the back porch with a paper bag.

"And chicken," Sebastian amended.

"Mmmm, a delicious combo-chicken and ice cream," Oliver teased, trying to struggle out of his yoga position to grab Lydie's foot. "Oh ouch, I'm injured," he whined when Lydie danced away from him and he sprawled across the deck.

"Deep in serious conversation?" Sebastian asked, kissing Abby's forehead.

"Yes, I was asking Oliver if he'll wear a boutonniere that matches Ezra's dress to the prom, I mean wedding." She winked at Lydie.

"When do I get to meet Ezra?" Lydie asked. "When your firs- born arrives?"

Oliver played at grabbing her foot again, but she side-stepped him.

"How come I'm the butt of the jokes?" Oliver complained. "Sweet innocent little Oliver always getting picked on by the cool kids."

"Don't tell Ezra you're not a cool kid." Sebastian chuckled.

****

"Is it a good idea to confront Victor right after the wedding?" Sebastian asked when he had Oliver alone. They had gone to the shed to box up some wood that Oliver needed to build a DJ table for Ezra.

"I think it's probably the best time. We'll be protected at Ula; all of the witches will be there so he can't weasel out of the truth."

Sebastian sighed.

"I just don't want it to ruin the day for Abby."

"It won't," Oliver insisted. "The wedding will be great and we won't say a word to him until the next day after you guys are long gone on your little honeymoon. By the time you get back, Victor will have confessed, hopefully we'll have the amulet back, and we'll wait for you to return before we ax it to death."

Sebastian smiled and shook his head.

"Oliver, you are a true optimist. Despite everything going wrong that possibly could in the last six months, you still believe that things will go according to plan."

"I prefer to look on the bright side, my friend."

"You and Ezra might just make the perfect match-opposites attracting and all."

"Ezra this, Ezra that. I feel like I'm surrounded by grandmas trying to marry me off."

Sebastian grinned.

"I think it just feels good to focus on something fun and normal, you know? A new love interest, Oliver's got a girlfriend, that kind of thing."

"Oh, I get it, believe me. I just wish we were doing it to Lydie instead of me."

"Lydie's thirteen!"

"What thirteen-year-old girl hasn't noticed boys?"

"Lydie."

"Yeah, you're probably right. Still, I have faith that this is going to work out. By this time next week, you'll be married, and we'll be a lot closer to eliminating this curse."

"I hope you're right, Oliver. I really do."

"Listen," Oliver closed a box and turned to face Sebastian. "I've been wanting to ask you this and the timing just hasn't felt right. It's probably not right now, but I have to ask. When you met with Kanti in the woods, was Dafne in there at all? Could you sense her?"

"Well, when I was blacking out, I don't know, but the few times I met her after Julian and I worked out how to stay conscious, the truth is, no. At least, I think no."

"What did Kanti say?"

"Well, she believed I was in a trance so we didn't sit and chum about the weather. She repeated phrases about bringing my sister back from the dead. She told me again and again that I would have the power of the universe at my fingertips."

"Did she tell you that she would appear with the Vepars? That you'd have skin-walkers crawling all over your property?"

"No, but Julian suspected she might. I had hoped not, but we had a plan and I felt like we'd be okay."

"Except we weren't okay. Dafne died."

"I know," Sebastian sighed. "And I'm genuinely sorry, I am. I never wanted that. I believed that once Kanti gave me the amulet and I broke away she would lose her hold on Dafne's body and Dafne would come back."

Oliver closed his eyes and tried not to think of Dafne dying every night in his dreams.

"I wish she had."

****

"It feels surreal," Abby admitted. She stood in her bedroom wearing the long satin wedding dress that Helena had made. Her hair fell in chestnut curls down her back.

"It's perfect," Helena said. "You and the baby both look gorgeous."

Abby laughed and turned to look at her profile. There was a prominent rounding at her mid-section. At five months along, the baby had finally begun to reveal herself, though still not so prominent that people commented. In fact, on Abby's moodier days, she felt bloated and frumpy rather than glowing with child.

At that moment, wearing the shimmering pearl dress, she felt beautiful, baby bump and all.

"Yeah," Lydie agreed. "You look like a princess."

"Is that allowed?" Abby joked. "A pregnant princess?"

"In your fairytale, it is," Helena assured her.

"Hair up or down?" Abby asked, gathering her hair and propping it on her head.

"Beautiful both ways," Helena told her. "But I think down, it gives you that wild look. Below the neck regal goddess, and above the neck wild warrior."

"Definitely!" Lydie added.

"How's Adora doing?" Abby asked. "Will she be able to attend the wedding?"

Helena shook her head.

"She's not walking well yet and sleeps most of the day. Faustine has set up a separate chamber for her in the tower so that she's surrounded by her air element."

"Maybe we could do a transfusion?" Abby asked, referring to her own blood, which had helped heal Helena.

"Yes, after your honeymoon, I'm sure that would be helpful."

"How can I be getting married in three days?" she asked.

"It's exciting, isn't it?" Helena murmured. "Now, shimmy out of that dress. I'm going to pop back through the mirror and do a quick hem and it will be finished."

"I thought the mirror was for emergencies only," Lydie teased.

Helena narrowed her eyes at the young witch.

"This was an emergency."

****

After Helena disappeared through the mirror and Lydie went in search of Baboon, Abby slipped off to her room. She sat on the window seat that looked out over the bay and pulled out her journal. Journaling had always been a solace, a place to unleash her thoughts, but in the last year, she'd barely lifted a pen. She had taken her journal when she fled Nick and Lansing and the life that left her gasping for breath. She had even opened it a time or two and glanced back over the previous entries. She read about her frustrations with Nick, her feelings of ambivalence in the relationship, her desperation to run away from it all. A dozen or more entries ended with the words "Why do I feel like I'm faking my own life?" It had been one of the questions, maybe the question, that ultimately drove her to pack her bags that fateful August morning and flee to Sydney's lake house. It had felt like a big decision. It wasn't one of those tiny choices like running to the supermarket for bananas that transformed her life forever. She knew the moment she left, she would not return. She had no idea, however, about the life waiting for her. A beautiful life, she realized, feeling the soft nudging of the child within her. A terrifying life, too.

She had packed away the old journal and purchased a new one. She bought it from True Self, the new age bookstore in town that offered tarot readings, sold crystals, and always smelled of lavender and eucalyptus. The woman had been generous and sweet as she guided Abby toward the journals. She was not a witch, but what Elda would call an empath. Abby could feel the woman feeling her. An emotional exchange that Abby would not have sensed before becoming a witch. The woman had shown Abby a wall of leather journals with images burned into their surfaces.

A caramel journal, embossed with a black tree, tiny birds fleeing its branches, had caught her eye. She took it home and struggled to write her first entry. Eventually, she had found herself writing letters to her baby rather than anecdotes from her day.

She usually started each entry with My Love-but that morning, without even realizing it, she had written, Dear Vidya. She stared at the entry now, relishing the thought of her daughter's name.

"Vidya," she said out loud.

She tried to remember where the name had come from. Had she heard it? Read it in a text at Ula? Nothing obvious drifted to her mind and she knew that, like many things, an answer to her question might never surface. Elda said that witches and people were meant to ask questions they may never get answers to. Questions were the spark for growth and evolution. Answers were an end to a story that was never meant to end.

CHAPTER 28

"What do you think of the name Vidya?" Abby asked Sebastian that night as they lay in bed.

Sebastian rolled onto his side and smiled, knowingly.

"What? Why are you looking at me like a sly fox?"

"I love it and I knew that you were going to choose it."

Abby widened her eyes.

"How?"

"I had insider information," he admitted. "Claire told me in the dream wood."

"You didn't tell me that!"

"I know. Claire told me you would arrive at it on your own and, honestly, I was curious to see if that would happen. How did it come to you?"

"I don't know," Abby admitted. "I was writing a letter to the baby in my journal and realized I'd addressed it to Vidya. Where's the name from, I wonder?"

"Not my life," Sebastian admitted. "I don't have any great-grandmothers named Vidya that I'm aware, but in this strange world, who knows."

Abby laughed.

"Yeah, me neither. Though I was thinking about the Sanskrit word Avidya, which Elda told me means 'lack of knowledge of the true self.' So maybe Vidya is actual knowledge of the true self, knowing oneself?"

"I like that," Sebastian decided

"Middle name Claire?" Abby asked.

Sebastian studied her face.

"Vidya Claire Hull," he said. "A great name."

"Yes," Abby agreed, realizing that soon she would no longer be Abigail Daniels, but instead Abigail Hull. That too felt right. Like her old journal that no longer suited her new life, she felt a name change was also in order.

****

"We'll be seeing you two lovebirds tomorrow," Oliver grinned.

"Is this going to be one of those gushy weddings where everyone cries?"

Lydie asked, tracing her finger along the edge of the huge gilded mirror propped in the hallway.

"Probably," Sebastian smiled. "But only the boys, I'm sure you girls will be dry-eyed."

"With Helena in attendance?" Lydie giggled. "Don't count on it."

"Okay Lyds, safe travels through the never-sphere. I'll see you in a few hours." Oliver wrapped Lydie in a funky maneuver that combined a hug and a headlock.

Lydie hugged back and then wrestled away.

"Au revoir," she said, giving them a quick salute and falling backward into the mirror.

"Is she going to come crashing out the other side and give Faustine a heart attack?" Abby asked.

"Probably."

"No mirror travel for you?" Sebastian asked.

"Nope, can't leave my magic bus behind and I need to swing by my post office box. I try to make it twice a year in case the IRS is after me."

Abby gave Oliver a hug and Sebastian offered him a fist bump.

Outside they heard a car pull into the driveway.

"Jim, I hardly think it's appropriate to bring fast food. I'm sure they've cooked a meal," they heard Abby's mother shrill.

Oliver widened his eyes and Sebastian pretended to grab Abby's hand and pull her into the mirror.

"If we move fast, we can all be in Ula in half a second," Sebastian coaxed.

"Surely you're not trying to escape your future in-laws?" Oliver joked, peering around them toward the door as if a ghoulish beast might burst in.

"If my dad had any hair left, it fell out on this drive." Abby sighed, picking up the black cloak bewitched to obscure the mirror. She threw it over the top and Oliver adjusted it into place.

"Why did your parents drive up together?" Oliver asked. "Attempting a reconciliation?"

"Doubtful," Abby muttered. "Honestly, I don't know. My mom called me last night and said 'Abigail, your father and I will arrive tomorrow. Is there a suitable place for us to sleep?'"

"I told her we'd roll out a couple sleeping bags in the shed." Abby grinned.

"You did not!" Sebastian laughed. "Did you? Please tell me you didn't?"

"Okay, I thought it really loud, but kept it to myself."

"I'm gonna make a run for it," Oliver told them.

They walked outside to greet her parents.

"Hi Mom, Dad," Abby called.

"This is a great house," her dad said, popping the trunk and grabbing a large gold pull-behind suitcase-her mother's no doubt. "What'd it go for? Half a million?"

"Jim," Becky seethed.

"Hi, Mr. Daniels," Sebastian shook his hand and took the suitcase. "Mrs. Daniels," he offered her an awkward one-armed hug that Becky leaned away from.

Oliver opened the door to his van.

"Hi, Abby's parents, nice to see you again. On a deadline, but I'll be seeing you tomorrow." He tipped a hat he wasn't wearing and threw the van in reverse.

"This is very nice," Becky commented, sizing up the house and turning to scan the property. "The color is rather strange though, and that widow's walk up there gives me the absolute creeps." Becky shuddered.

Sebastian caught Abby's eye and gave her a look that said, "play nice."

"Let me give you guys a tour," Abby said, beckoning them toward the front door.

****

"G'day." Oliver smiled as he murmured the Australian greeting with barely a thought.

The post office clerk beamed at him and she looked mildly disappointed when he turned toward the post office boxes rather than stepping to the desk.

He hadn't checked his mail in four months. He rarely received correspondence, but a couple times each year his brother or parents sent him a letter and he relished their every word. Though his family believed he lived in India, he had given them the post office box in the UP, with an unlikely explanation about regularly traveling there for wilderness meditations. The box had popped into his mind when he told Ezra about missing his family and he'd been unable to shake it from his thoughts. Dropping the stack of mail into a bag, he returned to his VW bus and rifled through the contents. To his delight, cards had arrived from his brother and mom. A third envelope caught his eye, written in painfully tight, nearly perfect cursive. He set it on the dash and ripped open the card from his brother.

The picture on the cover revealed Oliver's brother with his wife and sons standing next to a giant Christmas tree. *Christmas in New York* announced huge red block letters above the smiling family. Oliver could see that Jeannie, his sister-in-law, was pregnant with a third child. They wore funny Christmas sweaters sewn with google-eyed reindeer. His brother wrote that he missed him, hoped that next year he would visit for Christmas, and announced the rather obvious news that another baby was on the way.

The card from his mother was more generic with a smiling Santa Claus on the front. What the card lacked in personality, she had made up for by writing a novella inside. She outlined the previous months in detail, from his dad's unruly ulcer to the new dining room table she bought. She reserved the end of the card for how much she missed him, pleading with him to visit and finally with the question that she always asked, "What did I do wrong?"

He cried while he read the cards and when he finished them, he tucked them inside his shirt to feel their words against his chest.

He picked up the third envelope and glanced again at the writing. It looked familiar, but the sender did not immediately come to him. Ripping it open, he pulled out a single sheet of thick cream stationary. He recognized it immediately from the library at Ula.

Dear Oliver,

Perhaps when you read this, I will be sitting beside you. I will have told you, "Let's get that letter and burn it," because as you know, I am thorough and would worry that it is unsafe, even in your post office box. Maybe you will laugh at me and insist on reading it before I can light it on fire, which I will do as you hold it in your hands. There is another option, a more likely one, I fear, and it is that I am no longer of your world. My story is long-the tale of a witch is rife with tragedy, is it not? But how can I pass out of this life without leaving that story behind? So I have written it in detail in a journal, which I hid at Ula. Ula is great for hiding things, all those secret passageways you used to sneak into with Lydie during our games of hide and seek. I would practically have fire coming out of my ears, I'd get so angry with you. I will miss the two of you most of all. Before you came to Ula, I was a broken woman. It was only through your humor and Lydie's innocence that I learned to feel love again and I am grateful eternally. I have left something else in the journal, another letter that outlines what I have been up to. You're onto me by now, I'm sure. I am reluctant to mention names in this letter. The paranoia in me wins out yet again. Therefore, I will refer to the entity as K. I have learned much about K in the past year and things are not as they seem.

Do you remember the secret passage that led from Lydie's room to the library? At the second bend, reach to the ceiling. I will say no more, you were always a better sleuth than me.

Despite how all of this may seem, I loved all of you. Everything I did was to protect you, to protect Ula, and I now know that I was chasing phantoms, the wrong ones. I love you. In the journal, you will also find letters to each of the witches of Ula. I wanted to write them just in case, maybe we'll be burning them together later, by the light of the library fire, drinking a cup of Bridget's cocoa and celebrating life.

Dafne

Oliver, not realizing he'd been holding his breath, let it out in rush. He read the letter again and then a third time. Dafne had left a journal. Dafne had suspected that her death was imminent. He tucked the letter back into the envelope and leaned his head back.

****

"Why would Dafne hide it in the passage by my room?" Lydie asked, gazing at the stone wall hung with a purple tapestry that Helena had made for her. She looked again at the letter that Oliver had received from Dafne.

"I don't know, Lyds," Oliver admitted. "Maybe she wanted us to remember better times."

Lydie nodded and swallowed the lump gathering in her throat. It hurt to think of Dafne. It hurt most of all to think of Dafne in the years before Abby and Sebastian arrived at Ula. She was never a bowl of cherries, but she had a lighter side. Helena used to lovingly call her the Tender Dragon. Dafne had put a lot of effort into easing Lydie's transition into Ula, and as a fellow fire element, she believed it her duty to show Lydie the ways of fire.

Lydie remembered nights on Oliver's balcony. Dafne performed fire tricks and Oliver poked fun at the outlandish displays. Dafne liked to say earth elements were jealous of fire elements, but Lydie knew they were teasing. Oliver was the only witch who truly connected with Dafne until Lydie came along. Dafne felt protective of Lydie and wanted to help guide her.

"She wrote all of us letters?" Lydie asked, slightly afraid to read hers. It would make her cry and miss Dafne and wish to turn back time.

"It seems that way."

Lydie pushed the tapestry aside and fit her fingers into the grooves between two bricks. A tiny metal hook stuck from the cement and she flicked it with her finger. The stone wall shifted, swinging slowly in and back, revealing a passage behind the wall.

Lydie lit a small ball of fire. It floated before them as they walked into the shadows. Sebastian paused at the second turn and reached for the ceiling. He felt a large stiff envelope fastened to the stone ceiling, He tugged and it pulled away.

"Got it," he whispered.

Lydie's eyes looked wide and tearful in the light of her fire.

"What will it say?" she asked.

Oliver shook his head.

"We'll know soon enough."

****

They could have read the letters and the journal alone, but Oliver had tired of secrets. He wanted everyone in Ula to know about Dafne's journal so they gathered in the library and opened the envelope together.

"I feel like Abby and Sebastian should be here," Lydie broke in.

"They arrive with Abby's parents this afternoon," Julian reminded her. "And we can't exactly have this conversation in front of her mom and dad. After the wedding will be soon enough."

"I second that," Oliver said. "Let's give them a peaceful wedding and honeymoon before we wreak more havoc on their lives."

Oliver passed out the letters, setting the one addressed to Abby aside. Helena cried as she read her letter. The only dry eyes in the room belonged to Julian as he did not receive a letter since he'd been away from Ula for years when Dafne disappeared. After they finished reading their letters, Oliver held up one more.

"This letter is addressed to the coven. Does anyone want to read it out loud?"

"I will," Elda said, sniffling into a handkerchief. She dried her eyes and stood.

Dearest Coven-

I hope that in writing this letter, I'm offering all that I know of the curse that plagues my bloodline. In the midst of the damage I've done, I am attempting to set things right. Such powerful witches you are, and I have no doubt you've already discovered a great deal about this curse. I blame myself for not confiding in you sooner. Together we could have overcome this, but I hated and judged myself for having loved Tobias and even more for having abandoned my child. I did not want you to see me in that light and I arrogantly believed I could thwart the curse on my own.

As I write this letter, I am preparing to travel to France. Will I attempt again to wipe Sebastian's memories? I do not know. I am reluctant to admit that I have considered killing him. It is wrong, yes, but could it end the curse? Could it save Abby and all of you? My only hope is that you receive this information in time for it to be of some use.

I visited the L'Obscurite and obtained a book by Joseph Yarrow. How did I know to seek this book? The Lourdes, in one of her rare lucid moments, told me that the original owner of that book contributed to the curse on our bloodline. I do not know his name. Only that he kidnapped the girl Kanti, tortured, and murdered her. The information in that book outlines an Egyptian ritual for immortality. This man was desperate to live forever. He was not a witch, but sought power by any means possible. The girl Kanti was the origin of his magic. The Lourdes has compiled a great deal about this curse, which may surprise you. How can an insane witch trapped in a forest retrieve any information? Every potion she received, she used to those ends. She wanted to perpetuate the misconception of her evilness, and don't get me wrong, she's often malevolent and cruel. But she hoped to learn of the outcome of her abandoned child, and in searching for that child, she discovered the curse and a history of the girl Kanti.

If I am gone when you read this, go to the Lourdes. I have given her the book on

Yarrow. You shudder at this revelation, but I kept my word. She told me the name of the book and where to find it. In return I gave her the book after I read it. The witch Ethel in New Orleans believed she tricked me by ripping out the pages regarding possession, but I am not a fool. As Elda will tell you, a simple spell to reveal that which is missing produced those pages for me. Do not punish or contact the L'Obscurite in retaliation for her actions. They are a dark and ominous group and they will not soon forget a confrontation.

When I first learned of the curse, Kanti was the only entity I could discover. I am her descendant, as was the Lourdes, and Abby. There are many, many more and I will tell you a strange and unsettling truth: Tobias, Alva, and I believe Sebastian, are descendants as well. We come from that original duo - Kanti and the man who stole her. If this man did, in fact, follow Yarrow's instructions, he has committed a great many murders to fuel his immortality. He has created multiple objects, much like relics, that house the spirits and the magic of the witches he has slain. I know of only two-an amulet and a dagger.

Kanti is not the ultimate enemy. I believed that she was when I set out on this search. I now know that she is held hostage in the world between life and death. Her spirit continues to give energy to the man who took her life. After reading Yarrow's book, I realized that I could help Kanti come back in physical form. I'm sure you think me crazy that I would make such a choice, but let me explain. There is no entity in existence more desperate to destroy this man than her. She may be the only way to eliminate him, and in turn, the curse. I do not believe that Kanti created the curse. Yarrow speaks of lineage as the most powerful energy that a single person can possess. Each child carries an imprint of the original creator's energy. If Kanti is allowed to come back, she will destroy him. How does she come back? Through possession. She must possess the body of another and I intend to offer myself for this cause. Please try to understand why I have made this choice. I am atoning for my mistakes. Perhaps I will end this curse after all.

Yours Truly,
Dafne

Elda folded the letter and held it to her lips.

"Kanti didn't create the curse," Faustine murmured. "I have suspected as much. Since reading Yarrow's book, I have thought the curse is part of Clyde's immortality. It is like a refueling every hundred years."

"A refueling?" Oliver asked, skeptical.

Helena stood, her face puffy from crying.

"This is a lot to digest and there is still much to do for Abby and Sebastian's wedding tomorrow. I suggest we return to our wedding tasks and give this a couple of days to settle and make sense. I don't want our home to be filled with the energy of sad contemplation."

Elda returned her letter to the envelope and nodded.

"Yes, Helena is right. We will put everyone in a funk if we stay in this cerebral darkness. Let's find the joy in the present moment. Tomorrow there will be a wedding, a celebration of love, and we owe it to Abby and Sebastian to honor that ritual with our whole selves."

Oliver glanced at Lydie, half expecting her to argue, but she too looked ready for a break from the heavy revelations of Dafne's letter.

CHAPTER 29

Sebastian stood beneath the ornate wooden archway. Julian had carved it from driftwood he found on the Lake Superior Shore. It was pale, bleached by years of sun and water, and smooth to the touch. Helena had draped the arch in white silk. It blew in the soft breeze that flowed off the water.

A sea of emotion coursed through Sebastian, not all of it joyful. Sorrow tugged at his heart, beckoning him to look into the face of that pain and see his family, absent, from this most auspicious day. His mother would have run her fingers through his hair so that it stuck up in funny directions. She would have laughed and insisted that the pictures would be more memorable that way. His father would have been the serious one. He would have given Sebastian a memento to carry, a handkerchief or a pocket watch, something traditional and weighted with the Hull men who had come before. Claire would have been giddy and bouncing around the garden, chatting with the flowers. She would have fawned over Abby and insisted on braiding a flower into her hair.

A blue and black butterfly landed on his outstretched hand. He lifted his finger close to his face and thought of his sister's words in the dream wood. "Think warm breezes and butterflies," she had said.

"Hi Claire," he whispered.

The butterfly spread her wings wide, revealing a pattern of blue spots that nearly made the shape of a heart on her shining wings. Helena stood behind him and he saw her watching the butterfly as well.

Sebastian turned back to the witches before him. They faced the edge of the garden where Abby would emerge from the forest below. Her father stood, waiting. He wore a dark suit and clutched nervously at his tie. He turned frequently to scan the faces of the witches and offer polite smiles and nods before quickly turning his gaze back to the steps.

Abby's mother sat in a chair close to the arch. She gazed around the space with an awed, and perhaps, suspicious expression. She wore a long heather gray dress and a string of pearls. Sebastian felt her eyes study him regularly as she looked at the garden. When they made eye contact he smiled and offered her a thumbs up, and she returned a polite nod.

When Abby appeared, he felt every muscle in his body constrict. She looked ethereal in a long silk dress that flowed and shifted with her movements. Her gown seemed to slide and shimmer over her body like a living thing. Every inch of her looked beautiful, but most of all her eyes, soft and brown and huge as she walked toward him. He saw in her eyes everything he felt reflected back to him, love, desire, and fear.

****

Abby took a deep breath. She clasped the teardrop crystal around her neck and felt the cool, calming energy slipping into her fingertips and traveling her body.

"I am getting married," she said to the quiet forest. The trees did not speak, but she felt their stolid encouragement.

It amazed her that she could feel so nervous and yet serene at the same moment. She had spent the last ten months with Sebastian. She had kissed him and teased him and talked with him for hours. She now shared a human being with him. A tiny little person who would soon join them in the world. And yet nerves buzzed through every cell of her body. She reached a self-conscious hand up to her hair.

Helena had pulled her curls half-up. Lydie had placed a pearl comb in her hair and whispered to Abby that it belonged to her own mother. Abby was laden with 'something olds.' Her mother had given her an antique bracelet that belonged to her grandmother. It had tiny diamonds embedded in a delicate white gold band. Elda had offered Abby the teardrop crystal, an heirloom from her own original coven and a special piece of magic.

She lifted the hem of her dress and walked slowly up the ancient staircase to the floating garden. The flowers quivered in a hundred brilliant colors. She felt them smiling up at her. Her dad held out his arm as she stepped into the garden.

"You look radiant," he told her.

She smiled and felt the first tear slip down her cheek.

The witches of Ula and Chicago, as well as Abby's mother, sat in white folding chairs wrapped with gold silk. Lydie and Helena had spread white rose petals down the aisleway. Abby slipped off her sandals and walked barefoot. The earth settled her nervous energy.

Abby trained her eyes on Sebastian's and tried not to trip. His blue eyes sparkled in the sunlight and as she drew closer she saw them fill and spill over. He blinked away the tears and turned to her dad. They shook hands and then her father took a seat next to her mom. Abby saw that her mother had started to cry. Her cheeks were stained with tears and mascara.

Abby walked into Sebastian's arms. He hugged her and she rested her head against his chest. She could have stayed that way, breathing in the scent of him and forgetting that they stood in front of all the family they had left in the world, ready to commit the rest of their lives to each other.

Helena cleared her throat.

In the chairs, Lydie giggled and Oliver coughed.

"Okay, okay." Abby laughed pulling away from Sebastian. They turned to face Helena.

****

After the ceremony, Faustine led Abby and Sebastian to the stone slab at the lagoon. The other guests had been ushered back to the castle for a cocktail hour.

Faustine would perform the magic ceremony apart from her parents. It was enough that they had come to Ula and experienced the castle and the floating garden. Her mother had commented on more than one flower not native to Michigan, but hadn't pushed the issue.

At the slab, Oliver, Lydie, and Helena joined them.

"Sebastian place your arms around Abby's waist and clasp your hands together, carefully weaving all of your fingers tightly. Abby place your arms around Sebastian's ribs, beneath his arms and weave your fingers together."

Faustine unrolled a ball of hemp and handed a long piece to each of the witches. For a moment, Lydie's turned to fire and then resumed its original shape. The others did the same, Oliver appeared to hold a rope of steel, Faustine's was a long silvery piece of water and Helena's became sparkling and transparent. When they each again held their lines of hemp, they started to chant. Faustine tucked one end of the hemp into their clasped hands. The witches circled Abby and Sebastian braiding the strands together.

The elements of each twine sent a surge of energy through Abby. When Lydie's rope touched her, her whole body lit with warmth and passion. She felt fiercely protective of the man before her, the child within her, the witches surrounding her. At Faustine's rope, a cool serenity stole through her body. With her own element, water, the ball of blue flame at the base of her spine lit and traveled throughout her body into Sebastian's. She could see his eyes bulging and his face changing with the sensations. When Oliver's rope wrapped more tightly around Abby, her feet seemed to cement to the earth. She felt hard and heavy and strong. At Helena's rope, the weight released and buoyancy drifted through her. A thousand thoughts crossed her mind. She felt akin to great poets and scholars for an instant, and then it all washed away. Replaced with the miraculous sensation of peace. Everything would be okay.

****

Elda started the glasses clinking and Sebastian leaned in to kiss Abby again. Her lips felt raw from all the kissing, but she savored every moment. She wanted the night to last forever. Sebastian cupped her face with his hands.

"My wife," he said, looking into her eyes.

"My husband," she whispered back and tried to feel the gravity of those words. Husband. She, Abby, had married that beautiful stranger standing in Sydney's driveway only ten months before.

A long table draped in crimson linen, had been set on one of the stone balconies that protruded beyond the cliffs of Ula. The lake stretched toward the horizon, which had already begun to glow orange as the sun made it descent. Slender black candelabras held white candles that flickered with tiny shoots of orange flame. Bridget had outdone herself. Huge platters of food ran the length of the table. Smoked meats, fresh cheese and fruit, hot buttermilk biscuits, glazed and caramelized asparagus, Brussels sprouts, collard greens, and more. Never in her life had she so loved food and to have such a feast laid out felt like a whole new celebration. Adding to her delight was the look of pure ecstasy on Sebastian's face when he first saw their dinner. For an instant, she thought he might jump up and down like a child.

As they ate, the table buzzed with conversation. For the most part, the witches stepped carefully around the curse, sticking to neutral topics. Abby knew that after she and Sebastian slipped away for their honeymoon the following day, Faustine intended to confront Victor.

She glanced down the table at Victor. He held Kendra's hand clasped loosely in his own. Kendra and Dante were lost in conversation, but Victor looked distracted. He appeared tired and thinner than when she'd last seen him. He had worn black jeans and a black t-shirt, not one to follow tradition, but fastened a tiny red flower to his chest. In the tumult of the day, Abby had not spoken with him alone and she was grateful for that. Before the event, Faustine performed an intricate spell to conceal all their thoughts ensuring that Victor would not realize that they were onto him.

Sebastian nudged her.

"Everything okay?" She could see that he'd caught her watching Victor.

She nodded and took a sip of her sparkling cranberry juice.

After the food, Ezra set up her equipment and began to play music. All of the witches danced, even Faustine, who seemed incapable of more than an awkward sway until Ezra played Moon River and suddenly he and Elda twirled around the balcony in an old-fashioned waltz. For an instant, they were all transported to another place and time. Abby could imagine Faustine and Elda as young witches, in love and idealistic, ignorant to the suffering that would find them through the years. Abby clutched Sebastian more tightly as the dark thought passed through. Sometimes moments of great joy brought the possibility, the inevitability, of suffering to the surface in a whole new way. For that long moment, as she watched, transfixed on Faustine and Elda's graceful turns, she felt crippled with the fear of what lay ahead.

And then, as if on cue, Ezra cut to an upbeat country song and the mood shifted once again. It was more than the music, the food and the merriment. All the witches had cast their energy over the space. The air buzzed, objects randomly lifted from the tables and floated around, bursts of fireworks exploded from nowhere in the sky above them. Abby's parents watched it all in dazzling, and perhaps drunken wonder. During a long slow dance, Abby's euphoria produced a soft pink mist that shrouded the entire room. She didn't intend to, but Sebastian nodded toward her fingers where the mist had slowly begun to seep out. It enveloped the entire room.

****

Helena had outdone herself in the honeymoon suite. White silk tapestries hung from the ceiling and fell over the bed. White rose petals covered every surface. A thousand candles burned from the fireplace mantel, table tops and the floor. They fell into bed laughing and drunk on their love.

After they made love, Sebastian pulled Abby close against him and encircled her in his arms.

CHAPTER 30

It was after two a.m. when Ezra finally cut the music. Only she, Oliver, Dante, and Helena remained on the veranda. They had stopped dancing hours earlier and shifted to deep conversations about the evolution of magic.

"I really, truly, believe it is our responsibility to use our magic in meaningful ways to help humanity," Dante stated for the fourth time. He was drinking a cocktail that he referred to as the Kitty Kraze and his energy seemed to only grow in intensity as the night grew darker.

"What's in that thing, anyhow?" Helena asked, yawning.

Dante winked at her.

"It's a secret, but I can tell you there's a bit of rum, vodka, pomegranate juice and magic."

"Magic! Is that a meaningful use of your magic?"

"Touché," Dante laughed, raising his glass. "Shall I make you one? I believe you will deem it meaningful."

"Not for me," Helena laughed, standing and stretching her arms overhead. "I'm off to sleep."

"I second that," Ezra said. "But Oliver, you may need to show me the way. I'm afraid I've forgotten where my room is."

Oliver grinned and pushed away from the table.

"It would be my pleasure," he told her, taking her hand and leading her back through the dining room.

Victor watched the witches finally retire. He had waited in the shadows for more than hour. He had to be certain that all the witches were in their rooms before he could make his move. When he heard Dante's door click shut, he returned to his own. Kendra appeared to be sleeping soundly. However, she had crawled into bed that evening with a snake. She barely felt the bite, of course, but Victor saw her eyes bulge for a moment before they closed and she slipped into a long, deep sleep. She would not awaken for two days, and even then, he would have to summon her back from unconsciousness.

He opened the black crate, carefully punctured to allow the snakes to breathe.

"Come here my beauties," he whispered to the snakes wriggling inside. The serpents began to slither up his arms and coil around his biceps. When he had ten of them, he left the dungeon room and returned upstairs.

He stopped at the bedroom doors of every witch in Ula, except for Abby and Sebastian and her parents. A quick incantation muted the sound as he slid open their door and slipped a snake inside. He visited Faustine's door last. He would be the most likely to awaken. Telepaths tended to have sensitive minds, easily roused from sleep.

He took an added precaution at his door, pulling a small pouch of honey-colored powder from his pocket. He blew the powder through the keyhole. A little push to ensure they slept soundly. After two minutes, he performed the incantation and slid open the door. In the dim light, he could see both Elda and Faustine in the large wooden bed. He added a second snake and closed the door.

****

Abby and Sebastian left early to drive back to the lower peninsula and catch a flight to Beaver Island where they would spend two nights for their mini honeymoon.

"They must have partied late last night." Abby giggled. "I don't even smell coffee. Bridget normally has a full breakfast laid out by six a.m."

Sebastian grinned.

"I saw Helena hitting the champagne pretty hard. Best we let them sleep it off, yeah? I wouldn't mind a rowboat ride back to shore. It'd feel like the first time we ever came to Ula."

Abby smiled.

"Yes, let's."

They crept out of the quiet castle and climbed into one of the rowboats. The lake, as smooth as glass, reflected the morning sun. The early April day was cool but sunny. Abby tilted her face to the sky and breathed the chilled air deeply.

As they rowed away from the castle, she gave a little wave, though she doubted any of the witches were awake to see them go.

****

"And now the real honeymoon can begin," Abby murmured as they parked the car next to their house.

Their honeymoon on Beaver Island had been fun, but Abby loved home and each time she left, she looked forward to that first step across the threshold more and more.

"Wait," Sebastian told her, trotting around the car. He opened the front door and scooped her into his arms.

"Wow, you made that look easy?" she laughed, knowing her pregnant body was slightly more cumbersome to handle.

"You're light as a feather, my love," he told her, nuzzling his face into the crook of her neck. He set her inside the door and began building a fire in the living room hearth.

Abby unpacked their stuff and took a long bath. Her low back ached from the all the driving. The heat lulled her and she allowed her eyes to drift closed.

Kanti reached her hand for the soft, warm weight that should have pressed close to her belly. Her fingers brushed the prickly fabric of an empty wool blanket. She grew frantic, pushing blankets aside. She searched the bed, and then the floor, convinced the baby had fallen and rolled away. The hard-packed dirt floor was empty. The hut was empty.

She ran into the night, her chest constricted with a terror that enraged her. How? How could someone have stolen the child as she slept? She had learned to sleep shallow, to be always alert to any sounds, smells, shifts in the night.

Before she took a step into the dark forest, she smelled the fire. It called out to her, bold fingers beckoning her through the black night. She found him where the forest gave way to the beach. The earth had been scrubbed clean and a pyre erected in the center of a wide circle. Her baby, their baby, lay in a stiff wooden box in the center of the blaze.

Kanti had not loved her child at birth. When she first stared into those unnatural blue eyes, she had hated the being who had emerged from her own. Now another emotion took over. Love did not explain the desperate, fierce rage that coursed through her at the man who put her fragile child into the mouth of the hungry fire. She gazed into the flames and began to sing.

Abby startled awake in the bathtub, sitting up and sloshing water onto the bathroom tiles. The water had grown cold and her candles had burned to small puddles of wax on the bath's rim. She blinked and tried to get her bearings, shivering in the cool water. She had fallen asleep in the bathtub, but why hadn't Sebastian woken her? It was unlike him to leave her unattended for so long. She reached her energy beyond the bathroom and into the house. She expected to sense him in the kitchen cooking dinner, but felt nothing. Had he gone outside? Perhaps to the shed?

Climbing from the bath, she dried quickly and slipped into a pair of jeans and a t-shirt. The dream of Kanti had disoriented her and she took several minutes to successfully put on socks and shoes. She searched the house, but found no sign of Sebastian. She encountered the same emptiness in the shed. The sun had already set and the sky held the early dark blue of the descending night. She could see the full moon, huge and white, rising over the trees.

Hurrying back toward the house, she noticed a sheet of paper stuck to the front door. Her heart sank as she studied the page. It was one of Victor's charcoal drawings. It revealed a dense wood and in the center a ring of witches standing in terror. She recognized all the witches from Ula and Chicago. In their center stood Victor and at his feet lay Sebastian.

"Sebastian?" she screamed, suddenly frantic. She ran into the house and back through every room, bellowing his name.

She knew that she would not find him. Somehow, Victor had escaped Ula, or worse. And now he had also subdued Sebastian. Abby thought of her mother's terrified words: "It's all coming true."

"No," Abby whimpered and clutched her belly. She glanced up and stared at her own terrified face in the hallway mirror. Her hair was disheveled and still wet from the bath. Fear made her face look sallow and her eyes wild.

"I won't give in to this," she shouted. She ran to her room and found the crystal of water that Elda had given her before the wedding. She needed her element now.

CHAPTER 31

The ring of fire had consumed the trees around it, but did not spread. It held hard and close, lighting the faces of the witches inside. Faustine had fallen to his knees, his cloak pressed against his face. Lydie's face glistened with sweat as she tried to fight fire with fire. She sent bursts of flame from her fingertips, but it fizzled and died the moment it left her. Dante and Marcus reached for one another, their black sooty faces mirrors of terror and grief. Kendra too had fallen. She wept openly and called out to Victor, begged him to stop, but he ignored her, ignored them all. Only Ezra remained still, motionless, the rage in her face like a mask of defiance that the blaze could not penetrate. Oliver stood across from Ezra, staring hard at the ground as if willing it to open. Helena stood, eyes closed, speaking incantations and gesturing as if performing magic. Elda clutched the stone around her neck, and she too whispered incantations. Julian paced and spun in a circle, staring at the flames, and then at Victor, seeking a way to escape.

Sebastian lay in the center of the circle at Victor's feet, unconscious.

Abby stood, rooted, frozen, watching her friends with such horror that it sucked the breath from her lungs and left her gasping in the smoke-filled forest. She was alone to witness this. Victor had planned it that way, all part of the ritual that began that fateful day in the woods when the dagger sucked hungrily at her blood. It took a piece and it left a piece behind. Now, in her greatest moment of need, she could do nothing. The dagger tucked in the belt at Victor's waist and amulet glistening on his naked chest gave him absolute power and control. When the ritual ended and her friends lay a pile of ash on the forest floor, Victor-no, Clyde-would rise again more powerful than ever before.

Abby's hands shook as she reached to the water crystal at her throat. It filled her body with a cool power that invigorated her, but did not eliminate the wall of fear in front of her face.

She thought back to the story that Dafne had left behind. The detailed retelling of that fateful night in the woods, a hundred years gone. Dafne had tried to save her friends, but Tobias had used her very own power to eliminate them. But Victor did not have access to Abby's power. Unlike Tobias, Victor had not fathered Abby's child. They did not share that link.

He drew his power from another source.

The woods surrounding Abby whipped and roared. When Victor realized she was there, he would begin to use that wind against her. She dared not climb into a tree for fear he would blow her out of it. She stayed in the shadows and called to the water of the lake. After several minutes the first deluge appeared. It fell upon the fire and the witches inside. Some of them cried out in relief.

Victor did not shift from his place in the circle. He did not even turn to look for her. He lifted his arms overhead and the wind began to greet the water as she called it. It drove the water back and into the ground. She could not draw it past him to reach the circle.

She conjured rain from the sky, calling upon her element and raising her hands and voice in a desperate plea.

The rain fell in sheets and the sky cracked and thundered. Streaks of lightning drove across the black sky. The rain did not find the witches. Victor had created a bubble of air that blocked it from reaching the fire.

Abby started to cry when Lydie fell to her knees. Helena reached for her, screamed at Victor, but he did not blink. Victor seemed to have left his body. Abby could barely recognize his face.

She had not lived long enough in the world of witches to know advanced magic. She did not have spells for breaking the dark magic that Victor used. He had access to the power of every witch in the circle. Each time they attempted to use it against him, it fed the fire that would consume them all.

"I'm a part of this curse," Abby whispered, the smoke starting to burn her eyes. "Clear and free, keep this smoke away from me," she whispered waving her fingers in front of her eyes and drawing on her element to make the magic known. The smoke dissipated and she could see.

Clyde could not survive without the continuation of the bloodline. He had raped Kanti to ensure that she passed along a child. Abby was now the bearer of the next child in that long lineage of cursed kin. She touched her belly and swiped at her eyes. She had only one option that she believed, prayed, would force Victor out of the circle. Once she did it, she would be powerless. If the witches in the circle had grown too weak to perform magic, they would be powerless to stop him.

Abby sprinted through the Ebony Woods. She raced out of the trees and into Sydney's moonlit yard. The sight of the house gave her a little jolt of pain, but she ignored it and slammed through the door into the garage. She snatched a ski rope from the wall and raced back into the woods. Her sided ached and her head had begun to pound. She returned to the ring of fire and this time, she did not hide in the darkness. She moved into the light. Victor turned to watch her. A huge, wicked smile stretched across his face. He looked like a monster in the firelight.

"He is a monster," she whispered.

Sebastian had begun to stir at Victor's feet. He crawled onto hands and knees, but Victor held a hand above him, immobilizing him. Sebastian looked up, slowly taking in the circle of witches surrounding him and just beyond them the ring of fire, hungry and snapping at their clothes and hair. He followed the direction of all their gazes to Abby.

She walked to a tree and threw the rope over a high, thick branch. She tied a noose in the nylon rope, her hands trembling and sweaty.

"There's one way to end this curse, Victor," she shrieked. She placed the noose around her neck.

"No, no, no," the screams of her friends came back to her, Sebastian loudest of all, but she ignored them.

She climbed up the tree and found a thick branch. She slipped the rope over her head and pulled the noose tight. She couldn't drop and let the rope catch because it might break her neck. She had to lower herself by holding onto the rope above her head and letting the slack out. Her hands slipped on the rope as she slid off her branch.

Victor-Clyde-watched her with mocking and then angry eyes. She could see the dilemma playing out in his head. If she died, he would die as well.

"Abby, please no, God no," Sebastian screamed, struggling against the magic that held him down.

Abby lowered herself down the rope. Her feet still hung several feet above the ground. She took a final deep breath and let go of the rope above her head. The noose held, growing tight around her neck as the slack released. Hot white pain drove through her head as the rope pulled tight and cut into her skin. The pressure was unimaginable, she felt as if the rope would pull her head clear off her neck. Her legs kicked at the air and she clawed at the rope struggling for breath. Victor, the circle, the witches, even her child ceased to exist. She couldn't breathe, the pain was excruciating. What had she done? She was dying. She felt her eyes bulging in her head, tiny blood vessels bursting. She gasped for breath, but could not breathe. Dizzying black spots blotted out her vision of the forest. The firelight began to fade and she felt her body slowing down. She wanted to struggle, to tear the rope from her neck, break the branch that held it, but her body had grown so heavy, weak, it was impossible. She couldn't think, let alone conjure her power. The black spots grew thicker, muted out the edges of the world. The forest disappeared.

****

"No, no, please," Sebastian screamed. His eyes and nose burned and he dug at the earth with his fingers, clawing the soil, searching for a rock, but knowing he'd never be able to lift it if he found one. Victor held him down, using his element of air to create an invisible wall that Sebastian could not break through.

He watched Abby struggle against the rope. For an instant, he thought it would kill him. He felt his heart being ripped from his chest. He would die there with her, and that would be better than living for a single breath after she had gone.

The pressure holding him suddenly disappeared. He sprung up with such intensity that he flipped onto his back. He rolled over and sprang to his feet. The circle of fire had dissolved. He saw Victor, a blur, as he raced toward the tree and slashed the rope with the golden dagger. For a confused moment, Sebastian thought Victor had attacked Abby, but then she fell in a heap, the rope swinging above her. Victor had already vanished into the dark forest.

Oliver darted into the woods and Julian followed.

"Get him," Lydie screamed, tears pouring down her face. Elda went to her and crouched low. She wrapped her arms around her and pulled her into her cloak.

Sebastian took Abby into his arms and pressed his ear close to her face.

"She's not breathing," he howled.

Helena pushed him aside. She took a deep breath and Sebastian felt the air sucked from the space around him. Helena opened Abby's mouth and sent the enormous burst of air into Abby's body.

Sebastian's rage and fear boiled over. The tree that Abby had hung from split down the middle crashing into the forest.

Ezra dropped down next to Abby.

"She's still in there. Come on back, honey," Ezra pleaded as Helena breathed another blast of air into her.

Faustine gently pulled Helena away and placed his hands on Abby's chest. His hands jumped as if shocked. Abby's body jolted on the forest floor, but she remained motionless.

"Here, let me," Elda exclaimed. She pulled the water crystal from Abby's neck. Using her fingernail, she slit the fine glass and held the crystal above Abby's mouth, allowing the water to drip down.

Sebastian moved closer, he pulled Abby back into his arms.

"Please, Abby, please, wake up."

He rested his forehead against her heart. A buzzing started in his ears, and for an instant, he was blind. A streak of warmth passed from his body into Abby's.

"She's breathing," Ezra declared, touching Abby's chest.

Sebastian pulled back and saw the tiny flutter of Abby's chest. He rested his forehead on the ground and cried.

CHAPTER 32

"The last thing I remember is crawling into bed. I'd had a bit of champagne, but…" Helena muttered.

"He used snakes," Lydie said, looking up from her notebook. She sat at the base of the sand dune in her dream room, her legs pulled up to her chest and the notebook propped open on her knees. Her hair had been singed, but not burned off completely. She now had a curled bob. Her face looked red and shiny, as did most of their faces, but already the burn ointment that Helena made had begun to heal them.

"Snakes?" Oliver asked, desperate to remember the night, but coming up blank. Like Helena, he recalled dancing and drinking. Afterward, he and Ezra had returned to his room to be alone. They had fallen asleep shortly thereafter and he didn't have any memory until he woke in the Ebony Woods surrounded by a ring of fire.

"Yes, I woke up to pee and there was a snake an inch from my nose. I'm not sure if I screamed," Lydie remembered.

"Snakes?" Ezra asked, examining her arms and legs for a snake bite.

"I see it," Oliver told her. He scooted closer to her and touched a spot on the back of Ezra's neck. The skin was puckered with two small red bumps in the center.

"Ouch," Ezra muttered, putting her hand on the bite. "It's sore."

Oliver touched the back of his own neck.

"Mine must be somewhere else."

"Why would he use snakes?" Helena asked, lifting her skirt and examining her own legs.

"He's been interested in them lately, Dante confessed.

He and Marcus sat in Lydie's treehouse on the little porch, their legs dangling over the side.

"Yeah," Marcus agreed. "We took a group of kids to the zoo a couple months ago and you could barely drag him away from the reptile exhibit."

"Serpent House." Oliver sighed. "An island overrun with snakes. I'd say it's an interest he developed through Clyde."

Ezra rubbed her thumb and forefinger against the bridge of her nose.

"You were right," she told Oliver. "You suspected him and I didn't want to believe it."

"You didn't have all the information," Oliver told her. "After Australia, we knew someone had stolen the amulet. It had to be someone who'd come to Ula."

"But we had no idea that he'd been drawn into the curse," Helena said.

"Because Sebastian didn't give in," Lydie said, pushing her pencil against her lip. "Sebastian was meant to be next, but he fought it."

"So, it took Victor instead," Ezra sighed. She looked beaten. Her shoulders sagged forward. Her hair had mostly burned away, a few black and gold spikes stood out on her angry scalp.

"Where's Kendra?" Helena asked.

"In her room," Dante responded, gingerly touching a spot on his shoulder that showed a slick looking burn.

"This is going to be very hard for her," Marcus agreed.

"Abby sacrificed herself," Ezra said, changing the subject.

"It was horrible," Oliver murmured. "She shouldn't have done it."

"We'd all be dead if she hadn't."

****

Abby woke to the sounds of trickling water. She lay for another moment, eyes closed, paralyzed. Her last memory of the Ebony Woods, Sebastian and her friends in the fire, caused her breath to catch hard in her chest. She fought to suck in air.

"Abby, honey?"

Sebastian's voice allowed her lungs to open and the breath to whoosh in.

She opened her eyes.

He stood above her, his eyes searching. They were in the healing room and she breathed deeply the smells of lavender and eucalyptus.

She reached up and touched his cheek.

"You're alive," she whispered.

"Because of you."

Abby touched the tender skin of her throat. She felt the raw rope burn, already healing.

"It worked, then? He broke the circle to cut my rope?"

Sebastian frowned and nodded.

"You shouldn't have done that, Abby."

"You'd rather I let you all die?"

He grimaced and looked away.

"Honestly, yes."

"I would have died with you, Sebastian. Don't you see? The Lourdes and Dafne both died when they lost the people they loved. They'd have been better off taking their own lives and ending the curse."

Sebastian looked ready to argue, but closed his mouth instead.

"Is the baby okay?" she touched her belly, knowing that her daughter was, in fact, okay.

"Yes, Helena listened to her heartbeat when we got back-strong and fast. No bleeding. She seems to be just fine."

"Is everyone else okay? What happened after I lost consciousness?"

Sebastian sighed.

"Are you sure you're ready to talk about all this? Wouldn't you like a little time?"

Abby shook her head.

"I need to know."

"He did exactly what you thought he'd do. He broke the circle and ran for the rope, slashed it and disappeared into the woods."

"He got away, then?"

Sebastian nodded.

"That's okay. We know his weakness now."

Sebastian scowled at her.

"That's not a weakness we'll be exploiting again."

Abby smiled and smoothed her fingers over Sebastian's lower lip.

"Don't worry, husband. No more suicide missions."

"Everyone else is okay, though. Physically anyway."

"The Chicago witches?"

"They're all here. Kendra seems to be taking it the hardest, which is to be expected."

"Poor Kendra." Abby sighed. "So, he just ran?"

"Like a coward."

"I worried that he'd try to retake the circle, that maybe he'd weakened everyone."

"He's not stupid. It's Clyde running the show now and he's all about self-preservation."

"Knock-knock," Elda called from the doorway.

"She's awake," Sebastian told her, smiling.

"Yes, I thought she might be. Faustine sensed her coming back online so to speak."

Abby laughed.

"Happy that my hard drive wasn't wiped out."

"And lucky too," Elda told her, clicking her tongue. "That was a huge risk, Abby."

"I know, Elda and if I was a better witch, I might have done differently. But honestly, I couldn't find another solution. I knew that he'd have to stop me or face the end of his own life."

****

Abby and Sebastian stayed at Ula for three days. They had discussed the curse at length. When they returned home, Oliver, Ezra, and Lydie accompanied them.

"It's not safe here," Oliver told Abby when they were alone in the kitchen. "Victor walked right in the front door when he took Sebastian."

"Correction," Abby said. "Sebastian invited him in and Victor set a snake on him the moment he turned his back. Julian and Faustine placed new spells against Victor. He can't get in."

Oliver tilted his head and gave her a look of exasperation.

"We're not alone here, we have you guys. Plus, we have the mirror, we can escape to Ula in seconds if we need to, but you know what?" She took a drink of iced tea and slammed the glass on the table a little too hard. "We're not going to escape. We're going to end him."

Oliver grinned and shook his head.

"I like your fighting spirit."

"This place is gorgeous Abby," Ezra said, walking into the kitchen. "Can I take a walk in the woods?"

Abby said yes at the same time that Oliver said no.

Ezra looked back and forth between them.

"I'll come with you," Oliver said.

Sebastian and Lydie had taken a game of Scrabble to the porch and Abby heard Lydie insisting that 'smeat' was a word.

"It's like smite, but plural," Lydie argued.

"Okay Lydie, but if you get smeat, I'm putting funner right here."

Abby chuckled and walked upstairs. She pushed into the nursery and smiled. Though Helena had strongly suggested they stay at Ula, Abby wanted to come home. She loved walking into her baby's room and imagining the future giggles she would hear from the little bassinet. She'd also made a habit of flicking the little white birds and smoothing the blanket in the bed.

She leaned forward to touch the purple fabric and paused. Something bulky was tucked beneath the baby blanket. She peeled back the fabric and gasped, stumbling back from the bassinet. A crude-looking doll, hand-sewn, lay beneath the blanket. Blank obsidian eyes stared back at her and the grossly stitched red mouth opened in unspoken accusation.

Abby knew the doll. In her memory, she saw it dangling from a chandelier as she and the other witches entered the land of dreaming.

Ethel and the L'Obscurite.

Behind her, Abby heard the door click shut and a low cold laugh.

AUTHOR'S NOTE

I love characters. For me that's the heart of writing and reading. I would love to hear about your experience with my characters and what other fictional characters you love. Reading has truly shaped my life and there's nothing more amazing than connecting with other readers who share passions similar to my own. I write as J.R. Erickson, though my legal name is Jacki Riegle. I live in Northern Michigan with my excavator husband and my beautiful little boy.

Don't forget to check out the next book in the Born of Shadows Series. Visit my author website www.jrericksonauthor.com for more information about upcoming book releases.

Made in the USA
Middletown, DE
08 November 2025

Made in the USA
Middletown, DE
24 April 2021

With gratitude,

Krystal Kelley

EPILOGUE

Cracking our crystal code, collectively is an important and special evolutionary process at this time in history. I believe coincidences, synchronicities, a natural order, music's role in our lives, all of these facets of this human life are woven together with our past and our future.

We all have our Corona stories to tell. I'm now listening to stories from all over the world about how we, as humans fit into the vibrations of Mother Nature and the universe. Collectively, lets co-create a future through conversation and storytelling and music. Please follow my journey at krystalkelley.com as I interview wisdom keepers, shaman, artists, musicians, all the change agents who cross my path. We are all connected by water, by the crystalline structures within water, connected in a crystal grid. For me, this journey gets more exciting as each new portal opens up. I'll document as much of the shift as I can.

without pain. If I hadn't felt that pain and confusion, the lack of pain would never have felt this good.

What amazing power my mind holds when connected to my heart!

I follow that power to leave The Surfer and create a new reality with my children and my future.

The coincidences have led me down zigzag roads to these red rocks underpinning a pink sky. A world once black and white has ignited into vibrations of colors from multi-dimensional rainbows.

My soul is singing, my dragon tail is wagging, my heart is connecting and my mind is scripting a beautiful future of heaven on Earth.

the sun. The orb grew bigger and bigger. It was growing with love. Love for Drei. Love to heal those negative emotions. As the orb grew, it was pushing those pins out of my chest from inside my body. I stopped walking and closed my eyes. The orb grew so large, it exited my body from my chest. I held my hands wide. I opened my eyes. The giant ocean surf, with the sun reflecting in the waves looked just like the warm orb I saw in my mind's eye. I think I see Crooked Beak wave his wing and disappear into the sun. I blink. Crooked Beak is gone and I know at once that he was protecting me.

I took a deep breath and stopped, holding the air mid-breath. I was expecting the shooting pain, but there was none. I breathed in deeper. Still no pain. I exhale, surely expecting some pain. Nothing! I realize my arms are still spread wide, so I drop them by my sides. I say a silent prayer to Crooked Beak and vow to never forget his guardianship of my life.

It's a miracle. No doubt about it. I don't feel an ounce of pain. I feel pure JOY!

I catch up with my daughters. We walk back to our beach house. It all seems magical, there is no pain and it has only been two weeks since I fell like a ragdoll. I feel unbelievably powerful and full of love for this glorious Earth we get to experience—and *except broken bones. Well, then, this is clearly from an outside source. But, where from? I KNOW I didn't throw myself down those stairs. I look into the mirror again. Past my reflection, in the background, I see a rag doll. The doll is sitting in a basket. The basket is in the corner of a room, but no room I've ever been in. All over the doll's chest are a spiral of needles. Needles like the pains hitting my chest! Cold chills cover my body. I suddenly know at once what happened to me, **VOODOO**.*

I jolt awake.

The sudden motion jolts pains into my chest. Keenly aware of the spiral from the dream, I know this is no coincidence.

That afternoon, the girls ran in the Dunes and on the Beach. The Surfer was still in Seattle. I was walking along the beach, thinking about my dream. My ribs were still killing me. It was hard to laugh or sneeze. A long, slow stroll was what I needed.

I knew exactly who was responsible, Drei. I don't blame her, she was motivated by fear and jealousy. Those emotions don't run strong with me. I feel compassion for those struggling to battle negative emotions.

I envisioned an orb of light encircling my heart. It was radiating from my heart with the warmth of

CHAPTER 9

WESTPORT

I do not remember the details about how we moved all our items. It was a daylight moon as the kids and I pulled into our new home in Westport. The home was a modern beach house. It sat on the sand dunes, as close the Pacific Ocean as was allowed to build. It was the closest thing to a dream home I could imagine. Inside had tastefully chosen, modern amenities. It is rare that I go into a house and think that I would have chosen each detail. Usually, as a designer, I nit-picked the details and loathed some choices. This home was perfectly ap-pointed and my only neighbor was Mother Nature.

Purely, like a dream.

I look into a mirror. I see a reflection of pain. Where is it coming from? I am seeking biofeedback from within my body, neurologically. My subconscious scans for sources of fatigue or disease. Nothing

My mind only has questions right now. So many questions!!! It was time to meditate for answers, but we had to move to Westport.

I don't want to explain to this nurse about a crazy crow trying to get into our house; me, turning into a demon & falling like a rag doll down the stairs. I am only seeking medical attention. I'm not looking for a psychological analysis of this situation. I know in my heart there is an explanation, but first, I must take care of my injuries.

I can tell the nurse wants to ask me more questions, and is skeptical about me, but she does a physical exam and orders some X-rays.

I had some broken ribs, as I suspected. My back and neck were all fine. She gave me a prescription for painkillers and told me the ribs will heal in 6-8 weeks. She handed me my prescription and a pamphlet that was for a meeting of abused women. I looked up at her.

"I'm not assuming, I'm just giving you resources if you need them." She said before I could ask her about the pamphlet.

"Oh, thanks. It's not like that. I really did just fall down the stairs." I wince as I walk out the room. I know I did a horrible job of lying. Sometimes, the truth is a little too hard to explain. Besides, I don't know what the truth is. I doubt I'll be able to find a pamphlet with information for meetings with people who have unknown demonic episodes.

CRACKING THE CRYSTAL CODE

I called the doctor and got an appointment with the nurse practitioner. It took me two hours to slowly get upstairs and into my car to go to the doctor's office. I wonder in my head why my husband had to go to work and not help me? I was clearly in tons of pain. I discount my feelings and tell myself that I really scared him.

"What happened to you?" The nurse practitioner is sitting in front of me, taking notes.

"Umm, I fell down the stairs?" I answer with a questioning statement.

"You fell down the stairs?" She asks, skeptically.

"Mmmhmm" I mutter.

"Hmm, so was alcohol involved?" She asked as she wrote something on her notes.

"No, my husband said I was sleepwalking." I wasn't planning on telling her all the details, but it seemed as if she knew I wasn't telling the whole story.

"Hmm, do you have a history of sleepwalking?" She asks.

"No. Never." I say simply. "I'm just in a lot of pain, do you think we can do X-rays?" I'm growing impatient.

KRYSTAL KELLEY

body sideways. It was as if you were hurled into the basement stairwell. I watched your body fall like a rag doll and land on the bottom landing. I thought there was no way you didn't break your neck. Again, you looked like a rag doll at the bottom of the stairs. Your body contorted in a very unnatural way. I ran down the stairs. I was going to check your pulse, but as I touched your contorted neck, you sprang up! It scared me to death. I wasn't sure if you were a demon or what. You walked into this room and laid on the couch. You have been out cold until now."

"How long was that?" I asked curiously.

"Hmm, about 12 hours now." He looked at his phone.

"I don't think I can walk up the stairs, do you think you could grab my phone for me? I should call to see if I can get in to see the doctor. I'm pretty sure I broke some ribs at the very least." I moan. The pain is not good.

"Sure. Then, I'm going to head into the office. Meg will get the kids from school, right?" He asked me.

"Yeah." I roll my eyes at his disconnection with the kids.

it wasn't any language I had ever heard. The closest sound I've heard sounded like playing a record backwards. It was the weirdest fucking thing I've ever heard. But then, it got weirder." His hands and voice are shaking.

I don't know why, but I had an archaic memory of that voice in my head, but it was from another lifetime ago. It wasn't from this dimensional life. As if projected from deep inside a long tunnel, only echoes of the sound reverberated to me. This puzzled my mind, but I had to refocus my attention to this mortal, human form I held.

"Wait, where are the kids?" I asked, suddenly panicked.

"I took them to school in the morning. You were dead to the world. Anne told me what time their school started. I realized that I have never taken them to school." The surfer explained.

"Did you tell Anne what happened??" I asked.

"No. I haven't told anyone. I told Anne you were sleeping in. I don't ever want to tell anyone this story. It was pure evil." He is clearly shaken up. "But, let me finish," he says. I nod, The surfer continues, "So, after you demonically said some forgotten language, you launched, not jumped, launched your

KRYSTAL KELLEY

It was unlike any way I had ever seen you move. I asked you again, 'what are you doing?' You didn't even turn your head. You slowly walked out of the room. I got up to follow you. You walked down the stairs slowly, but surely. I followed, silently behind you." The Surfer stopped talking. It looked like he had seen a ghost.

"What happened next?" I'm almost scared to ask.

"You stopped walking. You were just standing in the kitchen, looking out the back door. I tried to look around you and I didn't see that your gaze was going anywhere in particular. I asked you again, 'what are you doing?' This time, though, I tried to make my voice more forceful. You turned. You didn't look like yourself. I mean, it was your face, but no expression I had ever seen you make. I said, 'Krystal?' And then it happened!" His voice was shaking.

"What happened?!" I hoarsely shrieked. Pins and needles were pricking me from all over INSIDE my body. I didn't know where all this pain was coming from and I was growing irritated by the pain and the strange story.

"That's when you said, **'SNSKDJHFHFKSMDM-DKFKDNFKKGVNJF'** in the most demonic voice I've ever heard. It wasn't your voice, Krystal. And tired—no, drained of energy. I went to bed with my clothes on. I need to know what happened last night." I feel a tiny bit of strength returning, but the pain is not subsiding.

"Uhhhh, This is the weirdest, craziest thing I've ever witnessed. Even more strange than when I watched a shaman drink cobra blood in Indonesia." He explains, still sounding unsure.

"Okaaay" I say, thinking it must be pretty crazy. I knew the cobra blood story and that was a pretty wild one. "I don't care how crazy it sounds, just tell me." I prod.

The Surfer explains, "When I was sitting in the office, there was a crow outside the window and it seemed like it was trying to peck its way in. I even went outside and tried to get it to shoo away. It dive-bombed me and almost got inside. I shut the front door and locked it. The crow was sitting right on our front porch. It kind of gave me the chills."

He continues, "I was too distracted to finish up my work, so I went to bed. I couldn't really fall asleep. I was tossing. Sleep was not hitting me. I turned over again and you sat up. I thought you were sleeping. I asked you 'what are you doing?' As you were now walking slowly out of the room. I've never seen you move so slowly. It was as if you were in a trance.

It's painful but I manage to sit. I place my feet on the floor and I can tell it's a carpeted floor. I still don't know where I am. I try to reach up to fumble for a light switch, but as I try to lift my arm, a pain pulls it back down. I reach with my left hand and my fingers hit a switch.

LIGHT

The light blinds me for a few moments. My eyes adjust and I realized that I'm in my basement. I'm so confused.

I hear slow footsteps coming down the stairs. The Surfer slowly, cautiously looks around the corner.

"Are you alive?" He looks at me with fear in his eyes. Not fear like he was worried, like he was AFRAID of me. His face looked tired, older.

"Wha—-at haaaappened? I-I-I feel like I got hit by a truck!" I was speaking slowly because each breath is stabbing me from inside.

"I don't know how to describe what happened. I think you were possessed or something. I don't know how you survived that fall" He seems almost scared to be saying this out loud.

"Ok, just tell me what you remember, from the beginning. The last thing I remembered, I was getting

The lights flickered and I felt even more drained. It felt how I was after I had talked to Drei at Freshy's a while back. Ugh, what an awful experience! She really rubbed me the wrong way. I hadn't really thought about her since then, but I suddenly was really happy that I was moving far, far away from her.

I was so tired I could hardly make it to my bedroom. I muttered good night to The Surfer as I passed by the office. I crawled into bed with my clothes on.

*** *** *** *** *** ***

My next memory, I wake up. As I breathe in, the pain is filling up my body. I feel like I got hit by a truck.

Seriously!

I'm in pain! Is it my back? My neck? There are sharp pains digging into my chest as I try to breathe. I finally open my eyes and look around. I'm in a windowless room. It's dark, very dark.

My heart is racing like a razor blade in my chest, everything hurts.

Where am I? I try to sit up.

CHAPTER 8

THE RAG DOLL

The very next evening, The surfer returned from a business trip. He came home after I had put the kids to bed, but it wasn't late. He had more work to finish up, so he went straight to his home office, upstairs.

I sat in the living room and there was Crooked Beak sitting on my front porch looking right at me. "What are you trying to tell me??" I ask him aloud through the glass.

"Huh?!" I hear the surfer ask from upstairs.

"Nothing! I'm reading aloud" I lie.

I looked around at my living room. We sure did a nice job with this remodel, but we now have boxes everywhere! I had been packing all day and I suddenly had no energy.

CRACKING THE CRYSTAL CODE

Crooked Beak was perched on the fence between her and I. I almost felt like he nodded his head in an upward nod when I waved at Anne. She looked like she was thoroughly enjoying her gardening. I put it all out of my mind because I'm thoroughly enjoying being in this one moment.

I envisioned a story in my head called 'Rise of the Couch Empire.' It is a parody of American Life. An empire of people sitting on their couches accomplishing nothing each day. Ironically, at the end of the story, Ish, the main character became an artist and musician. She focused on creating an America where people were finally happy. Happy, just like my 'secret-life' happy *and* people from Denmark.

Crooked Beak looked in from outside as we sat and told stories in the living room. I noticed him a few times, subconsciously. Also, subconsciously, I acknowledged and respected the fact that he was there, keeping a watchful eye on my home.

"Yeah, my friends in high school all knew Krystal. Some of them thought it was weird that you were so much older than me, but I didn't care. We had a lot in common." Zac explained. "Krystal hired my friends and I to move furniture for her staging company."

Zac is stirring the butter that has now melted in the boiling water. "I think it's time to start adding the magic!" Zac is excited.

I grab the bag of "trash" my cousin had dropped off. I reach in the bag and pull out a healthy, potent, marijuana plant and place it in the boiling water. Zac takes the bag from me and says, "Let me do this. Why don't you and Jude go in the living room and talk about writing or whatever. I got this."

"I'm not going to argue with that!" I say. "I wouldn't mind sitting down for a few minutes, I feel like I've been on my feet all day! Thanks Zac!" I give him a shoulder bump as I walk past him to sit in the living room.

The warm smell of marijuana slowly permeated the house and the neighborhood. It was heavenly. I looked out the window and waved at Anne who was just below my open window,, gardening.

I laughed too, "That's right. He would grumble all the time to me from across the hedge about how much money private school was for 'The Boy'."

"So, did you water her flowers?" Jude asks Zac.

"I sure did. Twice a day as instructed. I wanted to make sure I didn't disappoint Krystal." Zac laughed.

"When I got home from vacation, I had it in my head to be prepared to see dead flowers. I was pleasantly surprised when I came home to find that my baskets seemed to have grown during some of our hottest days of the summer. I was impressed with 'The Boy'.

He knocked on my door the day after we got back and was looking to get paid. Sophia was in the high chair and I didn't want to leave her by herself, so I invited 'The Boy' inside. He sat in my kitchen while I found some cash to give him. He ended up sitting all afternoon chatting about life. I found out he had a real name other than The Boy and that he had so many friends because he sold them weed. He said his weed sales paid for all the wild outfits he would wear. He was telling me how much he loved shoes and had every version of Air Jordan's ever made. I told him about my weed cookies and that I had a secret obsession with Air Jordan's myself, so we had a lot in common."

walking back from school. He had his backpack on and I was getting the baby out of the car. Just as I saw him, I thought, 'maybe he can water my hanging baskets'". I asked him.

He was all in. I invited him over and showed him where the watering can was and I told him to water them twice a day."

"Right." Zac chimes in. "During this same time, I had noticed Krystal. I had noticed that she had a baby and a husband and a super nice house. She seemed really young to have all that. Also, Krystal was not a typical first-time mom. She would carry her baby around wearing high heel shoes.

I noticed that she had a lot of friends who came by her house. At first, I thought it was because the baby was born. After a while, I got a little curious as to what was going on next door." Zac explains. "A lot of people would come grab something off her front porch and take off without knocking on the door. A reverse delivery, of sorts. She had housekeepers and gardeners. That seemed really posh to me because my grandpa was extremely frugal. He wouldn't pay anyone to do anything around our house. He always told me that he spent all his money on sending me to private school." Zac laughed.

social spectrum. There were cheerleaders with nicknames like "Bambi" on their sweatshirts. There were gangster-looking kids with big gold chains and white tennis shoes. They usually drove cars and were clearly older than 'The Boy.' There were nerdy-looking girls with pigtails and eyeglasses who came to visit. All his friends were super random." I take a pause to start unwrapping pounds of butter wrappers to put into the water as it was boiling now.

Zac chimes in, "yeah, I still have random friends." He laughs as he gives me a punch in the side of the shoulder.

"It's true, we are random friends, that's why I want to tell Jude our story. My best friends are always the most random ones. I mean, I met Jude because I plowed into him on the sidewalk! That's pretty random!"

Jude laughs, "That was random! How did you two start being friends as a middle schooler and a new mom?. I'm intrigued."

"Right. So, it was summer time and we were going out of town for a week. I was worried that my hanging pots in the front would go dry while we were gone. I had parked in front of my house one day and got out of the car, just as 'The Boy' was

Jude seems slightly annoyed by Zac's comments. "We met when Sophia and my son started Kindergarten together." Jude explains.

"Oh yea, you are the other writer she talks about." Zac's memory is triggered.

Jude smiles, "Yeah, I am the writer." He seems pleased.

I give Jude a little back story about Zac and I.

"Jude, Zac and I used to be neighbors. I moved in next door to his grandpa's house when Sophia was a baby. Zac was in middle school. He was raised by his grandparents. His grandpa only referred to him as "The Boy". 'The Boy's' outlandish outfits caught my attention first, I remember a pink collared polo shirt paired with pink sweatpants, complete with pink Chuck Taylors. It was as if each day of the week, he had a color scheme. It was fun to watch when I was at home with a new baby."

Zac and I are synchronistically tending to the large pots. It was clear we had done this many times before. I continue, "I started to notice he always had lots of friends stopping by. I know, teens all have friends, but most teenagers I've encountered, have friends that dress and act like each other. 'The Boy's' friends were different. They criss-crossed the front door. He comes in with his oversized sweat-pants. The pockets seem to be weighing down the waist because they are full of a janitor-sized-ring of keys and an overstuffed wallet. The outlines of both were readily apparent in the jogging pant pockets. His tee shirt was oversized. It was adorned with a large gold chain. His shoes are Nike Air Flight 89's. His Jean Paul Gaultier cologne preceded his hug. I'm standing at my kitchen counter and Jude is sitting on a stool at my kitchen island.

"Haaaaauh!" I'm trying to say hi, but Zac's hug took my breath away. He squeezed me in a big bear hug that took me off my feet. He drops me back down on the ground in a big friendly way.

"Alrighty! It looks like you already got started, I was worried you lost track of time and started do-ing something crazy like writing." Zac teases me all the time. Jude could tell that Zac was very comfort-able in my house. He started opening up my fridge and helping himself to a large glass of milk.

"Zac, this is my friend Jude. Jude, this is Zac." I say.

"How long have you known Krystal? Zac says, "I've never heard her talk about you before."

simultaneously dragon lifetimes downloaded into my collective memory. I imagined in my head that I still had my dragon tail if I thought about it hard enough.

"Of course you're a dragon." Jude does a funny little giggle because he just imagined me in his mind with a dragon tail on. He almost wondered if he was seeing things....

I am getting out two industrial-sized pots and all the other supplies that go into this process. It's a pretty simple process, but there are a few points where I need help. I do such large batches, it takes a few extra hands to pull it off without burning myself. I rarely have any trouble finding helpers. In fact, most of my friends will ask me when butter day is and they will just come hang out with me. They get high in the living room while the butter is brewing. We have so many funny conversations about things that are not happening.

It's a ton of fun, I love my cookie business. I meet loads of interesting people and have such deep conversations with all sorts of personalities. I think it's fun that Jude is getting a sneak peek into my crazy life.

Just then, my front door opens with some GUSTO. A power to be reckoned with--Zac walks through my my cousins. He told me he had a gift for me and it would help him in his business, it is a very symbiotic relationship. See, his weed growing endeavors were exploding. He had a green thumb. But, getting rid of the clippings was difficult because you can't put it in City compost bins because marijuana is illegal. So, to make a long story short, he drops off trash bags full of weed clippings every month on my front porch. I boil it down to make butter and then I bake chocolate chip cookies out of it. The cookies are really popular. I sell them for $5 each. It's my side hustle."

"So, you sell houses and weed cookies. Now I get why you do interior design! It bridges your business and creative sides. I knew you were cool." Jude says. He looks a little flabbergasted as we walk into my house.

"Oh, so *now* I'm cool." I tease, "Haven't I been cool this whole time?" I'm genuinely wondering.

"Totally, but ever since the first day I met you, you keep surprising me. Like, every story you tell me is not what I was expecting." He explains. "You are quite a fascinating and mythical creature."

"I'm a dragon." I explain. I suddenly knew that I was a dragon in one of my lifetimes. It's like, as if the words uttered out of my mouth while once a month. She gets the entire neighborhood high. Most of the neighbors have no idea what house it's coming from. Krystal makes weed butter and the smell is amazing, I swear I get high just walking out my door! I like to keep the windows closed because I don't want the kids to come home and think I'm smoking a joint in the house." Anne makes a dramatic motion to walk away and waves her hand.

"Have fun you guys." she says walking away.

Jude turns to me and is smiling, "So, you bake edibles!" he sounds excited. "I love edibles! Ever since I stopped drinking. I've found them hard to come by though. Now I have my source!"

"I am a source!" I tell him!

I explain the whole background of my 'secret' business, "I've been making weed cookies since about the time Sophia was born. The surfer didn't like me smoking weed after she was born, but I really used weed as a medicine. Even my psychic told me not to stop using weed, it comes up in my cards as my medicine. It makes me more calm. I'm very high strung and sometimes I don't know when to slow down, so weed makes me naturally more calm. I didn't think the surfer's judgment of weed was fair, so I was complaining about this dilemma to one of listens in. She knows exactly what I'm talking about.

Jude looks bewildered, "So, what is this 'work'?" he asks with his fingers as quotation marks.

"Oh, he doesn't know what he's getting himself into?" Anne plays along and suddenly becomes quite dramatic like she is going to let him in on a big secret. "Today is butter day!!" Anne says excitedly.

"Butter day?" Jude looks disappointed in the 'secret' so far.

"Yep, today is butter day. The 'trash' got dropped off on my porch yesterday, so I'm ready to go. I already went to Costco yesterday for all of the supplies." I explain.

"So, I have like one hour before I need to close up all my windows then?" Anne asks seriously.

"Yeah, the smell will start wafting outside around 11:00" I look at my phone to gauge the time.

"It's my favorite day of the month!" Anne says excitedly, "Don't be surprised if I start gardening in your yard this afternoon" Anne and I start laughing.

Anne looks at Jude and she says, "You are going to have such a fun afternoon. Krystal does this about into." I warn him. I can tell that he thinks I'm kidding, but I'm not. I'm not a very "normal" person when it comes to my extracurricular activities. Only my closest friends know my "secret life".

Actually, I don't know what he is thinking he is getting into, but I know he will be surprised by where his day takes him.

We encountered Anne on the sidewalk just in front of my house. Anne pauses and gives me one of those, who's-that-guy? looks. I decided that I better introduce her to Jude. "Oh, there's my neighbor." I say to Jude.

"Hey Anne," I say casually as she gets closer to us. "This is my friend Jude, he is going to help me today." I explain. Jude looks at me with a questioning glance.

"Ok, just so I know when to go outside, what time are you starting your 'work' today? Anne asks using her fingers to show the quotation marks. Now I can tell Jude is really wondering what my 'work' is. I try to keep the mystery going for a few more moments.

"Oh yeah, Zac is going to help us too. The extra hands will make light work of it." I explain as Anne and sudden it came to me, but I'm confident in my decision and I'm very excited for what this will bring me. I think I'll be able to focus on my writing in that tiny town. There are only about 2,000 people in Westport. I think that sounds quaint." I ramble on with excitement.

"I think that sounds dreamy." Jude says. "What are you doing right now?"

"Like, right now, right now?" I answer with a question.

"Yeah, Drei is at school all day and I have nothing planned. What are you doing right now?" Jude asks again.

"I'm planning on going back home and 'working'" I explain with my fingers as my quotation marks. I'm wondering what Jude is asking of me?

I have some 'work' to do, but I don't exactly feel like explaining all my work to him (it's a very long story) and I usually talk to him about imaginary stories, not always real life things.

"Well, do you mind if I come hang out for a while?" He asks.

"Sure. I'm totally cool if you come back to my house, but you have no idea what you are getting yourself

CHAPTER 7

MY 'SECRET' LIFE

"I've hardly gotten to know you and I heard you are moving" Jude says on our now ritualistic walk to school.

"What?! Word travels fast. I'm not even sure my husband knows yet." I joke. I'm shocked he has heard we are moving. I've told Meg and Anne.

Hmmmm.

Anyway, it is a fact and I know I'll be moving soon.

"Well, the kids know. They are the ones who told me" Jude explains.

"Ahh, that makes me feel better. Yes, I did tell the kids." I admit. "Yeah, we are going to move to Westport. I've had a complete epiphany of where my life needs to go right now. It's crazy how fast

all be happy then. I will have my family and he will have his ocean.

Sublime.

Or so I think.

where I was and I wasn't sure exactly why. This process of relocating could help me realign.

Perhaps some unknown questions from some unknown answers could become clearer with a new perspective.

I almost forgot about the strange meeting with Drei. As I trotted up the street, now out of breath from running, I saw my house with the fence in front.

Who did I see sitting there?

Crooked Beak.

Why was he there?

I felt like he was protecting me from something, but it creeped me out. I burst in the house announcing to Meg and the kids that we were moving to the beach.

"Is the surfer cool with this?" Asks Meg. She looks skeptical.

"He will be" I declare. I know in my heart of hearts there is one thing the surfer loves and that is the water. It's almost sad, I'm pretty sure he loves the ocean more than his family. Oh well, I think, we will

Two balls of light, or swirls of energy appeared in front of me!

Something within me knew I was looking at myself from another dimension; the pulsing energies were my own. They were torn apart yet I knew together they could be so much more powerful. A voice asked, "How do I reignite my own fire?" The smaller of the two balls of light was weakened, and the larger floated away towards the West. My mind realized what my heart knew: that bright light of my dreams was actually me and I was ARG, I was the power within the power that was calling me.

I cracked the cosmic egg of my existence and I knew there was so much more for me to learn. I was suddenly embarking on a quest. I got up from the overturned log I was sitting on and I ran all the way home. Yes, I ran. I don't typically run, but I had this revived energy inside of me, I felt like I could burst with love.

I knew it wouldn't be hard to convince the surfer to move to the beach. We had purchased a property out in Westport years prior and it had just sat there, basically a depreciating asset.

This seemed like a natural change for us. Besides, I could feel change coming on, I wasn't happy *some garbage on the street; just do something really small that might make someone's day a little better. Sometimes it is the little things that actually do matter...wait, its always the little things that are the truth.*

Who knows how long I walked and thought. At some point, I decided to sit and think.

I sat,

I sat,

I sat,

I sat

and I sat.

Unwinding.. I felt myself slowing down and letting the noise of this fast life slip off of me. My mind calmed and I felt my heart beating again. Unwinding...stillness. I took my mind off of my vision, and looked without intention of seeing.

All at once, I saw sparkles in the distance, the water of Elliott Bay in front of me glistening like I had never seen before. The sun peaked out and I noticed dragonflies buzzing around my head.

KRYSTAL KELLEY

Sometimes we think we know people. Sometimes people surprise us & we don't know them anymore. Oftentimes this is good, but there are times people disappoint. Disappointment is far harder to deal with than when we are surprised in a good way. Good surprises us & brings us up to a new level... often to a level of love. It's positive.

On the other side, when people surprise us in a negative way, we begin to hate, to loose perspective and trust in our own judgement, we get resentful that we trusted a truth that doesn't exist. That resentment can lead to a lot of hate, but deeper than hate...to wanting that trust back...which is what I believe leads to revenge. This is strong & evil. People will go to great lengths to regain what they believe is truth...even if others have to hurt...but it doesn't matter because so much hurt has already been caused to us prior...the hurt will cause the truth to prevail....but the bottom line is that it doesn't, it causes more hurt because truth is buried in the hate.

What could change this awful spiral? Surprise each other with positive actions. Even little things like a smile can make a person's day. Surprise people with good. Offer a piece of gum to your sister or brother; Tell someone they have something in their teeth (precedes embarrassment); say hi; pick up

Meg, I don't know how I could do it all. I don't think Jude has met the surfer. I call him that because he doesn't think of anything except surfing. His head must be full of water!" I make a bad joke and neither of us laugh.

I can't tell what is going to happen next. I feel my energy completely drained. I suddenly feel really tired. I want to get home. I look at the time, "Drei, it was really nice chatting, but I have another meeting I need to get to. Can I buy your coffee?" I offer.

"Oh, thank you. You don't need to do that." Drei says.

"I'm happy to" I lie. I pay the tab, grab my book and walk home. I said no good bye to Drei and didn't look back in her direction. She was not worth my energy. I had to go recharge somehow.

A nap?

A walk?

What the fuck just happened?

I feel so drained, I want to nap, but my intuition is telling me something else. I decide to go on a walk. I have a dialogue with myself as I walk:

She seems unamused. I don't blame her, it's a bit of a boring story. It's only the work I do, it's not my soul work. I definitely don't feel comfortable explaining my soul work to this dark force.

"Hmm, interesting. So, I hear our kids are in the same kindergarten class. Do you have other kids?" Drei seems to be interrogating me now.

"Yes, another daughter, she is two years younger than Sophia." I answer. I don't need to ask about her kids because I know all about them. Jude fills me in all the time on our walks to and from the school.

"Are you married?" Drei prods.

"Um, yeah. Of course, I'm married to their dad." I tried to explain, but my marriage always felt less connected than my bad business partnership. We weren't emotionally wrapped up, we were convenient partners for now. Again, I didn't need to explain any matters of the heart with Drei.

"Oh, I didn't know you were married." Drei explained. "Jude never mentioned the girls' dad."

"Yeah, he travels a lot. My nanny, Meg is my rock these days. Trying to juggle a busy work schedule with family life is really challenging. If I didn't have last sentence strangely and looked me directly into my eyes.

I shivered. I remembered her dark presence as she had shadowed my reading page earlier. I desperately wanted to change the subject. "So, how did this voo-doo metamorphosis into interior design?" I half smile, hoping to turn this meeting around.

She glared at me smugly and says, "Well, once I had kids, I decided not to pursue my dark arts anymore. I went back to school for interior design. I'm almost done with my degree. Where did you get your interior design degree?" She asks, but still not friendly.

"Oh, I don't have an actual interior design degree. I have a degree in communications and international studies from U-dub, my undergraduate studies had a focus on Canada. I learned interior design with my business partner through the trials and many, many errors of doing it ourselves. My business partner and I had creative differences, so she started her own separate business a few years ago. Now I run my staging business with my employees. My theory with interior design is twofold. First, I try to make the space better than before I arrived. Second, I believe good design always allows for somewhere to set your drink, no matter where one sits." I explain my work to Drei.

KRYSTAL KELLEY

creatively challenging people who stretch my mind into new dimensions. I have zero interest in sleeping with him! I'm happy to hear what she has to say.

My mind slips into a small imagination bubble. Perhaps I've been reading too many graphic novels, but the Sandman series by Neil Gaiman has invaded my psyche. The two of us, Drei and I, are sitting at the coffee shop and we are suddenly hand drawn, Sandman-Esque characters. It's POWER vs. FORCE. I'm this light power and she is a dark raven. I personify POWER and she personifies FORCE. It's a battle.

"………Native American heritage" I realize Drei is running down an oral history to me of her life-before-Jude story. She must have noticed I wasn't listening because she repeated the last sentence again, "So, my parents are Native American and when I was a teenager, I was really gothic" she explained.

"I could see you being gothic." I intertwine into her story, just so she knows I'm listening and to make sure I keep listening. It seems as if I'm battling a wandering mind today.

"I got into the darkest of dark magic. I spent more time as a teen talking to ouija boards than I did talking to live people. I was really into voo-doo. I used to make dolls and *I'd use them*." She says this

Just then, a dark shadow walked in front of my sun-filled book and stopped, looming over me. Startled out of my deep reading material, I cautiously look over my shoulder.

"Oh, hey Drei!" I try to act like I didn't forget we were meeting. Luckily, I just happened to go read at the coffee shop at the same time I had told Jude I'd meet Drei for coffee. I neglected to put the appointment in my calendar, which means I completely forgot. I was saved by the fact that I scheduled it to fit into my likely day.

I set my book down. "Have a seat, it's fun to, um, socialize with you" I grope for the words...I'm not sure if I like her body language. 'What is this meeting for anyway?' I think to myself.

"Yeah, I wanted to tell you a little bit about myself." Drei was abrupt and it seemed this wasn't going to be the friendliest of meetings. She wasn't being confrontational, but she was cold. I figured out right away, this was one of those jealous, **bitch-stay-the-fuck-away-from-my-husband** kind of meetings.

"Hehe" I giggled out loud. Oh shit! Did I just do that? "I would love to hear all about your perspective" I say out loud, no explanation for my giggle at all. I have no interest in this woman's man, I just like

CHAPTER 6

POWER AND FORCE

I was sitting at Freshy's Coffee, unexpectedly engrossed in a book suggested to me by Jude. "Power vs. Force" it was called. It was a fascinating explanation of energy transfer. The author gives the reader tools to navigate decision-making. Powerful decisions basically have a win/win/win result, while a forceful action or decision has negative effects on someone or something. I think of it like this: if you have an egg and something cracks it from the outside, the egg dies. That's Force. If something cracks it from the inside, life begins. That's Power.

The way the author, Dr. Hawkins broke down power and force, it made perfect sense in my mind. In fact, I felt as if I was a powerful thinker. Empathy floats high in my awareness and I prefer lighter, more upbeat patterns. I mean, we all have a dark side, it just matters how you balance the light with the dark.

"Did you see his feet? They are kind of zig zag. And his beak is totally crooked. It's a good name for him." Anne says.

"Yeah, Eloise came up with that one." I laugh. "I gotta get to work. See you later." I shove the last bag into Anne's stuffed car and get into mine. As I'm driving away, I wave goodbye to Crooked Beak.

"Haha, we should double check. I just can't stand the clutter, so I start throwing everything on my porch. Sometimes, I throw away things we need." Anne confesses.

"Hmm, I haven't noticed." I joke. Laughing to myself about Anne's predicament.

"Have you noticed that crow that is stalking you?" Anne asks me as we are carting bags to her car.

"Yeah, it's Crooked Beak. He's my new friend." I explain nonchalantly.

"Well, he certainly likes you. When you are gone, he sits and waits all day on the fence. When you walk into your house, he flies up to the porch, then hops across your roof. It's like he is literally following you. When you walk out to your backyard, he watches you from the back fence. I've been mesmerized by his loyalty for the past few days, it's remarkable." Anne seems mystified.

"It certainly is strange. Maybe he is protecting me from something." I theorize. As soon as I say it, I wonder if I might be right. I wonder what or who I need protection from. I really do think Crooked Beak is some sort of mystical warrior. "I can tell he has battled demons before." I say to Anne.

KRYSTAL KELLEY

happened in a funny way." I giggle thinking about how random that was.

"Well, it was certainly the most entertaining evening we have had in awhile" He admits. "Drei wanted me to ask you if you will have coffee with her tomorrow?"

"Sure, what about 10 o'clock at Freshys? I'm planning on working from there anyway. I'll be there until at least two." Freshy's is my work-from-home-away-from-home coffee shop. It also happens to be a few blocks from both of our houses.

"Sounds perfect. I'll let Drei know!" Jude waves goodbye.

As I walk back in my front gate, I see the crow again. I've now also named him Crooked Beak in my mind.

"Hey!" Anne yells at me from her open car door. She sends her kids to private school, so they have to drive to school. "Can you help me carry all these donation bags to the car?" Anne asks me.

"Sure," I say. "But, are you sure you haven't put your cat or anything else important in them?" I tease her.

CRACKING THE CRYSTAL CODE

feathers are topsy-turvy too" I notice and announce it to the girls. I feel like he is a friend.

"I'm going to name him Crooked Beak" announces Eloise as she waves goodbye to the crow.

We laugh as we are walking down the street to school. We see Jude at our street corner. We were late today, so I'm surprised to see him.

"Typical Monday" I say to Jude as we walk up to the corner. "I helped my neighbor find a wayward shoe this morning, so we are late."

Jude laughs, "We slept in. Nothing altruistic about our tardiness."

"Thanks for coming to our house on Friday. Drei really liked you." Jude says.

"It was fun. Drei is interesting, it was nice to meet her. I didn't get to chat with her too much." I say back.

"Drei can be a bit cold at first. She doesn't warm up to people very easily" Jude explains. "But she thought your fishnet stocking situation was hilarious."

"I wasn't really trying to be funny." I explain. "I was expecting to change incognito, but then it just because she would buy her neighbor lotto tickets every week. I wrote an offer that day and Anne brought it with that evening's lottery drawing. That's how we became neighbors.

We looked through two bags each and I finally found a small green sneaker. "Is this it?" I ask.

"Yes! Thank you! You are a lifesaver" Anne runs in her front door and I can hear her three kids making a commotion inside.

I turn to head back to my house. 'I hope the kids are ready for school' I think. The same crow is perched on top of my porch as I walk in my front door. I notice, but have no time to process any thought about it.

The kids are not ready for school. Eloise is being a mermaid in the bath and Sophia is drawing. I frantically get them dressed and we head out the front door—late for school.

"Mom, look! We have a crow friend." Eloise announces as we pass by that crow sitting on our fence. "Look," she says again, "he has a crooked beak."

I look at the crow and sure enough, his top beak is bent upward in a very crooked way. "His tail

Monday morning is the first time I see him. In fact, he was the first thing I saw as I drank my coffee and looked out at my front fence. A crow sitting on my fence, not an entirely strange occurrence, except for the way he was looking at me.

I open my front door and walk onto my oversized porch. In fact, this front porch was the primary reason I bought this house. I sit down on my cozy outdoor couch. I sip my coffee and continue to watch this crow watch me. I'm a little surprised he hasn't flown off yet. "Good morning!" I say out loud to him.

"Huh?" Says a voice to my left. I look over and there is my neighbor, Anne on her front porch rifling through a bag. Anne was always donating bags of clothes. I often wondered how she had any clothes left judging by the bags on her front porch.

"Good Morning" Anne says to me. She must have thought I had said good morning to her. She continues, "I accidentally placed one of Thomas' shoes in a donation bag. Now I can't find the pair in these bags and he has no shoes to wear to school." She looks stressed.

I laugh. "Do you want help?" I ask her. Anne and I are friends. In fact, I had told Anne that I liked her neighbor's front porch one day. She told me that the owner needed to sell her house. Anne knew

KRYSTAL KELLEY

CHAPTER 5

CROOKED BEAK

Awakening.
Epiphanies.
Balls of energy appearing before me,
follow them.
Purging old beliefs, feelings and unhealthy habits.
Purging.
Purging.
Purge into the garden,
swirling into one of those dark feelings:
Hate, anger, jealousy and fear.
combatting those inner demons,
shaken to my core.
Transmute the dark into light.
Honesty is key to making this story real.
This is my gift,
my calling to write.
My creative way to share,
To make the world more beautiful than before.
I return to Mother Earth,
the gifts she gives me.
She provides life,
She recycles the dark for us;
a filter in her soil
gives birth to beautiful flowers.
My writing is blossoming.
my true cosmic code calling—
from the depths of my soul.
Lifetimes of memories sprouting,
channeling through me.
A waterfall flows onto this crystal screen,
I call it my life.

It's a giant prism, like a diamond pulsing. I realize this prizm is inside my being, beating like my heart with a pulsing light. ARG is with me at all times.

There is a gentle voice. It is of a woman. She says, "A-R-G has deep meaning. 'A' stands for the Alien aspect of life. The out-of-this-world events that are unexplainable. They are the magic, like a fungus dust creatively powers the Alien part of ARG.

The "R" is for Robot. The mundane, minutiae of everyday life that must get done. Commitments are met by the Robot inside of me. I am you and you are me.

The "G" is the God part. The meta-physical, spiritual side that one only knows within themselves. Once enlightened, a perfect balance of A-R-G within this prism, there is peace, love and harmony."

Her voice fades away and I am laying in a dense forest. Fairies with golden wings wake me up with a bright, white light.

leggings down right in front of everyone. I slip the boots back on and announce, "I'm ready to go dancing! Thank you for the nice evening and it was great to meet all of you." I stuff my leggings in my coat pocket and give a wave as I walk out the door.

I can hear laughter and lively conversation as I get into the Uber waiting for me.

Kate's birthday is full of dancing and karaoke. I get home late. Meg and her boyfriend are watching a movie.

"How was your night?" Meg asks, looking at me peculiarly. "Wait, were you wearing that when you left tonight?"

"Ha! No, it's a funny story," I explain as I pull my leggings out of my coat pocket. "To make a long story short, I undressed in front of everyone at Jude's house." I giggle.

"I can only imagine!" Meg says. "The kids were great. We are going to get going, it's late."

"Goodnight!" I say as they walk out the door.

ARG visits my dreamspace again.

"I missed something," Drei says.

"What's so funny?" She asks me.

"Well, I had a wardrobe predicament today. I was coming to your house tonight, but I'm also going dancing and probably karaoke after." I explain. "I didn't want to wear a going 'out' dress to a staying 'in' night."

"Oooh, that is a predicament" Drei agrees. "You picked out a cute outfit" she says looking me up and down.

"Well, I haven't shapeshifted yet" I say and giggle again. Now, I'm kind of excited to show her my 'genius' wardrobe idea.

Drei just looks at me.

I reach inside my black cowboy boot and pull my footless legging up my leg revealing my fishnets. I don't realize it, but everyone is watching me. I look up, my face turns red. I'm a little embarrassed that I'm all of a sudden the center of attention.

"Ha! That's a funny idea" Jude is laughing. "You are one strange chick!"

Just then, my Uber arrives. My embarrassment fell away quickly. I kick my boots off and pull my

KRYSTAL KELLEY

"How do you do all that with two children?" she asks dumbfounded.

"I'm efficient." I giggle "and I'm very busy."

"Hmm, Jude said I would like you, but I didn't believe him. I'm surprised, but he was right. You are cool. I want to talk about interior design with you sometime. Maybe we can get coffee." Drei says.

"That would be nice." I say, thinking that perhaps her coldness was just an insecurity and maybe she just takes time to warm up. Drei pours me a glass of wine and I take it into the dining room to hang out with the more-friendly crowd.

The friends Jude and Drei have invited are nice. Conversations range from discussions about the super bowl halftime entertainment scheduled this year to pot cookies.

The time went by fast. "Oh dear, it's 9:30 already!" I exclaim when I look at my phone.

"What time is your friend's party?" Jude asks

"10. I need to order my Uber." I say. "It's downtown and Kate is one of my best friends. I don't want to be too late." I chuckle thinking about my fishnets under my leggings.

first impression is not so great, but my curiosity is tickling me. I got up and walked into the kitchen.

Drei seems surprised at my forward behavior, but everyone else seems totally cool with me. For as warm as Jude seems, Drei is like ice. It makes sense, I suppose; opposites attract, yin and yang. A lot of couples are like that, but I'm curious to know more about her.

Drei and her friend stop talking as I walk into the kitchen. "Hey Drei, It's really nice to finally meet you. I walk with Jude everyday to school with the kids, I'm surprised this is the first time I'm meeting you." I say in a friendly way.

"Yeah," Drei explains, "I'm going back to school studying interior design. I'm going to be a designer." She says 'designer' with a snobby undertone.

"That's what I do." I say cheerfully back. She looks at me, surprisingly interested now.

"Jude said you were a writer." she seems confused.

"I am a writer, that's my soul job. My day job is being a real estate agent and I own a design company in SODO with a business partner. Most of my design work is new construction. This city is growing so fast, it's a profitable niche." I explain.

KRYSTAL KELLEY

I walk to Jude's house, it's only a few blocks away. I knock on the door. A woman with jet black hair opens the door. She is dressed in a long dress, it's the shape of a potato sack. "You must be Krystal." she says smugly as she opens the door wider and motions for me to come inside. "I'm Draven, but you can call me Drei" she says.

"Nice to finally meet you, Drei. I've heard so much about you from Jude." I try to make small talk, but she walks into the kitchen.

"Hey, Krystal! I'm so glad you could make it." Jude cheerily greets me. He is standing at the dining table with a guitar in his hand, his leg is propped up on the chair. Some other people I don't recognize are sitting around the table and they all seem more cheery than Drei, so I sit down at the table. Jude introduces everyone to me. I don't remember any of their names, but it's jovial at the table. I see Drei in the kitchen talking to another woman through the open kitchen door.

"Oh, I'm so rude." Jude announces. "Krystal, can I get you something to drink?"

"No, thank you." I say to him. "I'll make myself at home and grab something in the kitchen." I'm really curious what his other half is like. So far, her

CRACKING THE CRYSTAL CODE

dress with fishnet stockings. I think teal will look awesome next to the red dress I know Kate will have on.

My predicament is this: Before Kate's party, I'm supposed to go to Jude's house. I have never met his wife and I know it is a mellow evening "in" that I was invited to. I can't show up in fishnet stockings and a teal dress, I feel like it would make the wrong statement, especially to his wife. *But* I'm planning to get an Uber from his house to Kate's party and I don't want to change in an Uber car. I don't want to stop at home to change because that is right at the girls' bedtime and Meg will be putting them down. If I walk in the door, it will disrupt her entire routine.

I meditate on this situation and I have what I think is a genius idea. I put on my fishnet stockings, then I put black leggings over the stockings. Next, I put a hooded zip-up over my dress to downplay the cute dress. I look in the mirror. It's a cute outfit, but not too cute for night "in" and underneath, I'm ready to go "out".

Proud of my solution, I kiss my daughters good night and say bye to my nanny, Meg. Sometimes, I feel like Meg is my roommate. Her boyfriend is visiting and watching the girls with her. They will have a great evening.

KRYSTAL KELLEY

CHAPTER 4

WHAT SHOULD I WEAR?!

Thoughts are patterns.
Identify the patterns your mind makes.
Interpret the form,
Your personal archetype.
Are these the same patterns you want to see in your future?
you can alter the pattern.
visualize how you want the new pattern to feel.
An altered mind is a mind edited, inspired;
An enlightened perspective.

It's Friday afternoon and it's Kate's birthday. Kate is one of my best friends and she is fancy. When she goes out, especially for her birthday, she wears red. Red lipstick, a red dress, red earrings and gold shoes. She's stunning and that is only one of the reasons why I love Kate. The real reason I love Kate is her big heart. I'm planning on wearing a teal cannot. You are the bridge, you have the deep powers of teaching and healing. The golden circle around your pupil is a crown of knowledge. Your compassion, determination and kindness guide your empathy to help others."

I listen, but don't fully understand.

I'm standing in my kitchen doing the dishes, then I'm diving into the soapy water. I'm spinning around inside the watery, holographic void, there are so many moving parts, some seem good and some seem evil. I'm groping, looking for a stepping stone. I know they are there because I've seen them from the shoreline.

I've seen these images before, but I'd rather not get wet right now. I can still make it across, swimming. I just have to find those stones in the dark water. I adjust my vision and creatively stay dry. Everything is clear and easy now.

I see the shore, like a wave of a shining essence that is all encompassing.

Bright, white light.

The following morning, on the walk to school, I shared my ARG journal with Jude. "I think you are tapping into those lost memories" Jude seems excited.

"We are having a few people over Friday night. Can you join us?" Jude asks me.

"Sure. I mean, what time? It's my friend, Kate's birthday Friday night and I was supposed to go dancing with her." I explain.

"We were thinking around 7" Jude says.

"Perfect, Kate's party doesn't start until 10, so I can stop by." I make a note in my google calendar and head off to start my work day.

I talk to Ellie, she is on her way to Costco. Then I talked to Kate. She was at Costco. While I was talking to Kate at Costco, Kate got a text of a picture of herself from her friend who was also at Costco watching her talk to me. That's how my day went.

That night, more dreams.

My dream is laid out, just like a hologram.

Projections of ARG tell me, "You are a Starseed. You personify Spiritual Knowledge and Cosmic Wisdom. Your magnificent dark blue eyes can see dimensions others

As it turns out, Aliens do exist. In fact, now I'm friends with them, well one of them. ARG is her name. Her language was easy to learn because it was embedded into my DNA. I call it 'The language of Subtleties'. I've met other wisdom keepers, shaman, medicine women in my travels since and I've heard it referred to as telepathy, psychic awareness, a living vibration of no words. I think there are many forms and ways to describe this ancient language.

ARG's channeled message to me:

Atmospheric Evolution is what we want for us all. It might seem tumultuous, remember, Mother Nature is very random. A natural order can seem out of place, only time will tell if you can find a parachute as you race through the air in freefall. If the parachute fails, resourcefulness will build your wings midair. When those wings get too heavy, gravity will collide with time and space and cushion the landing.

Creativity allows all to prevail; eternal happiness.

Gender, race, age;
all transcend to
ONE

KRYSTAL KELLEY

to reconnect the lines from my life force energy (my soul) towards my future. It was inspiring.

Somehow, I pulled that energy right up into my heart. Most people don't allow themselves to feel this sense of aliveness. It was a bit scary and felt a little out of control. However, it was also the most *in control* I had ever felt. This cosmic force exhilarated me. It projected me into my own universe where I could create my own future. I didn't belong to an artificial matrix that wanted to deconstruct my natural order. I was sent into a vortex.

My mind is reeling that evening. It's like a portal opened up in my universe and I started writing things down that I didn't know I knew. A cosmic egg of wisdom seeded in my mind somewhere was cracked open and information was flowing out of me like a burst of water. I wrote stories, poems, equations, symbols. Sometimes, a lot of the time, I couldn't even read my own writing. It's like something channeled through me onto paper. I was just a vessel. Electricity was inside of me, bursting out.

A cellular symphony was radiating from me, causing this vortex of power around me. Coincidences and "crazy" things kept happening. I couldn't make up the stories I was living.

wanted something "extra" with Jude. I didn't. I just wanted to feel inspired to write more. To actually *do* something with my writing. I wanted to publish a kid's book I had been working on about a little bird who poops art. I used to take pictures of bird poops when I'd go on long walks. They were like an organic rorschach test. My girls and all the neighbor kids loved looking at my "splats".

I was amassing quite a collection of splats. A hummingbird, a heart, a bear riding a unicycle, smily face, I had pages and pages of splats on my phone camera.

Anyway, When these cosmic vibrations began to hit my physical body, it started to resonate in the energy of original creation. At first my mind said to avoid this energy, it is weird or wrong. This is inappropriate. But, something else in me got more excited than normal to dig into my journals and start telling this "new" version of my story. It's like I was starting to draw some sort of invisible line from my past to my future and back again, like a huge infinity symbol.

Basically, I felt like I didn't care what other people thought, I'm doing this for me. All of those people's feelings are conditioned to a "right and wrong." I wanted to move beyond this conditioning

"I guess I do," Jude says humbly. "We do live in Seattle and I suppose it is possible to bump into rock stars on the street corner." He looks at me with a flirtatious glance. I roll my eyes and laugh.

Unbeknownst to me, I had become friends with a pretty famous writer. Now, I understood why one of the Kindergarten moms had asked me how I knew Jude. Everyone else knew he was a rockstar, except me. Honestly, I didn't really care. He was funny and we inspired each other to write. It didn't matter that writing wasn't my day job. Writing was my soul job. Jude confirmed that for me synchronistically.

My friendship with Jude was cosmic, our chance meeting sparked inspiration in both of us. Here is where I need to pause to explain what I've learned about creative energy. Many people confuse creative energy with sexual energy. I had clarity in my mind, but I felt that not everyone had my same sense. I have an old soul that is energized by cosmic vibrations.

Imagine, two stars in the vast universe collided. It's magical, but it can really shake things up.

Jude and I meeting, coming together, creatively to inspire each other to write, it shook up our lives a bit. I could tell by the Kindergarten moms' sideways glances on the playground, that people thought I

Jude stops walking and just stares back at me. "I think aliens do exist," he declares. "And I think you were abducted. You need to figure out how to trigger those memories." Jude gets super serious. I haven't seen this side of him before. "Krystal, my bandmates and I were in the middle of producing our next album, but I had writer's block and we had to stop production. I've been so depressed that I was letting them down. Your story and coincidence has me excited to get back home to start writing again." Jude explains. "Krystal, I'm so glad I met you, you are an inspiration. You need to NEVER stop writing." Jude says emphatically.

"Wow. Thanks! You keep talking about your bandmates. Would I know your band?" I ask Jude. We talked and texted several times every day for the past few months. "I'm embarrassed I've never really asked what you do. I mean other than write. I know writers don't make money. *I* have a day job." I giggle.

"Haha" Jude looks embarrassed too. "My day job *is* writing. I told you, I write songs."

"Oh, I thought you wrote songs for fun. I didn't think it was actually your profession. I mean, who makes a living writing??" I ask.

and my back is sore from sitting on the floor of my closet. I've been reading for hours.

I looked at the clock and realized that I had to go to school pick-up. I ran out my door so as not to be late to pick up Sophia.

At the end of my block, Jude is standing, waiting for me. "Did you find the ticket?" he asks me.

"No, but I found my journal. It's actually interesting, because there are three days missing in my entries. Back then, I was writing every day." I explain to Jude as we walk to the school together.

"Back then you wrote everyday?" Jude teases "You write everyday now too. Have you ever stopped?"

I roll my eyes.

"I texted my bandmate in Portland and he told me what day that flight was on. It was March 17th. What are the three days missing?" He asks.

"I'm fairly certain it was somewhere between March 16th to the 19th" I answered. "I know I attended the baseball game on Tuesday, March 19th, 1996. It was the Mariners vs. the Padres at 1:05pm. I went by myself, but met up with two friends, Jeff and Todd, at the game. Since I was alone, I don't have anyone else's recollection of those three days."

a notecard by my Grandpa Jay. My plane ticket showed I flew in at 5:55pm. Grandpa was really excited when I showed up in a limousine. I wish I had a picture of the smile on his face when he saw me. I'm pretty sure all their neighbors think Jay and Keka's granddaughter is some sort of movie star.

March 16th, 1996

Grandpa made me fresh squeezed orange juice this morning, it was amazing. Like drinking liquid sunshine. Then, we went to the Renaissance Festival. I went to watch a jousting match at a faire in the desert with Grandma and Grandpa. What a strange event. Everyone was dressed in medieval clothing, I felt quite out of place in a tank top, jean shorts and chuck taylors. I didn't have an iguana as a pet or anything to "fit in" there. It was fun though.

March 19th, 1996

I wrote 'PEORIA SPORTS COMPLEX, home to Seattle Mariners and San Diego Padres. 16101 N. 83rd Ave, Peoria.'

Hmm, that was odd. Judging by my journaling, I was writing everyday. Especially when I was on a trip. I realize that my neck is starting to pinch

In the morning, we walked to get breakfast. I bought it because Dustin was homeless and had no job. We went swimming in the ocean and layed in the sun all day. I just hopped on a bus back to the airport to meet Annette. Dustin went another way. On the way to meet up with Annette, I met William on the bus, who invited Annette and I to Chip 'n Dales Strip Tease! Well, what more could I have gotten out of 24 hours?

(I have no idea, but not too much more!)

I read on: There was sailing to Catalina Island on a small, 14-foot boat; surfing in Oceanside; hiking up Mt. Rainier, snowboarding down, topless; free admission to DisneyLand; taking a limousine to "Trailer Village". I wrote, *"If you ever want to feel like royalty, hire a limo driver to take you from the airport to a trailer park. It was the best $35 I had ever spent"*

Then, I found what I was looking for! My trip to Arizona when I was potentially abducted by something!

March 15th, 1996

"303 N. Lindsay Road, Mesa" I had jotted down in my notebook. "Space 46, 'Trailer Village' was handwritten on

Honolulu. My only option is to wait for the 194 to arrive. (that must have been the bus number?) I got to the gate and trip like some drunk up the escalator!

Phew! On to San Fran, barely. I slept the entire way because I had gone out to Jeff's before I left and barely got any sleep.

In Honolulu, I had 24 hours to wait for Annette, so I lazily walked around, trying to decide what in the hell I am going to do with 24 hours in a place that I am totally clueless about. By myself.

I see a guy smoking who had a backpack and he looked just as aimless as me. I didn't smoke, but I asked him for a cigarette. Later, I gave it back to him. Dustin was his name.

We hitchhiked to Waikiki with a guy named Brad in an open air jeep. Then we sat on the beach with ⅕ of Jim Bean (yes, I wrote Bean, not Beam) we asked someone to buy for us outside a store. Then, I slept on a park bench, Dustin slept on the ground. I shivered all night and I thought I was going to die a number of times, but it was fun. (How did I think that was fun?)

brought in pack in my mouth, then drank a swig of rum. Everyone else did the same thing and we laughed so hard.

We went back to the beach and slept for a while. After a while, we walked back to that Oriental restaurant. They were really cool, so we told them we felt bad we got drunk in their parking lot earlier. They gave us our meal for free.

At the end of the trip, Marshal declares he is going to write a book called "A Little Sompin-Sompin in San Francisco." I can't wait to read that story!

I look at my phone and check the time, I've been reading my journals all morning. I eat some lunch and then dive back in:

12/17/1996 (I'm 19 years old)

Hawaii Trip

It all started Tuesday Morning, early. Amy Rose couldn't drive me to the airport because she forgot she had to work. So, I take Joe Metro. (That's the public bus, I didn't take the bus much in college, so I know this was a challenge for me). I need to transfer downtown to get to Sea-Tac, but the damn bus was late! What now? If I miss my flight to San Francisco, I will miss my flight to me say here that this is the Ghetto of SF. That night we heard squealing wheels, 2 gunshots, sirens and police with flash lights went running past our tent--and we lived! Amazing (what, for real, were we thinking?!?!)

San Francisco didn't seem like a safe place to camp, so we took the Greyhound to Santa Cruz. The beach we ended up at was like a dog beach or something. This one dog, Boss, was a pit bull and most annoying. When we were playing frisbee, he would chase it and steal it. You know how owners match their dogs? Well, Boss' owner was perfect for him.

We found a park across the street from the beach and pitched our tent. We awoke to someone yelling at us "You guys better move that tent before the cops show up!"

We walked 5 miles to another beach. It was cold and rainy. So, we had a bright idea to walk BACK 5 miles to town. Marshal was 21, so he bought a fifth of rum. We went to Taco Bell and bought one, bottomless coke. We sat in Taco Bell, passing around one cup of coke for hours. We walked out of there SO drunk. We finished the bottle of rum in a parking lot of an oriental restaurant. (I can't believe I used that word, 'oriental'.) I didn't want to drink straight rum, so I put powdered lemonade that Rachel had

$100 plane tickets, roundtrip. *Rachel* (my roommate), her friend *Marshal* and *Adam* (My boyfriend's roommate) ended up going. *Tyler* (my boyfriend at the time) was supposed to go, but I made him REALLY mad, so we just thought Marshall could use Tyler's ticket. They told us it was $120 to change the ticket. But, then, Teddy, this nice ticketing lady let Marshal get on plane anyway. It was a miracle!

I had a bright idea in SF. We went to the police station. Marshal filed a false police report, saying that he, "Tyler" had lost his wallet on the beach. We all signed as witnesses. The copy of the police report allowed Marshal to fly back as "Tyler" with no questions asked. Outside of the police station, a prostitute asked Marshal if he wanted a little "sempūr-sempūr".

We tried to call Dave, who was Adam's friend. Dave was a high school friend of Adam's. He was going to Berkley and was supposed to be our lodging for the weekend. Adam came back from the pay phone looking lost. Apparently, Dave had flown to Seattle for the long weekend and we didn't have a place to stay. Luckily, Marshal had brought a tent.

We went to Golden Gate Park and played on Ocean Beach until dark. We pitched our tent in Golden Gate Park. Yet

San Francisco, May 23 1996 (I was a freshman at UU)

Memorial Weekend

My eyes were burning and my throat was starting to hurt. An American, sitting next to me, started yelling at the smoker. Him, yelling in English. Her, yelling back in French. The situation got worse every hour, at least 3 cigarettes. It was incessant. I wasn't mad though. The American next to me was fuming. He finally said, "I dare you to light up ONE MORE CIGARETTE!!" He was red in the face. She answered smugly, with some French phrase I didn't recognize. Then, she flippantly, lit another cigarette and blew the smoke right at his red face.

That was it! He launched at her like a beast. The flight attendants tackled the man as he was attempting to punch the woman. I was caught in the crossfire and was trampled by the commotion. They put the American in handcuffs and he sat at the back of the plane. The French woman continued smoking her cigarettes, only to take a break as the service cart rolled around. I just sat there, rubbing my elbow that was surely to have a huge bruise on it.

That was just the flight there. I could write a book about that whole trip.

The next day, I crossed this page with a big "X" and wrote over the top of the entry, *"HE'S A NERD"*

Apparently, Jasn and I didn't have a very long relationship. I laugh at my seven-year-old self. Ironically, my husband (and soulmate) is named Jason. Talk about foreshadowing!

I'm beginning to wonder if I write or if I channel the future?

I keep reading, all afternoon, I read journal after journal. I realized that I am kind of an odd person. I do really random things with my time.

April 10, 1993 (I was 15 years old)

My Trip To France.

The airport in France looks like The Jetson's, so high tech with moving sidewalks. Fools you right when you arrive because the cities are sold old. On the flight there, I sat on the edge of the smoking section. (OMG! I forgot they used to allow people to smoke in designated areas on international flights back then.) *A French woman, sitting behind me, was chain smoking. For hours!*

The first entry:

1984, October 1

(I wonder how I made an entry before my Grandpa gifted me the book? Clearly, I didn't know the exact date. I'm guessing I knew it was October and 1984, but not the day. I'm also wondering why my Grandpa gave me this book in October?? My birthday is in May and it's not Christmastime. I have no recollection of Grandpa randomly giving me presents. I do remember that my Grandpa was a mindful and thoughtful person. He had a kind heart. I loved walking to the store with him and as he lit his cigarette, he would say every single time, "Don't tell Keka, this is our little secret. And don't tell your mom I gave you candy." Then, he would hand me a piece of candy. Grandpa and I would walk along, him smoking his cigarette; and me, sucking on my candy. As we walked, he would tell me wonderful stories.)

Ahh memory lane. Here was that entry from 1984:

2 grade I hade a boy friand and his name is Jasn. I love him very mush. I learned math. And I lend to kalre. I like school. Vary much I Like it so much. The Math. I hav a lots of frinds.

any way you could find out what the actual date was?" Jude asks me.

"What?!! That's crazy! A few weeks ago, I did NOT believe in aliens, now I skeptically think I was abducted and you are telling me your bandmate says he was abducted in the **same** timeframe in the **same** area? This really is a coincidence!! I think I kept my Mariner's ticket to the spring training game. I could look at what date was on the ticket. It happened the morning before the game, so it should be the same date. I'll look today for the ticket." We waive bye to each other and I hurry home to look for a fifteen year old game ticket.

At home, I can't find the ticket, but I dig out all of my old journals. I spent the entire day reading through years worth of writing.

10-4-84

In my grandpa's handwriting, *"To Krystal FROM Grand ma and PaPa Jay"*.

In my handwriting, on the other page reads:

Krystal Kelley's Book. Dear Diary. I am 7.

"Since that party, I've been researching other people's stories about alien abductions and I'm beginning to think it explains a lot. I'm a little skeptical about if I REALLY think aliens exist, but it won't leave my mind. Ever since Chris suggested it to me, I've been having the wildest dreams." I explain my emerging thoughts. The whole time I'm telling this story, Jude is silently listening with his mouth half open.

"What year did this happen?" he asks when I finally finished. We had stopped walking and were standing on the street corner talking. The same corner we had bumped into each other a few months before. I think for a second, calculating years in my head. "1996, I'm pretty sure this happened in '96." I answer.

"You said it was springtime?" he asks

"Yep" I answered. I'm wondering why he is asking me all of these questions.

"That's a strange coincidence," he says.

"What? Were you abducted by aliens in spring of '96 too?" I ask jokingly.

"No" he answers, "but, my bandmate was." He pauses, "And he was flying over Arizona. Is there

I chit-chat with Jude as we walk the rest of the way to school together. Our kids coincidentally were in the same class, so we walked together and chatted everyday after that. It turned out we were both writers. He wrote songs, I wrote stories.

Jude and I became creative friends, we would walk and talk every day to and from school. I had a lot of fun chatting with Jude because he was a dreamer like I was. We both had vivid imaginations and neither of us would ever say an idea was silly or wrong.

It was about a week after the party where Chris had suggested the alien abduction to me. Jude and I had just dropped off the kids at school. I'm not sure why, but I had aliens on my mind and I had no one to talk to about it. I turn to Jude and I say, "So, apparently, in college, I was abducted by aliens." I expected him to laugh and dismiss my comment. Instead, he asked, "Really? Where?"

"Some highway in Arizona from Mesa to Peoria." I answer.

"Explain to me what happened." he says. I retold him the story about the bright light and how Chris helped me realize that I had some memory loss afterwards. I had lost track of time.

I was walking my oldest daughter to her first day of kindergarten. It was misty raining, in Seattle and we have a lot of ways to describe which type of rain is happening. Misty rain is like a wet fog. Dew drops form, but they form slowly. I had my sunglasses on. I think the mist blurred my vision a little because I literally bumped into another parent as I rounded the corner of the sidewalk. He was leaning down tying his son's shoe. "Excuse me" I said and giggled. It seemed funny the way we had both almost fallen over. I was slightly embarrassed, I literally collided into him.

I know Sophia was embarrassed. "Mom!" she said mostly under her breath.

Luckily, he laughed too. "I'm Jude" he said.

"Krystal" I said back."It's our first day of Kindergarten, so my mind was preoccupied or something, I just wasn't paying attention." I take my sunglasses off to wipe the blurred mist with my shirt.

"Do you always wear sunglasses in the rain?" He chuckled. I just put the glasses back on as he continues, "It's our first day of Kindergarten too. Maybe the kids will be in the same class." Jude is very friendly, a nice guy.

CHAPTER 3

DISCOVERING THE LANGUAGE OF SUBTLETIES

It's an ear-marked page
that I embody,
the beginning of absolutely no ending.
The middle of the mirror—
a true reflection of the flower sleeping.
nocturnal bugs are creeping,
Petals glow and tickle the moonlight,
igniting electricity in my dreams.
Powerful feelings that can alter my reality,
beyond any expectations within.
Flooding a passion;
my soul needs no watering.
fueled with an ethereal,
eternal spiral.

I spend the following days lightly researching UFO's and alien abductions. I was starting to think that Chris might be right with his prediction. My perspective is shifting, my mind is beginning to change.

We end up in a large field of grass bordered with steel cabinets to one side. Kate has on the wrong shoes. Laser beams begin shooting out from everywhere.

I hit the ground, Kate awkwardly runs to the cabinets and opens one. Inside is a full protective suit and helmet. She doesn't undress, the suit is now on her. She swims into the field dodging laser beams.

I can't see her anymore.

I'm all alone lying in the field of long grass as lazer beams are narrowly missing me. I scramble up from the ground and fumble as I open a cabinet door. Only, there isn't a full protective suit, just a helmet. I put it on.

I run in the same direction I think Kate went, but I am so confused that I don't know which way is which. I look up to the sky and I see all the stars line up to point me in a direction. The stars were literally moving into place, like a cosmic puzzle.

I follow the stars and the lazer beams slow down, as I'm speeding up. I'm now moving faster than the lazer beams towards the sky.

It's a bright, white light.

CRACKING THE CRYSTAL CODE

"I'm not bothered!" I insist. "Really, I'm intrigued. I want to know more!" I hand Chris my joint. "Want some?" I ask.

Chris takes a few puffs.

"It seems like you were bugged. You are never this quiet. You always have a wild or fantastical story to share with me." Ellie explains.

"I'm not bugged, I'm thinking. Chris's idea has sparked some new ideas of my own. I just have a lot of rhetorical questions racing through my mind." I tell them both.

"Ah, I have some good resources for you" said Chris. He gave me some good resources to read up on UFO research and alien abductions. I jotted them down in my notebook. Yes, I had my notebook at a party. I'm such a nerd, but I love writing and I never know when I might hear a bright idea.

That night, the dreams started flowing:

I am slowly walking through an endless art museum. I'm with my friend, Kate. She is wearing gold high heeled shoes and big gold hoop earrings. I'm wearing my hair in a ponytail and i have on tennis shoes. It feels as if we are in the same place, yet in different dimensions.

KRYSTAL KELLEY

I inhale as I look up at the sky. I exhale as smoke dances around my head. I look up, watching the smoke waft away, joining the clouds gently moving in the breeze. The sky is melting colors from pink to navy blue. Massive cedar trees, like fingers, or antenna poking through the meandering clouds.

I wonder what is really up there?

Beyond those clouds.

I don't really know more than what I know on Earth. Yet, I feel something deep inside of me that tells me I do know more. It's as if I can see it through a haze. How do I make enough wind to blow this haze past me? When will things become more clear? I just have so many questions.

Is there one quantum machine orchestrating this universe we live within?

Or is everything random? Like a drunkard's walk?

I start to think I have a narrow knowledge-base. Chris' theory is making me rethink my reality.

"There you guys are!" Chris says, walking over to the fire pit.

"Hey, Love. Why are you bugging Krystal with all your alien theories?" Ellie scolds Chris.

abducted." He said it so matter-of-fact, I was massively intrigued.

"How do you know that? I don't really believe in Aliens" I ask, skeptically.

"Well, Believe whatever you want. I've read hundreds of abduction stories and many have similarities to yours." Chris explained walking away, "I gotta get another beer."

This was a little mind-blowing. I don't quite know what to think, but I see Ellie across the room and I walk over to her. "Hey, your husband is trying to convince me I was abducted by aliens." I chuckle as I say it, realizing how absurd it sounds.

"Of course he is. He is such a punk." Ellie rolls her eyes at her husband grabbing another beer. "But I love him anyway!" Ellie laughs. "Let's go sit by the fire"

I follow Ellie outside. The crisp November air of the Pacific Northwest felt nice as we walked across the damp lawn to the fire pit, overlooking the Olympic Mountains. The mountains look almost pink with the setting sun reflecting off the newly fallen snow.

Ellie and I sit. We chit and we chat. I take a joint out of my pocket and carefully light the tip in the fire.

KRYSTAL KELLEY

I parked, but the next thing I remember is waiting in line for a Mariners spring training game."

He takes another sip of beer, "Who were you with?" Chris asks.

"I was by myself" I answered.

"You went to spring training by yourself?" Chris looks at me a little sideways as he sips a larger swill of beer.

"Yeah, it was spring break at U-dub. I got a cheap flight and my grandparents lived in Arizona, so I spontaneously thought I'd visit them. They let me borrow their car to go to the game." I explain, holding a full glass of wine in my hand. I haven't had a sip yet.

"You know what happened to you, right?" Chris asks me yet another question, as he tips his head back and pounds the rest of his beer.

"Uh, No, I don't. I've told this story so many times, but I've never had an explanation of that light. It was so bright and so unforgettable. What was it?" my curiosity is piqued.

"Well," Chris explains as he looks into his empty beer can, "it was a UFO. Judging by your lost recollection of time, my guess is that you were also

He takes a sip of his beer, and I continue, "All of a sudden, I see the brightest light I've ever seen, but it wasn't blinding. It filled the entire sky, all of my peripheral vision was filled with this light. And then, it went away as fast as it appeared. I felt like if I had blinked, I would have missed the light."

I looked at Chris. He nonchalantly took another sip of his beer and he doesn't look surprised at all. Now, I'm surprised because every other person I had ever told that story to was surprised. Except Chris. I wondered, "What does he know that no one else does?"

"What happened next?" he asked. Another sip.

"Um, hmmm. No one has ever asked me that. I don't remember what happened right after that." I answered, I'm a little perplexed. I had never really thought about anything after I saw that bright light. The light was the only memorable incident I had that day.

"Well, what is the next thing you remember that day?" He asks me, trying to be more specific about his question. He takes another sip of beer.

I think for a moment and say, "Uhhh, I was driving to Peoria. That's why I was on that road to begin with. Now that you mention it, I don't know where

CHAPTER 2

FLASHBACK

The first crack into my cosmic code happened 25 years prior, I was in the Sonoran Desert. I had told and retold this story many times to a wide range of listeners. But, it was Ellie's husband, Chris who was the first person to have an explanation as to what I saw.

Chris is an avid skateboarder and a connoisseur of art. We were at a party, and I was telling Chris about how strange things always seem to happen to me in deserts.

"I was in college. I was driving a green, 1976 Dodge Aspen down a long Arizona highway. I was between Mesa and Peoria. It was just before dawn. I was by myself, there were no other cars, no streetlights. It was as dark as dark gets." I explain to Chris.

I've been surprised before..." My sentence trails off as my mind begins a labyrinthine flight of plots and subplots a super power could explain.

I'm following a shapeshifting trip to the Mojave Desert, bumping into a pocket oracle, and mysteriously started playing music. Ironically, I've never played music before this point, but I discovered that I had vibrations lying dormant in my DNA.

I must take you back to the steps that helped me unlock my cosmic code and tap into a collective, interdependent world of symbiotic and synchronistic events.

I'm struggling. I think we all are. I mean, we are in a Global Pandemic, a war between Nature and Humanity. I'm shocked, yet not at all surprised. We are inhabiting a planet that seems to be dying. Humanity has apparently shot itself in the foot.

I'm a human, but I haven't always been one. I've also been a dragon flying in the sky, my scales millennia old. I've been my pure energy floating around in the universe, witnessing new worlds, like a fly on the wall. I watch worlds within worlds, within no walls of an infinite universe, unfold into my Akashic memory.

Regardless, the time is now. Right now, I am a human and I am struggling with wondering "How do I make a positive difference in this messed up world?" I owe it to my children. I want to inspire them to make a positive change in their lives. If I can ripple positivity to my three daughters, they can make a bigger ripple than mine, and so on. Then, one day, a tidal wave of positivity will envelope the planet in a crystal clear vibration that will bring a feeling of wholehearted love.

Again, this is why I struggle. My intentions are so clear, yet I have no idea how this vibration in my heart will ripple to yours. I suppose I don't need to know the answers to silly questions.

KRYSTAL KELLEY

CHAPTER 1

A MIND SHIFT

Like a constant humming in my ear,
I can't ignore it any longer.
I have these thoughts—
I'm thinking that if I'm thinking these thoughts,
I think they make me think I'm thinking.
I'm thinking these thoughts,
that make me think
there are possibilities.
ancient stories embedded in my mind,
an ever-present knowing.
that is how I have arrived today.
this predicament of thinking to myself
guides the humming in my ear.
the humming follows a thump in my chest,
my heart humming a hum.
hum,
hum,
hum.
hum, hum.
Who knows how this happened,
but it's always been this way
for me.

CRACKING THE CRYSTAL CODE

then, there is the space in our minds representing yet another dimension; I drift into my heart's center and realize, that it too, is a different vibration than our minds, this must be the third dimension. I run through time and pull ancient memories and future events, yet another dimensional shift when you factor in time. As these shifts happen, more portals open to more and more dimensions. I'm exploring these dimensions, one at a time, as energy shifts. The crazy thing is that once you move through dimensions, they stay with you. Some humans have an amazing ability to bridge dimensions. I believe these humans are called Shaman, medicine workers, artists, writers, musicians, poets, the change agents who push our evolution through compassion and kindness.

I'm gathering my mystical band of change agents on this cosmic train to the stars. A galactic revolution, one bridge at a time. Welcome aboard.

ARTIST'S STATEMENT

With one hand, I pick up a chunk of driftwood. In my mind, the wood looked like a little meditation stool. The part I grabbed, fell off in rot. Then, I used two hands. I wanted a comfortable place to sit on the pebbled beach, close to the water. I carried the wood down to the water and placed it in the large and small pebbled shoreline. I heard the waves, an eagle anointed me with a nod of his wing. I lean to sit on the driftwood-turned-bench; a new life for this old tree. As my butt hits the wood, all I can think is, "ah, so peaceful. The perfect day." Then, as the wood shifts under my weight, I fall, awkwardly tumbling on the rocks. I laugh out loud. I push the rock hard into the sand and let it naturally level out. I sit again, the wood is not at the angle or the way I thought I was going to sit on it, but it was surprisingly comfortable. I sit and enjoy the sun, the boats passing, the birds flying, and I think.

I think about how the clouds in the sky and the rocks beneath our feet represent one dimension;

Dedicated to Clean Water

CONTENTS

Artist's Statement 1

Chapter 1   A Mind Shift 3

Chapter 2   Flashback 7

Chapter 3   Discovering the Language of Subtleties 15

Chapter 4   What Should I Wear?! 37

Chapter 5   Crooked Beak 45

Chapter 6   Power and Force 53

Chapter 7   My 'Secret' Life 65

Chapter 8   The Rag Doll 79

Chapter 9   Westport 89

Epilogue 93

ISBN: 978-0-9834298-6-9

Mind Unwind Publishing, 2021

For more information: www.krystalkelley.com

FIRST EDITION

CRACKING THE CRYSTAL CODE

KRYSTAL KELLEY